First published in 2008

A catalogue record for this book is available from the British
Library

ISBN 978 1 84425 484 2

Library of Congress control no. 2008929388

Published by Haynes Publishing, Sparkford, Yeovil,
Somerset BA22 7JJ, UK
Tel: 01963 442030 Fax: 01963 440001
Int. tel: +44 1963 442030 Int. fax: +44 1963 440001
E-mail: sales@haynes.co.uk
Website: www.haynes.co.uk

Haynes North America Inc.
861 Lawrence Drive, Newbury Park,
California 91320, USA

Printed and bound in Great Britain by
J. H. Haynes & Co. Ltd, Sparkford

Risks

Boating and boat maintenance can safely be enjoyed but
involve risks and some dangers. It is vital that you follow
instructions provided by the manufacturers when using
boats, equipment, tools and materials for maintenance
and repair. Boat insurance companies are increasingly
expecting some types of maintenance and modification
work to be formally approved (or carried out) by qualified
professionals before the boat is used. Consult your policy
for details.

HM Coastguard (HMC) and The Royal National
Lifeboat Institute (RNLI) provide comprehensive safety
advice for boating. Readers are advised to consult and
follow their advice at all times: in particular you should
wear a lifejacket, and be aware of the dangers of booms
and winches and of navigational and weather hazards.

As can be seen in some of the photographs in this
book, some people decide to take the risk of not wearing
a lifejacket, and that is their choice. But as the RNLI
states, a lifejacket can only save you if you are wearing it.
People have been known to fall from boats in the calmest
of conditions.

The Boat Safety Scheme

The Boat Safety Scheme (BSS) provides an inspection
system, compulsory for cruising boats on inland
waterways. The Scheme's manual is also an excellent
source of safety information for boats used in coastal
locations.

Electrical, gas, fuel and safety installations

Readers are strongly advised that all work on electrical,
gas, fuel and other installations affecting safety should be
inspected by properly qualified engineers before use. Gas
installations must be carried out by an appropriately
qualified Corgi-registered engineer experienced in work
on boat installations.

Further information on safety

Details of how to obtain HMC, RNLI and BSS information
are included in the Appendix.

**Suggestions in this book concerning particular boats
and products do not guarantee or endorse the reliability
of particular companies or their products.**

Sailing Boat Manual

Haynes ®

Dennis Watts

BUYING, USING, MAINTAINING AND REPAIRING SAILING DINGHIES AND SMALL SAIL CRUISERS

1

Introduction

Sheltered sailing in superb scenery.

You don't have to spend a fortune

You don't have to be wealthy to enjoy sailing and you don't have to be rich to own a boat – but you can let other people think you are if you like! Either way, this book will try to get you sailing without spending a fortune. Indeed, a frequent comment by boat owners is 'The most enjoyment we ever had was in small and simple boats', where 'simple' means low-cost whilst still being safe and great fun for the whole family. New and experienced boat owners alike will find plenty here to help them enjoy using and maintaining a sailing boat.

This book is about sailing dinghies, open day boats and smaller sail cruisers with cabins, up to about 7.5m (25ft) in overall length – in other words, the sorts of boat best suited to the many shallow sheltered inland and coastal waters waiting to be explored by those who want to get afloat under sail without undue expense.

It's now much easier to find boat bargains. In the past sellers had to pay to advertise in just one or two specialist boating magazines, but today the Internet's boat-selling websites – often linked to publications – mean that sellers can advertise to a wider audience far more economically or even for free.

If you're capable of some basic do-it-yourself tasks at home you can adapt your skills to improve an inexpensive, neglected small sailing boat or even to build a new one from a kit and plans. New materials and methods

Smaller sail cruisers as well as dinghies can explore shallow creeks under sail.

have helped make domestic DIY much easier, and the same applies with boats. You don't have to be a shipwright to tackle many straightforward maintenance and improvement tasks.

A sailing boat can be renovated with basic DIY skills or even built from a kit, like this one from Whisper boat kits.

A Halcyon 23 sail cruiser rescued from decline, renovated and refitted ready for cruising.

Being captain of your own boat is a great thrill.

Personal experience

My Uncle Maurice introduced me to boating as a child. When I was very young he taught me to row – on a shallow pond, with the little boat tethered to the bank while he gave instructions. For a few minutes he fell asleep in the sun, lying on the grassy bank, and I became captain of my own boat! The thrill of that moment remains with me even now.

Later I crawled into and under the sailing boats that he renovated and refitted in his spare time throughout his life – sawing, drilling, gluing, scraping, repairing and painting. It was hard work, but well worth it when we set sail into the estuary aboard a brightly painted old boat rescued from decay in the corner of a boatyard. Buying a neglected boat in the autumn, improving it on suitable winter days, sailing it in the summer and selling it (for a good price) to buy another – and bigger – one is how he progressed over the years from dinghies to substantial sail cruisers.

When I became a boat-owner in turn I copied Uncle Maurice's routine, starting with a Mirror sailing dinghy that I built from a kit of parts and plans and progressing thereafter through the ownership, improvement and enjoyment of many boats of various types. Some of those I owned along the way are pictured in this book. You may want to try the same process, buying, improving and selling a succession of progressively larger boats until you have a sail cruiser with a cabin. It's rather like ascending the bricks-and-mortar property ladder. It's even possible to make a small profit each time you sell, to reinvest in the next boat.

Alternatively, you may be content with one small sailing boat that suits your particular needs. But whatever you decide, the aim of this book is to help you enjoy the experience.

Sailing for fun – not to prove something

Some view the sea as a challenge. It gives them the chance to prove how brave they are, to develop their character, to talk about their achievements. By all means have fun doing just that, as safely as possible; but perhaps the most enjoyment to be gained is through being able to relax in an entirely different environment, away from the stresses of normal everyday life. The concentration that's needed to sail a boat blocks out any aggravating thoughts and you find

Right: Sail silently into secluded bays and rocky coves.

that you can leave them behind on dry land. Surrounded by scenic coasts or inland waterways, fascinating wildlife, a broad seascape, breathtaking skies and friendly boating folk, you'll find that enjoyment and relaxation go together.

Arthur Ransome's famous *Swallows and Amazons* book series, about children enjoying adventures in sailing dinghies, is responsible for many people — young and old – being drawn to the fascinating environment of coastal creeks and inland waters. Some are keen to re-create the world found in Ransome's series of books, and this is not only possible but is likely prove a highly enjoyable and rewarding experience.

Drift away into relaxation

With its huge variety of inlets, estuaries, islands, sea lochs and bays, the United Kingdom has nearly 8,000 miles of coast, much of it sheltered and safe for

Inland rivers and lakes provide sheltered and interesting sailing.

Idyllic spots can be found for an overnight stay in tranquil surroundings.

small boats when used sensibly and carefully. In fact nowhere in the UK is more than 72 miles from the sea. Inland, few places are far from a safely navigable river, canal, lake, broad or reservoir.

Most of our ancestors actually arrived here in small boats, and as an island nation it's no surprise that boating comes naturally to many. Boats were the main means of long-distance transport in Britain before railways, motorways and air travel were even thought of. Now we use them for fun.

The phrase 'messing about in boats' will be familiar to everyone, but sailing involves much more than this. Skills have to be learned and precautions taken, but with a small boat and a gentle breeze you can take it easy in sheltered waters. You can explore shallow creeks, visit remote island beaches and, either in a tent or the cabin of your own small cruiser, you can enjoy an overnight stay in idyllic surroundings.

Family fun

Most children are fascinated by water, and getting afloat will thrill them. Much is said about children being over-protected from adventurous outdoor enjoyment, but if you work together as a family everyone can learn to sail safely. Some family members may require persuasion, but on a warm sunny day with a gentle breeze even the most cautious can be converted to the joys of sailing.

For older children and teenagers there's the thrill of racing sailing dinghies. This is as exciting and challenging as any sport, with all the health benefits of exercise and fresh sea air. Plenty of clubs, sailing schools and sailing organisations provide opportunities for youngsters. A particularly appealing spectacle is the host of red sails to be seen when dozens of Mirror dinghies are raced by young enthusiasts in 'Nationals' at locations such as Brightlingsea in Essex and the coast of North Wales.

Families used to camping or caravanning will find it easy to adapt to sail cruising, which will enable them to enjoy the adventure of anchoring or mooring overnight in remote and scenic locations.

Above: The whole family can enjoy getting afloat.

Above: Sailing estuaries and creeks, you can encounter some magnificent sights in both natural and man-made settings.

Below: Red sails line the horizon as young enthusiasts race their Mirror dinghies.

The exhilaration of high-speed sailing.

Excitement if you want it

Speed is relative. In a boat you're close to the water's surface, and your speed may seem slow compared with land, but the combination of balancing and coping with the unpredictability of winds, waves and currents whilst slicing through the water gives a thrilling sensation not experienced ashore. Adrenalin rushes abound if you want them. Sailing a dinghy in a strong breeze on a choppy lake or estuary is as exhilarating, all-absorbing, exciting and vigorous a sporting activity as you could hope for.

As in any other sport, developing racing skills with the help of a local sailing club can lead to national, international and even Olympic competition, where highly-skilled competitors from the UK always gain many medals.

A larger boat may be your eventual ambition, for either fast or gentle sailing according to choice.

Scope of the book

Any book has limits on its content, and the huge variety of boats and equipment available mean that sailing and boat maintenance is a vast subject. Many books concentrate on particular aspects of boat ownership and use, and go into great depth and detail on their chosen subject. This book by contrast covers a wide range of topics, but concentrates on those that are within the capabilities of the majority of sailing boat owners.

The emphasis is on simple and basic maintenance tasks. The very large and extensive topics of sailing dinghy and sail cruiser modifications and the installation of additional equipment are not included, as these would require a whole series of books in order to cover them adequately.

Having coped with the basic topics set out in this book, more advanced sailing skills and more complex boat improvements can be learned. You can go on to take courses in offshore sailing, navigation, advanced engine maintenance or boat building. You can also buy more specialised publications, such as books on modifying dinghies for racing, and the monthly magazines that thrive on topics such as the addition of the latest equipment. But you should always remember that, in the interests of safety, a number of practical aspects are best left to the professionals. These are indicated in the appropriate chapters.

Nautical terms are often confusing for new and experienced boat owners alike, and are therefore explained both in the text and in the detailed Glossary.

2 The parts of a boat

These diagrams identify the principal parts of a sailing boat. The Glossary has more detailed definitions, and explanations of most of the parts will be found in the appropriate chapters.

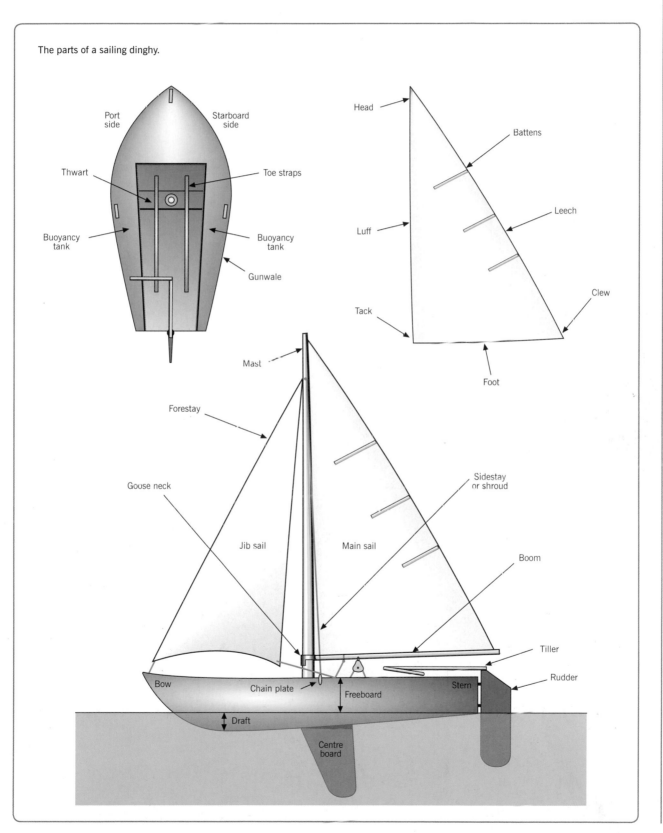

The parts of a sailing dinghy.

Port side
Starboard side
Thwart
Toe straps
Buoyancy tank
Buoyancy tank
Gunwale

Head
Battens
Luff
Leech
Tack
Clew
Foot

Mast
Forestay
Goose neck
Jib sail
Main sail
Sidestay or shroud
Boom
Tiller
Rudder
Bow
Chain plate
Freeboard
Stern
Draft
Centre board

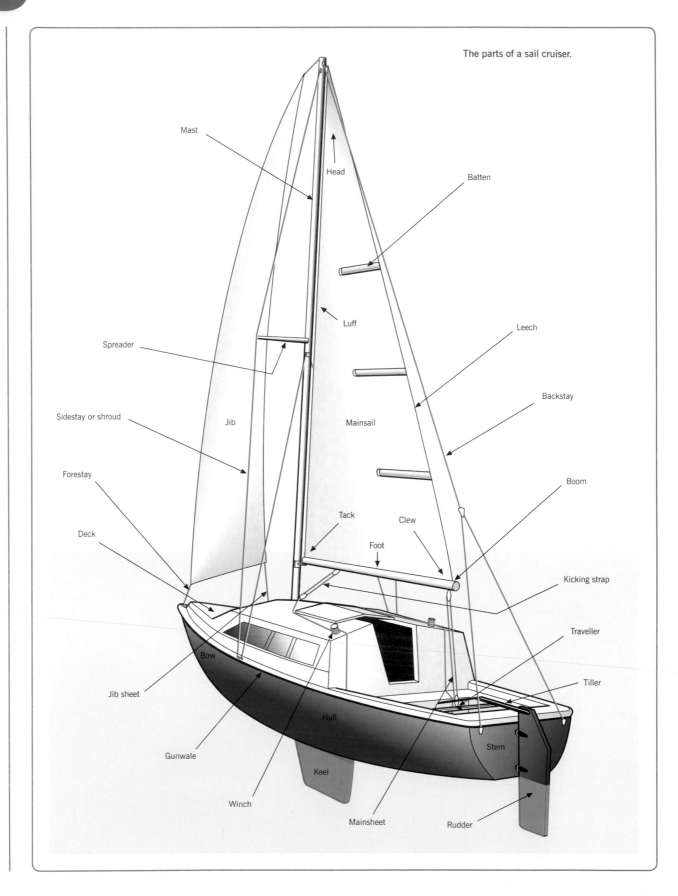

The parts of a sail cruiser.

Mast

Head

Batten

Luff

Leech

Spreader

Backstay

Sidestay or shroud

Jib

Mainsail

Forestay

Boom

Tack

Clew

Deck

Foot

Kicking strap

Traveller

Bow

Tiller

Jib sheet

Hull

Stern

Gunwale

Keel

Winch

Mainsheet

Rudder

Basic types of rig

Lug rig
A supporting spar extends in front of the mast.

Gaff rig
The mainsail is supported by a spar behind the mast.

Una rig
The sail is set behind the mast, and usually without any stays to support the mast.

Bermudan rig
The sail is set behind the mast and usually has a boom along the foot of the sail.

Bermudan sloop rig
With an additional sail in front of the mast, this is often considered to be the most efficient rig on all points of sail.

Gunter rig
In this case the features of Gaff and Bermudan rig are combined. The mast, though, is in two parts. The top part is held upright against the main part of the mast. The advantage is that the rig can easily be dismantled and the spars carried in the boat.

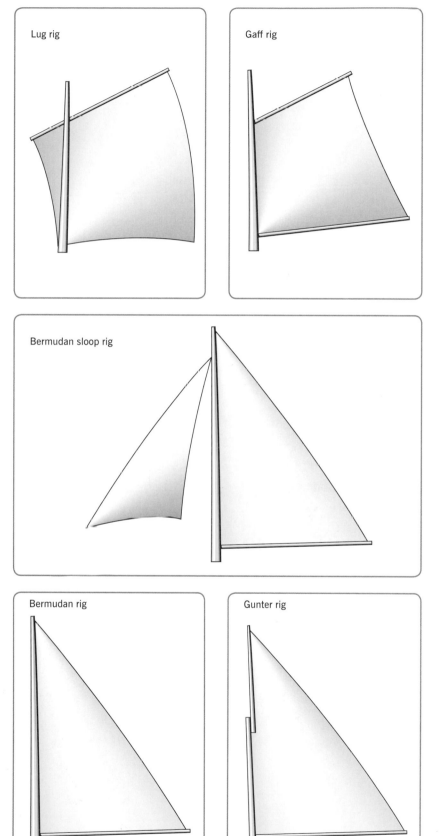

Lug rig

Gaff rig

Bermudan sloop rig

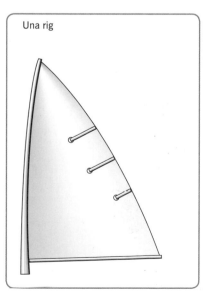

Una rig

Bermudan rig

Gunter rig

3 Choice of boat

Sailing clubs also organise races, with a safety boat ready to rescue anyone who has problems.

Sailing clubs usually welcome visitors and applications for membership, and often arrange sailing training courses.

attitude means that beginners are much more likely to be welcomed, helped and encouraged.

Some clubs have boats available for the use of members, and it could be worth becoming a member to gain experience by using a club boat, with assistance from members, before actually buying your own. Club and town regattas also provide great opportunities to see a variety of craft afloat and being put through their paces.

Enthusiasts for one particular boat type abound. They can be very helpful but also tend to get carried away with praise for their favourite boat, so keep an open mind and try to talk to owners of a variety of boats that interest you.

On most weekends and some evenings in the summer, sailing clubs, outdoor activity centres and sailing schools have events such as races and training sessions. These are

worth watching to see what sort of boating most appeals to you, and how to use particular types of boat. Later you may even get involved. Getting on the water in company, and often with a safety boat nearby to help anyone in difficulty, is very reassuring for beginners and experienced sailors alike.

Reading this entire book before making a choice will reveal a variety of boat types and the enjoyment potential of each. This should help with your decision regarding which type to seek and buy. The chapter on buying second-hand and the sections on repair and maintenance, for instance, contain much information about minimising the costs involved.

At this stage it's worth considering some more research and trying sailing in several different types if that's possible. Visit sailing clubs, sailing schools, outdoor education centres, boat shows and boat dealers or brokers. These often provide the chance of trying out an assortment of different boats. Hiring a suitable boat may also be possible.

Some sailing clubs have had the reputation in the past for being rather exclusive and not particularly welcoming unless a newcomer is already well known to existing members. This situation has fortunately changed in most clubs: the days when most clubs had waiting lists for membership have passed, and many now need to attract new members. This more enlightened and less exclusive

Above and *left*: A town or club regatta provides opportunities to learn about different types of sailing boat as here at Maldon Regatta.

Considerations

Age and agility will have an inevitable influence on your decisions. The young and the agile of any age revel in the thrill of dinghy sailing and racing with the sorts of boat that you tend to sit *on* rather than *in*. The Topper dinghy and the high-performance Laser dinghy racers are examples that provide thrills and spills. This type of sailing sharpens your reflexes and reactions to rapidly changing wind strengths, directions and water conditions. You get to know the consequences of your actions very quickly, or go swimming instead as the boat capsizes and the water comes up to meet you!

Sailing in a dinghy is often recommended as the best way to learn how to sail and gain experience, but this doesn't have to be in a high-performance racing dinghy. The risk of an unscheduled swim can be much reduced by choosing a larger, heavier and more stable sailing dinghy or day boat. This will appeal to those who prefer a more relaxing experience but with the potential for some excitement if the wind increases. Boats that you sit *in* rather than *on*, such as a Wayfarer, are good for learning to sail. Such more stable boats will be inclined to forgive mistakes and slow reactions rather than punish them with a dunking.

The amount of cash you have available will also have a big influence on your choice. The websites quoted below, in the following chapters and in the Appendix provide the current prices of new boats or the contact details for you to make enquiries.

The examples of sailing dinghies in this chapter and in later chapters are available new for a few thousand pounds or second-hand for often less than a thousand – perhaps only a few hundred – depending on condition. More on this is in Chapter 4. The larger day boats cost rather more, both new and second-hand. New small to medium-sized sail cruisers (about 5 to 8m length overall) are mostly between £9,000 and £70,000 depending on size and equipment included. But second-hand sail cruiser bargains can be found for a few thousand pounds.

When learning to sail, a Wayfarer dinghy provides more stability than other smaller boats.

A selection of sailing boats

The following examples cover some popular boats. A substantial list of websites for information on many more types can be found in Chapter 4.

Sailing dinghies

The Topper
http://www.topper.org.uk

The small Topper sailing dinghy has been in production for over 20 years and is popular with the young and the agile. As its name indicates, it's easily car-toppable. Being made of polypropylene it's virtually maintenance free compared with many boats, and it can be rigged and on the water faster than most. It's a boat to sit on and hang out of whilst skimming over the water – so it's not a family cruising dinghy, but is great fun if you can handle it safely without capsizing too often.

The Topper range has developed to include the Topaz Uno, which is also easy and quick to rig, and the larger Vibe with space for parent and child sailing.

The Laser
http://www.lasersailing.com
The range of Laser sailing dinghies is one of the best-known for racing. The high-performance Laser 2, with its trapeze for sitting out, is recognised for its speed and thrills. The Laser 4000 provides a high quality racing experience where

class rules ensure particularly fair competition by emphasising sailing skills.

The Laser 2000 is suitable for family cruising as well as racing. You can sit quite comfortably inside this boat, which has room for the children and equipment for a day out. Youngsters can be taught to sail in a reasonably secure situation. Alternatively, the versatility of this dinghy enables a quick change of rigs for racing.

The Laser Pico is popular for learning to sail and can be

The Mirror

http://www.ukmirrorsailing.com

The Mirror has almost certainly been the most popular choice of first sailing dinghy since the 1960s. Well over 70,000 have been built since television DIY expert Barry Bucknell designed it along with Jack Holt and the *Daily Mirror* newspaper that promoted it. It's still very popular as a reasonably stable boat for all ages and abilities, and is great for a family to just mess about on, whether rowing,

used by every member of the family. Its large cockpit area and high boom give it the impression of being a larger boat than it is. Stability is good for its size and yet its sailing performance can be exciting.

Above: An older marine plywood Mirror dinghy still going strong.

Left: The Mirror dinghy is quite easy to rig and launch.

A Mirror dinghy professionally built from the most up-to-date synthetic materials.

Above and *below:* Inflatable Tinker Star Traveller ready to sail. An electric outboard motor on the transom helps when exploring creeks and coping with tidal currents.

sailing or using a small outboard motor. It is also raced seriously, particularly by enthusiastic youngsters.

A particular appeal is its ease of construction in marine plywood from a kit of parts. Alternatively, ready-built Mirror dinghies can be bought, including ones made from GRP or the most up-to-date composite materials. It can also go on a car's roof rack, although it's quite large for many cars to carry on top. Trailing it is better. If you want to avoid using a trailer, then a folding or inflatable sailing dinghy may suit you better. A folding boat similar in many ways to the Mirror is the Stowaway Kontender (see below).

The website given above provides details of the large number of events and races organised annually for Mirror owners, as well as providing information on where to buy kits and ready-built boats.

Tinker inflatable sailing dinghies
http://www.tinker.co.uk

Whenever we visit a coastal or waterway location by road without a sail cruiser on tow, I like to have my old Tinker Star Traveller in the back of the car. It rolls up and fits in easily, so that even with racing sailing kit and a collapsible launching trolley it still leaves room for my wife and son!

These inflatable sailing dinghies are so strongly made that they're used as life rafts on ocean-going cruisers, where in an emergency the crew can rely on them to self-inflate and provide a lifeboat able to cope with stormy seas. This perhaps explains why my very old Tinker is still going strong and providing great fun for the family.

The Stowaway Kontender

http://www.seahopper.co.uk/kontender.htm
This folding boat was originally made of varnished marine plywood but is now available with its folding sections made of GRP. The sections fix together and hinge using high tenacity polyester. In its folded state, the Kontender can easily be secured to the roof rack of most cars. It can be made ready to sail in about ten or fifteen minutes, and its performance has been favourably compared with a Mirror dinghy.

These photographs show how the Stowaway Kontender is unfolded and assembled.

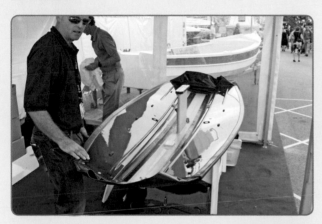

Motor sailing with electric outboard and inflatable Tinker.

an aluminium mast that slots together, but the more recent Tinker foldaway rib has a hinged GRP hull.

When fully inflated such boats are rigid enough to sail well. Stepping into one for the first time is a strange sensation, but once you get used to it you realise how safe and stable the design is. As well as sailing, Tinkers can be rowed, but I prefer using an electric outboard to explore estuary creeks.

The Wayfarer
http://www.wayfarer.org.uk
An example of a large, stable dinghy suitable for family sailing as well as racing is the Wayfarer. Originally designed by Ian Proctor and constructed in wood in 1957, later versions were built in GRP. Like the Mirror dinghy, it can easily be sailed by two people but can accommodate up to six quite comfortably. The Wayfarer remains a popular

This type of boat assembles like a combination of a folding boat and an inflatable. Most consist of a plywood floor and transom between two inflatable hull sections, with

Another make of double-hulled inflatable sailing dinghy is the Minikat, a small catamaran that collapses to fit into a large rucksack.

The Wayfarer.

choice and it's worth looking at the association's website for plenty of information

The Wayfarer is also big enough for cruising. Some adventurous enthusiasts pack enough supplies into the storage compartments for a week of cruising and camping in areas such as the Norfolk Broads. With a tent on the boat (the Wayfarer Association has boat tents for hire) you can make for secluded creeks or remote hidden waterways and spend your nights afloat before exploring areas that larger boats can't reach.

Day boats

Large open sailing boats, often referred to as day boats, can also be used for cruising and camping afloat. These are more stable and heavier than racing dinghies. Sailing performance can still be quite lively but there is much less risk of a capsize. The hull is strong enough to cope with beaching in calm conditions, in order to go ashore and explore. Many are sturdy enough to be kept on a drying tidal mooring.

The Yachting World Day Boat

http://www.cserve.co.uk
This is a large sailing dinghy built at Chris Somner Dinghy Services. Built in a classic style, it combines stability with seaworthiness and good performance. Its metal centreplate helps to keep it upright and young members of the crew can take responsibility for the small and easily handled foresail.

Yachting World Day Boat.

Drascombes

http://www.drascombe-association.org.uk
These are larger, very seaworthy and stable day boats particularly suitable for cruising, camping and safer racing. The best known is the original Drascombe Lugger, a design that was inspired by the working boats of north-east England and is reminiscent of Viking longboats. A sprayhood and tent can be rigged on board to provide shelter and more comfort.

Character Boats exhibited at the Southampton Boat Show include the Coastal Day boat.

A Drascombe Gig on Lake Bala.

Below left and *right:* Drascombes are available in several sizes and rigs. The Coaster and Drifter have cabins.

The rig is interesting, with two masts and a 'bumpkin' extension at the stern, which helps to increase the sail area. An outboard motor is mounted in a 'well' within the cockpit, making it easier to reach compared with an outboard mounted on the transom at the back of the boat.

As well as having its own website, the Drascombe Association publishes the informative *Drascombe Association News* quarterly; the quality of many of its articles rival those to be found in glossy boating magazines.

Character Boats

http://www.characterboats.co.uk
This is another range of day boats based on proven designs – this time from north-west England and Scotland. These boats have a shallow long keel instead of a centreboard, and the lack of a centreboard case makes more space available inside. Their traditional design and tan-coloured sails appeal to many, and the option of a sprayhood on a folding stainless steel frame provides some shelter.

Above: The Drascombe Coaster sailing well.

Below: Some day boats, such as this Character Boat, have removable cuddy shelters.

Small sail cruisers

If rather more shelter and comfort appeals to you, small cruisers are the next step up from day boats in terms of size, stability and accommodation. These are sometimes referred to as 'pocket cruisers', 'mini cruisers' or 'micro cruisers'.

A small sail cruiser takes longer to change direction and to respond to gusts of wind than dinghies do, which gives you more chance to correct mistakes; and with its keel and ballast to stabilise it there's much less chance of a capsize. Many people actually learn to sail in the relative safety of a cruiser. But should you try sailing a dinghy after learning on a cruiser, you'll need to take great care to adapt your skills and improve your reaction times to suit its much faster responses to wind speed and direction.

A very large range of good value second-hand sail cruisers is available through the media listed in Chapter 4. Perhaps because of this, the choice of brand new small cruisers is rather limited compared to larger and much more expensive sail cruisers.

The following are available both new and second-hand:

Drascombes

http://www.drascombe.org.uk/
The Drascombe Coaster is a larger version of the Drascombe day boat and has a two-berth cabin with cooker and toilet. A sprayhood and tent can be used to extend accommodation into the cockpit. Even though this boat is larger and heavier than the other Drascombes, it still has their shallow draft, which means that it can venture into shallow creeks with its centreboard raised.

West Wight Potter

http://www.theleisureboatcompany.co.uk
The original 14ft (2.4m) West Wight Potter with a small two-berth cabin can be found second-hand, while a newer 15ft

The 15ft (4.6m) West Wight Potter.

The P19 sail cruiser (above) and inside the P19's cabin (below).

(4.6m) version imported from the USA is also available along with a much more spacious 19ft (5.8m) model, the P19.

The P19 has four berths and as a new purchase is good value considering its size and the inclusion of a trailer, 5hp outboard motor and plenty of the equipment needed for cruising. The layout is typical of this size of cruiser. The fully retractable swing keel is wound up using a handle in the cockpit, reducing the draft to only 8in (20.3cm) – suitable for shallow creeks or grounding and going ashore on a suitably safe beach.

The Pippin 20.

The Pippin 20

http://www.pippin-yachts.com

At 20ft (6.3m) this sail cruiser has a different interior layout from the West Wight Potter and most other small sail cruisers. Its galley area, including a sink and cooker, are mounted partly across the centre of the cabin over a cupboard that divides it into two compartments.

Dolphin

http://www.dolphinboats.co.uk

At 21ft 8in (6.6m) the Dolphin Sasanka 660 is a little bigger than the boats described above. It has a lifting keel that provides a shallow draft for exploring creeks, and a well-equipped cabin that can accommodate up to six people.

MacGregor 26

http://www.macgregoruk.com

The 26ft (7.9m) Macgregor is an unusual sail cruiser. If fitted with a 50hp outboard motor it has the ability to behave like a powerboat, reaching speeds fast enough to tow a waterskier. Although this may not necessarily appeal to those keen on sailing, the boat is good value and has some interesting features, including twin rudders and the use of water ballast, which can be drained to make transporting the boat on a trailer easier.

Hunter, Crabber and Shrimper

http://www.selectyachts.co.uk

These three types are all available from Select Yachts. The 20ft (6m) Hunter 20 cruiser is designed to be easily trailered and launched. Its open-plan layout provides accommodation for four people. The Shrimper and Crabber ranges are solidly built in traditional style.

The Crabber, Shrimper and Hunter sail cruisers.

Another view inside the Pippin 20's cabin, showing the cooker and cupboard that divide it into two compartments.

A small selection of the many second-hand small sail cruisers frequently advertised

These are not normally available new unless a boatyard decides to build one from any moulds still available. The selection includes cruisers that are small, fairly simple to maintain and often advertised for sale second-hand.

The Lysander

http://www.lysander.org.uk

Most Lysanders were built in marine plywood from 1963 onwards. The original plans for this two-berth 17ft (5.18m) cruiser were produced by well-known designer Percy Blandford, and are still available from the owners' association at the web address given above. Some GRP versions were also built.

The Silhouette

http://www.soia.org.uk

A classic small cruiser is the Silhouette. The 17ft (5.18m) originals were built in marine ply but considerable numbers were also built in GRP along with larger and longer Silhouettes. The attractive shape of the deckline is a distinctive feature. Silhouette owners have an active association offering plenty of information at the above website.

Hurley cruisers

http://www.hurleyownersassociation.co.uk

The Silhouette (above) is sometimes referred to as the 'grandfather' to the range of boats built by Hurley Marine. The Hurley range of cruisers goes up in length in several stages from 18ft (5.5m) to more than 27ft (8.2m). These boats have a pleasing appearance and remain very popular. Some are used for both cruising and racing.

Leisure cruisers

http://www.leisureowners.org.uk

The Leisure range of sail cruisers has been particularly

A Silhouette III formerly owned and improved by the author.

popular and successful. The Leisure 17 sleeps two in comfort, or four who're very tolerant of each other, in a well-designed cabin. Larger versions were also built and the full range includes nine different lengths in total. Entering 'Leisure' into the search box on advertising websites such as http://www.boatsandoutboards.co.uk will reveal a large second-hand selection starting from about £1,500 for the 17ft (5.18m) version. A number are also advertised on their owners' association website.

The Westerlies

http://www.westerly-owners.co.uk

The cruisers known as Westerlies started with small versions, the first of which was the Westerly 22. This was followed by a large variety of very successful and popular sail cruisers of all popular sizes. The fact that so many small Westerly cruisers dating back to the 1960s and 1970s are still going strong shows how well built they were. Plenty can be found at reasonable second-hand prices.

Other sail cruisers often available second-hand include Eventides, Pandoras, the Halcyon, Skipper, Sailfish, Manta 19, Matilda 20 and the Prelude.

Some websites for small sail cruiser owners' associations are listed in the chapter on buying second-hand. These and the associations listed on the Royal Yachting Association's website have much information and many photographs that include all of the types mentioned above.

A Lysander – the author's first sail cruiser, renovated with the help of his wife.

Family sailing or a boat for one?

The above details provide points to be considered alongside the potential extent of family involvement. The main issue to resolve is: will you be sailing alone, with an enthusiastic partner, with a nervous partner, or with children?

Some family members may need encouragement to take part. Once scared by a near-capsize or some other event that an experienced dinghy sailor might consider exciting, they could be put off for life. This needs to influence your choice of boat. A course of sailing instruction followed by the purchase of a large, stable day boat or small sail cruiser may be the wisest course of action.

Family sailing requires compromise. It might be worth considering a small sail cruiser for the whole family plus a sailing dinghy, which can also possibly be used, if suitable, as a tender to reach the cruiser on a mooring. In this way you get the best of both worlds: suitably skilled and responsible children could use the dinghy in safe, supervised conditions, and so can the adults if so inclined. At the same time, less confident and less adventurous family members can stick to the comfort of the cruiser.

A caravan afloat?

Another consideration with a cruiser with a cabin is its 'caravan' appeal. Now, this is a very controversial point amongst dedicated sailing enthusiasts. They may feel that

it's sacrilege to think of a boat on a mooring as a facility for fun in its own right. But if it's your boat, you can use it how you like.

Many people enjoy a cruiser with reasonable cabin accommodation as a weekend retreat on the water. They may prefer a tranquil stay beside a riverbank, and only occasionally leave their mooring when conditions are ideal for a relaxing sail. A 'cottage afloat' is a term sometimes used and I apologise to pure sailing enthusiasts for daring to mention it… Nevertheless, it's a consideration to be taken into account, and a way to ease less enthusiastic family members into a frame of mind where they may actually agree to leave the mooring for a sail.

Hazard awareness – booms and winches

Apart from the water itself, there are some hazards to bear in mind when choosing a sailing boat with family use in mind. But don't let them put you off – such hazards can be dealt with.

On most boats the bottom edge of the mainsail is attached to a horizontal spar called the boom. This moves with some force from one side of the boat to the other –

One appealing aspect of ownership is keeping your boat in a pleasant and relaxing environment.

Take care to avoid the boom as it swings across the boat when changing direction.

hopefully in a controlled manner, depending on the skill of the skipper. However, there's always a risk of the unwary being hit on the head and even knocked overboard. Experienced crew will automatically duck whenever this is a risk, but other people can be injured if they aren't warned in advance.

This hazard can be avoided in two ways. One is by being absolutely sure that everyone is aware of the boom and avoids injury by keeping clear of it – staying seated helps.

Winches need to be treated with care to avoid getting fingers trapped.

The other is by choosing a boat with no boom and a loose-footed sail. Some sailing boats have no boom, examples including most of the Drascombe range. Of course, you can still get a slap from a sail but it's not as bad as a bump with a boom.

Inevitably, ropes abound on a sailing boat. Some items of equipment meant to keep them under control could ensnare unwary crew. Winches and pulleys designed to make them easier to handle can actually create a further hazard. Consider whether any of these are within easy reach of young children's fingers or may harm an adult unfamiliar with the operation and behaviour of the equipment. The main problem is hands and fingers getting trapped. Ensuring that everyone is aware of the potential dangers and choosing a boat with few such hazards will help.

Later chapters include more on safety afloat.

Where will you sail?

Slow-moving inland rivers, lakes, reservoirs and the sheltered safer coastal waters are the venues for the craft covered in this book. These minimise hazards and maximise pleasure for those new to sailing.

The availability of nearby water suitable for sailing and the distance to be travelled are considerations. Add up the time it will take to travel to the water and the time it takes to launch and prepare a trailed boat for sailing. Discuss this with existing owners of similar boats to get an idea of the time and effort involved. This can influence both the type of boat you choose and where you'll keep it. Consider, too, the types of boating that go on in nearby waters. If your local club specialises in racing will this suit you, or will you want to buy a sail cruiser and find an alternative base with access to suitable waters?

The exact locations most likely to be sailed will have a bearing on your choice of boat. Depth of water is crucial. Most sailing dinghies have centreboards that can easily be raised to cope with shallow water. Some sail cruisers also have lifting keels that can be winched up for shallow water, though unfortunately the raised keel and its housing takes up room in the cabin or in a day boat. Some boats with fixed keels, mainly cruisers, have more space in the cabin but require deeper water. A single fixed fin keel gives good sailing performance but needs the most depth whilst twin-bilge keels need less and provide a compromise.

The more exposed and colder the location for sailing, the more you may be inclined to choose a boat with some

Sheltered estuaries and creeks provide relaxed and interesting sailing. A desire to sail in shallow water depth will influence your choice of boat.

shelter: a 'cuddy' or small cabin. Alternatively, appropriate weatherproof clothing can overcome this problem, as in dinghy sailing. Remember that the temperature is almost always lower out on the water and that the wind chill factor is significant.

The mooring, launching area and local tides need to come into consideration here. The twin keels provide stability on a drying mooring but you have to wait longer for the tide to float your boat compared with a lifting keel.

A cruiser with twin bilge keels.

Moving on and upgrading to cruising

Many dinghy sailors, after having had much fun with their smaller boat, reach the stage where they'd like to go further afield under sail and enjoy some comparatively dry comfort whilst sailing. Availability of the necessary funds for the upgrade to a sail cruiser may be a problem, but reading Chapters 4 to 7 of this book may help to alleviate your problems.

Buying a bargain second-hand boat needing improvement could be the answer. This process can be taken a stage further if the practical side of boat ownership appeals to you. You should also bear in mind that second-hand boats tend to keep their value rather than depreciating like cars. A neglected boat substantially renovated, refitted and improved can increase in value sufficiently to cover the cost of materials and even produce a small profit when it's sold.

Over several years, this process of buying, improving, sailing for a season and then selling small boats at a small profit can eventually increase the cash available to buy a substantially larger boat. The author has followed this route successfully, progressing from dinghies to cruisers without having to find extra cash to invest. Obviously this takes a substantial commitment of time and effort. Some enthusiasts, though, even enjoy the practical processes of boat improvement so much that they spend much more time on this than out on the water sailing!

In the meantime, having decided on the boat type you want hunting for it should be enjoyed as part of the overall boating experience.

4 Buying a second-hand sailing boat

A mooring may be included with a second-hand boat, but don't rely on it.

Searching for and finding a suitable sailing boat can be a most enjoyable part of the boating experience. Walking along a sea wall or riverbank, watching all the different boats sailing by, arouses a strong desire to join them. Buying what seems the ideal boat is an exciting and emotional experience as you anticipate the pleasures and enjoyment of ownership and sailing. But try to keep in touch with reality. Ideally, you should read not only this chapter but also the rest of this book before you commit yourself to buying a boat. The extra knowledge will help towards making a wiser decision.

Where to keep it

Before buying a boat a most important consideration is where you'll keep it. Most boats of the size covered in this book will fit onto a trailer and could be kept in a suitable space at home. If this isn't possible, storage space at an appropriate club may be available. The availability of storage and moorings varies greatly according to location and should be arranged before purchase. Sometimes it's possible to take over a mooring or storage space when you buy a boat, but don't rely on it. More on storage and moorings will be found in Chapter 7.

Second-hand for choice and value

A large budget is needed to buy new, but for a fraction of the price of a new boat you'll find a much wider range of choice among the thousands of second-hand small boats advertised for sale. In fact there are many excellent boat

types that are no longer built, and the only way to obtain one of these is by buying second-hand. Just one example is the original 14ft West Wight Potter sailing boat with a small cabin. Second-hand, in good condition, these sell for about £1,400 at the time of writing, whereas a new boat of a similar design is over £9,000. Likewise, many types of sailing dinghies sell for hundreds of pounds compared with several thousand for new versions.

In addition a second-hand boat will often include many of the accessories and extras that have to be purchased separately when buying new. Equipment such as spare sails, anchors, outboard motors and their spare parts, mooring ropes, oars, fenders and lifejackets usually have to be bought as extras, so when they come with a second-hand boat they're a major asset and cost saving.

Much is said about recycling and its environmental benefits, and it is worth bearing in mind that buying second-hand recycles boats that might otherwise remain unused and deteriorate to the point where they would have to be scrapped.

Mooring included?

Some boats are advertised as having a mooring or storage space available to be taken over by the purchaser. This can be really worthwhile in an area where moorings are difficult to find. In fact, some people have been known to buy a cheap boat sold with a mooring simply to take over the mooring. The boat is then sold on separately, thereby releasing the mooring for use with a better boat.

The original GRP hulled West Wight Potter with some varnished wood superstructure, formerly owned and improved by the author.

A road trailer included as part of the deal is a big asset.

All this depends, of course, on the co-operation of the person or organisation that owns and rents out the mooring, so it's important to confirm that it can be transferred and what costs are involved. Sometimes there's a transfer fee and the annual rental charge may be increased above that paid by the previous owner. If the boat is stored at a sailing club, will membership and the storage space be available to you as the new owner of the boat?

Trailer included?

The inclusion of a road trailer with a second-hand boat is a big attraction, particularly if you're keeping the boat at home. A road trailer in good condition may add something to the second-hand price when included with a boat, but an appropriate new trailer would cost far more, possibly even more than the second-hand boat itself!

Where to look

In the past, it was difficult to find smaller low-cost boats and ones needing some work, since the cost of advertising tended to restrict them to adverts on club notice boards and in newsagents' windows. Only larger, higher-priced boats tended to appear in the glossy boating magazines. However, recent years have seen a huge increase in opportunities to advertise boats cheaply, often free of charge and to a very big range of potential buyers, mainly via the Internet.

Photos of boats for sale

Another advantage of using the Internet is the easy availability of photographs. Plenty of website adverts include pictures, and sellers are often able to supply more by email. It's worth asking for extra views of boats that genuinely interest you. For example, it's a good idea to see the interior of a sail cruiser as well as several different views of the hull and decks. Photographs of a reasonable resolution can be copied into appropriate software to be enlarged on your computer's monitor. That way it's possible to get a good idea of a boat's condition before travelling some distance to view it. But always bear in mind when looking at pictures that there's a tendency for photographs to be flattering if taken in bright sunshine or when the boat is wet after a shower of rain.

A website that's taken the approach of providing plenty of photographs to a particularly helpful level is www. boatshed.com. Advertisers have to pay a broker's fee, but the help provided can make it worthwhile for both seller and buyer. Someone is sent by Boatshed to take up to 65 photographs of the boat for sale. However, this site is mainly for sail and motor cruisers – you won't find cheap sailing dinghies here.

Before making a journey of any distance to view a particular boat always telephone to check it's still available. Even websites aren't always completely up to date.

If a particular type of boat isn't currently being advertised a 'wanted' advert can be placed on most websites, often free of charge. State where you are and how far you're prepared to travel to view the boat.

It's also worth keying 'project boat' into the search facility on boat-selling websites in order to find neglected boats available cheaply that are worth improving.

Internet auctions

The eBay auction website has a section for sailing boats under 'Sporting Goods'. More boats are – rather strangely – included under 'Car Parts and Vehicles', which is certainly worth searching on a regular basis. Sometimes a boat has to be sold in a hurry because of a change in family circumstances: unexpectedly inheriting a boat, for instance, can mean that it needs to be sold quickly, and eBay provides an opportunity to dispose of it fast – which means a potential bargain for the buyer.

A disadvantage of eBay is the short time available to visit and view a boat being auctioned. It's essential to inspect a boat before bidding, whatever assurances are given by the seller. Remember: bids are legally binding once you click on the bid button.

Boating magazine adverts

Don't forget to look at boating magazine classified sections. In fact you'll probably be tempted to buy magazines such as *Practical Boat Owner* and *Sailing Today* anyway, because they contain many interesting articles and trade adverts as well as listing boats for sale. Boating magazine websites with contact details for subscriptions are given in the Appendix. Their websites also include boats advertised for sale.

Sailing clubs and owners' associations

Sailing club websites often have a page of boats for sale. The Royal Yachting Association provides a list of sailing clubs nationwide. Just go to http://www.rya.org.uk/general/helpinfo and select 'club' from the 'find' box for contact details and websites for sailing clubs in your area. Most will have lists of members' boats of many types and classes for sale.

Associations for owners of particular types of boat also advertise examples for sale on their websites and in their newsletters. Some owners' associations that usually have boats for sale are listed below. The discussion forums on such websites are also a good source of advice. To find boats up for sale, in most cases you just click on 'boats for sale' or 'members' adverts'. If this option isn't available, select the contacts option and email to enquire if any boats are for sale.

The selection below is intended to demonstrate the range of sailing boats that can be found by visiting association websites. A full list is regularly updated on the Royal Yachting Association website – select 'class associations' from the 'find' box.

Additionally, try a Google search for particular boat types and classes to find other boating organisations currently advertising boats for sale.

Sailing dinghies owners' associations
- http://www.ukmirrorsailing.com
- http://www.sailenterprise.org.uk
- http://www.gp14.org
- http://www.tidewaydinghy.org
- http://www.wayfarer.org.uk
- http://www.laser2000.org.uk
- http://www.miracledinghy.org
- http://www.int505.org
- http://www.flying15.org
- http://www.gbrtopper.co.uk
- http://www.optimistsailing.org.uk
- http://www.420sailing.org.uk
- http://www.tinkerowners.co.uk
- http://www.albacore.org.uk
- http://www.cadetclass.org.uk
- http://www.cometsailing.org.uk
- http://www.heron-dinghy.org.uk
- http://www.ospreysailing.org.uk

Day boats and small sail cruisers owners' associations
- http://www.drascombe-association.org.uk
- http://www.devonyawl.com
- http://www.soia.org.uk (for Silhouette owners)
- http://www.lysander.org.uk
- http://www.eventides.org.uk
- http://www.leisureowners.org.uk
- http://www.hurleyownersassociation.co.uk
- http://www.pandora.org.uk
- http://www.westerly-owners.co.uk
- http://www.prelude-owners.info
- http://www.trail-sail.org.uk

Notice boards
Don't neglect the old-style advertising methods. Although Internet access is widely available, not everyone advertises on websites, so club notice boards and the windows of newsagents, chandlers, boatyard offices and supermarkets

Websites selling boats
The Internet is now accessible to virtually everyone. Even if you don't have access to a computer at home or at work, there are Internet cafes, and local libraries have expanded the number of computers available to the public, with assistance available if it's needed.

Some boat-selling websites not only provide free or cheap advertising but also publish adverts in printed form. Conversely, several boating magazines have website listings of their classified adverts. The most popular boat-buying and selling website is probably http://www.boatsandoutboards.co.uk, several reports indicating that it has more visitors than any other such site. However, it's also well worth searching in other websites, and a selection of these are listed below. A list of the sailing magazines' own websites is included in the Appendix.

- http://www.boatsandoutboards.co.uk
- http://www.apolloduck.co.uk
- http://www.dinghyshop.co.uk
- http://boatshop24.co.uk
- http://www.boats4sale.co.uk
- http://www.allatsea.co.uk
- http://www.ybw.com/ybw/boatsale.htm
- http://boatsforsalenow.com
- http://search.ebay.co.uk
- http://www.boatshed.com
- http://www.boatbrowse.co.uk
- http://www.boatsforsale.co.uk
- http://www.noblemarine.co.uk/boatsforsale.php3
- http://www.look4boats.com
- http://www.boatandyachtbuyer.co.uk

A great many websites specialising in general classified advertising also do an excellent job in encouraging the recycling of all manner of items, including boats. Many of them are online versions of the classified ads in local newspapers that wouldn't easily have been available to people outside their local area in pre-Internet days. There are also sites that exist mainly to provide free or cheap advertising. Some classified advertisement websites that include sailing boats are:

- http://www.adtrader.co.uk
- http://www.friday-ad.co.uk
- http://www.loot.com
- http://uk.freeads.net
- http://www.findit.co.uk
- http://www.preloved.co.uk
- http://www.classifieds.co.uk

A shop window may be the first place a boat is advertised.

A friendly welcome at the clubhouse is usual for visitors with an interest in finding boats for sale.

may still be the first place a bargain boat is advertised. Some sailing boat types are popular in particular locations and could be sold quickly this way.

Knock on the door of a sailing club and introduce yourself. As a non-member you'll need to ask a club steward or a committee member for permission to look at their notice board to see any boats for sale, but most will be happy to help. It's also worth asking members if they know of any boats likely to be up for sale in the near future.

Boat brokers

Dealers in boats are called brokers or yacht brokers. Most of them have a catalogue of boats for sale on their websites. Brokers selling boats usually concentrate on the more expensive vessels, as their fee is normally a percentage of the boat's selling price. This is charged to the seller, not the buyer. The percentage fee a seller has to pay to the broker may increase the price above that for similar privately advertised boats.

Boatyards, such as this one in Suffolk, often include a range of second-hand sailing dinghies and rowing boats as well as plenty of sail cruisers.

Investigate corners of boatyards for neglected boats. Some may have 'for sale' signs – as on the tiny white notice on this 'project' boat.

Most brokers seldom deal in sailing dinghies but will probably have plenty of sail cruisers. However, there are some who cater for a wider price range.

If a suitable boat is available, there should be advantages in buying from a broker, who can provide plenty of advice about particular types of boat. Bear in mind, though, that brokers are similar to estate agents, and are keen to sell you a boat; so if you go on a mailing list they often tend to assume (or hope!) that you can afford more than the figure you may have mentioned. On the other hand, you might receive details of the boat of your dreams before someone else gets a chance to buy it.

Brokers may be members of appropriate associations, such as the Yacht Brokers, Designers and Surveyors Association, which has its own website at http://www.ybdsa.co.uk. Such membership can increase your confidence in the services provided. These can include checking the paperwork that comes with many sail cruisers to ensure legality of ownership, and ensuring that deposits and payments are handled correctly. At additional cost, they should be able to arrange any necessary surveys and boat safety inspections, and provide transport facilities for the boat to be taken to its sailing destination.

Boatyards

These can vary enormously. Large boatyards may have a substantial brokerage business with plenty of boats to view both on hardstanding and on their moorings. Smaller yards may just have a notice board in their office window or on their gate, with a

few cards giving brief details of boats for sale. Some vessels in the boatyard may simply bear a handwritten 'for sale' sign.

Sailing dinghies are sometimes abandoned by owners who have lost interest. They might clutter corners of a boatyard and the boatyard owner may be keen to arrange for them to be sold and cleared away as soon as possible. It's therefore worth investigating and asking to see them. The response could vary according to the job on hand: a boatyard owner busy deep inside the hull of an old boat may give a short sharp reply, but catch him at a better time and he could prove to be the most helpful boat expert you'll ever meet.

Boat owners often ask the boatyard that provides them with maintenance services to sell their boat. The main advantage of dealing with a boatyard is the availability of skilled craftsmen who can deal with work you don't want to do yourself. Part of the deal might include the cost of hauling out and relaunching or servicing the engine. A further advantage is the possibility of being given priority when renting a temporary or long-term mooring or storage space at the boatyard.

Auctions

It might be possible to find a bargain by attending an auction, depending on the level of risk involved. Items are sold 'as seen', and much depends on whether you have sufficient opportunity to inspect a sailing boat and its equipment before the auction. Few boats are now put up for

A boatyard will have equipment to lift, launch and transport boats.

Boat jumbles are worth searching for bargain boats.

sale at real live auctions – mostly they're sold on website auctions, or are advertised in one of the ways described above.

Boat jumbles

Events called boat jumbles – the low-cost alternative to boat shows – can be fascinating. Major boat shows are an experience not to be missed, but they tend to include a high proportion of boats and equipment priced well out of the reach of many people new to sailing. The main attraction of boat jumbles is the range of low-cost new and second-hand equipment for sale, in addition to which there are usually a number of actual boats on display, which you can pay for in cash and take away on your roof rack or trailer. The bargains go quickly, so get there early and join the queue before the opening time, which is usually around 10am on a Sunday. The friendly atmosphere and fascinating boating conversations alone make boat jumbles worth visiting.

Some concern has been expressed about the quality and legality of a few items for sale at boat jumbles, but the police now often attend such events, acting as a deterrent to fraudsters and reducing the possibility of stolen goods being offered for sale. However, you'll still need to take care when buying equipment or boats to check that they're suitable and safe for their intended use.

A list of most of the main boat jumbles can be found at http://www.boatjumbleassociation.co.uk.

Finding a bargain

Privately advertised sailing boats and neglected ones in boatyards and sailing clubs' dinghy parks provide the greatest chances for finding a bargain. Occasionally a boat with a 'for sale' sign can be seen in an unexpected location such as the front garden of the boat's owner.

Damaged or neglected boats can be difficult to sell and are often called 'project boats'. The price may be very tempting and there could be much scope to reduce it further. Don't get carried away, though. Check the later

chapters on boat maintenance and repair to be sure that you want to take on the work involved. Having done that, an informed and level-headed decision can be made to spend your winter weekends renovating and refitting a project boat so that you end up with an outstanding bargain ready for summer sailing.

Sometimes a really shabby, dirty boat with green algae all over it is actually in sound condition – particularly a fibreglass boat, where rot isn't a problem. Where an owner hasn't had the time, inclination or ability to clean a boat, its appearance reduces the asking price substantially – or provides you with a good reason for negotiating a reduction. Careful use of a pressure washer, cleaning compounds and some paint or polish may produce a bargain boat.

Prices

There is no frequently updated guide to boat prices as there is for cars. Try to find several advertisements for the same type of boat and compare their prices, bearing in mind age, condition and the items included in the sale. The Internet has made it easier to establish the value of a boat. Putting the type or class of the boat into an Internet search engine such as Google will not only provide you with details of the

Look out for boats for sale in unexpected places. This one was in a field beside a country road.

prices currently being asked but will often indicate where boats of that type are up for sale.

The auction website eBay provides a list of boats recently auctioned, showing the final bid. Go to 'Sailing' and the boat listings and click on 'Completed listings' in the column on the left. This shows the bids that won particular boats and those that didn't meet the reserve price. This quickly helps to establish how much you might have to pay for a particular boat, and a printout of the page could be used to help negotiate a price reduction on a boat advertised elsewhere – if you're lucky!

When to buy

Understandably, the greatest interest in boat buying tends to be aroused when the weather improves in late spring and early summer – the start of the main sailing season. However, prices tend to be higher and less negotiable at that time, with plenty of buyers about.

By contrast, a boat advertised in late autumn or winter, by someone who needs to sell it quickly, is likely to attract fewer buyers and there's consequently the potential for a bargain to be found. One exception tends to be January each year, when publicity for the annual London Boat Show encourages thoughts of sailing in summer sunshine, and interest in boat buying increases for a while – until it subsides again when confronted by the reality of February weather.

Minimising risks

As with buying anything second-hand, there will always be some risk involved in buying a used boat. However, the risks can be minimised by adopting a commonsense approach and taking some precautions. The risk of being sold a stolen boat is small compared with road vehicles. For larger boats there are registration schemes, but small boats don't have to be registered like motor vehicles. Two websites listing stolen boats are http://www.stolenboats.org.uk and http://www.newtoncrum.co.uk/stolen.html

When buying from a private individual it's advisable to visit their home address to make the payment – ideally collecting the boat from there if it's on a trailer. A boat bought from a broker should come with some assurance that it's legitimate.

The Recreational Craft Directive was established by the European Union in June 1998. This introduced minimum standards for all new pleasure boats between hull lengths of 2.5m and 24m and required such boats to have a hull identification number. Part of the rules includes a requirement that the seller of a second-hand boat built since

Boat shows increase interest in boat buying.

June 1998 must pass on the paperwork – including proof of compliance, the hull number and proof of ownership – to a purchaser, so check that this is available before you buy.

As with many other EU regulations, the Recreational Craft Directive is changed frequently, and if you want to read the latest version full details should be available at http://www.berr.gov.uk. Put 'Recreational Craft Directive' in the search box.

Most small sailing boats built before the introduction of the Directive will have a number on their mainsail and probably on the hull. Ask the owner to show you where this is on the boat, and check the number against that on any paperwork the owner has. And ensure that the hull number matches the sail number. If it doesn't, you need to ask why. Outboard motors have serial numbers, which should also be checked.

VAT should have been paid on any boat built in or imported into the European Union since 1985. If paperwork and receipts are available with the boat they should show that VAT has been paid. Availability of such proof makes life easier in the future when selling the boat or trailing it for a holiday abroad.

Most sailing dinghies have a number on their mainsail.

Thorough inspection and testing

Buyers of second-hand boats are often advised to carry out a considerable number of tasks, stage by stage, to check a boat thoroughly – particularly the more expensive sail cruisers. These include viewing it several times, in and out of the water, trying sailing it in different circumstances, and getting a professional survey done. However, this is the ideal situation in a perfect world, and requires considerable co-operation from the seller.

Being more realistic, boats that have been widely advertised at a reasonable or bargain price will attract many enquiries and the seller will be inclined to accept the first buyer to put cash in his hand. A buyer who goes away thinking that he can take his time to make a decision frequently misses the opportunity to buy. It's a careful balancing act between rushing in and buying on impulse – which may lead to later regrets – and thoroughly considering the purchase before buying.

It makes sense to inspect the boat as thoroughly as you can on the first viewing, bearing in mind all the points raised later in this chapter and elsewhere in this book. If you're satisfied with the boat's condition, then a cash deposit can be paid to secure it before someone else does. If any doubts remain, you could try stipulating that payment will be subject to a satisfactory survey, with possible negotiation on the price if the surveyor finds any faults.

Ideally, arrange to take the boat out for a sail before buying.

Taking a friend with you when you go to view a boat is a good idea – preferably a friend who knows something about boats, though even someone with no relevant knowledge can help you check the various aspects mentioned below. Two pairs of eyes are better than one.

Surveys

A boat surveyor will charge several hundred pounds and is more likely to be involved when the boat is a substantial size. For boats costing more than a few thousand pounds it can be well worth spending this money. A serious fault may be hidden to anyone but a qualified surveyor, and you could be saved from wasting a large amount of cash. More likely, however, the surveyor will find some minor problems that will enable a reduction in the price to be negotiated. This reduction may well be much more than the surveyor's fee. Ensure the surveyor will provide a written report, including a valuation.

If you have any doubts about the safety aspects of a boat, either don't buy it or get a survey done to establish exactly how safe and seaworthy the boat and its equipment are.

A recent survey report may already be available from the seller. This can be useful – especially if an insurance company wants to see one before providing cover. Three websites listing registered and qualified surveyors are:

- http://www.ybdsa.co.uk
  (the Yacht Brokers, Designers and Surveyors Association)
- http://www.iims.org.uk
  (the International Institute of Marine Surveying)
- http://www.boatsurvey.com

Be aware of insurance matters

Another point to bear in mind is that many (although not all) insurance companies tend to want a survey report on an old sail cruiser before quoting for insurance or continuing to insure it when it reaches a particular age. This age is usually 15 or 20 years, though this can vary according to the make and type of boat.

It's wise to check the type of boat you have in mind with several insurance companies before viewing boats, to establish their requirements and get some idea of insurance costs. There is more on insurance in Chapter 6.

Inspection: what to look for

Fortunately, with sailing dinghies and smaller sail cruisers simply spending some time carefully looking over the boat and under the hull, and checking associated equipment, will reveal most problems. Plenty of the faults likely to be found can be repaired with sufficient enthusiasm, time, effort, DIY skills, some expenditure on materials and the help of this book.

In order to inspect the boat fully it must be out of the water and supported safely off the ground. Be absolutely sure that the boat won't fall on you before going under it.

Old antifouling paint can look shabby, as it's designed to dissolve in order to deter the growth of marine organisms on the hull.

Magazine reports

Sailing magazines have published a great many reviews and reports on new and second-hand boats. These can be purchased from the magazines via their websites (see Appendix) or by telephone. Boat report reprints from several magazines can also be ordered via http://marinedirectory. ybw.com/reprints/search2.jsp.

Reports should include indications of weaknesses that have emerged over time for particular makes and classes of dinghy and sail cruiser. These provide a pointer to aspects that warrant careful investigation when you view a boat. More reassuring are the positive comments on a boat's resistance to wear and tear.

Many makes or classes of boat have active owners' associations, such as those already listed earlier and in Chapter 3. Their list of committee members usually includes a technical expert willing to give advice on what to look for when inspecting their type of boat prior to purchase. Remember, though, that this person is providing help as a voluntary service, so don't be too demanding. Remember too that they'll be enthusiasts for that particular type of sailing vessel, so may be a little biased and unwilling to be too critical.

At the end of a sailing season most boats will look rather shabby so bear this in mind if viewing them in the autumn. It's surprising how many people put a boat up for sale without smartening it up. This can be an advantage to the buyer, as any defects may be easier to see if polish, paint and varnish haven't been applied.

The antifouling paint used to stop the growth of water plants and pests on the hull of a sail cruiser normally kept on a mooring will look very patchy and thin when hauled out. Again, this can make it easier to spot any problems with the hull. Antifouling paint is usually applied in spring within a few weeks or days of launching. If it's applied at some other time of year, before you go to view a boat, could it be to cover any faults?

Wood

An old wooden or plywood boat may be cheaper than a fibreglass one but there are more potential problems, depending on how well the wood has been cared for. Superb examples of beautifully varnished wooden boats can be found. These can be a delight to own for a real enthusiast. The important point to remember, however, is whether you want to spend the amount of time necessary to keep such a boat in the same condition: it's often said that at least an hour's work repairing, scraping, painting and varnishing is needed for every hour of sailing.

Wooden boats more recently constructed and thoroughly treated with epoxy resin are much more durable than older boats without this protection.

On older wooden boats not maintained by enthusiasts, rot, cracking of dried-out timber and fillers, possible attack by wood-boring organisms, delamination of plywood and poorly carried out repairs to damage are the main problems. These tend to be quite obvious on close inspection but are sometimes concealed under layers of fibreglass and resin or filler, applied in an attempt to strengthen, repair or replace rotten wood. Rotten areas may feel spongy. With the permission of the seller, you could try pressing the blade of a screwdriver on to suspect areas. If permission isn't given, be suspicious.

A well-maintained wooden boat looks superb but takes a lot of work to maintain.

Wood not adequately protected with paint or varnish or reinforced with epoxy resin can quickly rot and crack.

Bubbles under paintwork can lead to this situation, where rot may be well established under the paint.

It's very important to inspect the interior of a wooden hull as well as the hull and decks. Rainwater is a serious enemy of wood: where it has accumulated in such places as the bilges, perhaps concealed under the floorboards, wet rot can do considerable damage. Condensation shouldn't be as great in the cabin of a wooden sail cruiser as in the cabin of a fibreglass boat, but if it does accumulate in corners without enough ventilation to dry it out, rot can set in.

Black stains under varnished wood indicate water damage, which can be dealt with if it's only superficial, but the risk of deeper penetration and rot is substantial. Bubbles under paintwork can also show water damage.

The plywood in a boat should be marine grade or at least 'water and boil proof' (WBP). Many plywood boats will have been constructed by amateur boat builders using plans or kits. They should have used epoxy resin and marine plywood, but if marine-quality plywood hasn't been used water is likely to have penetrated at an early stage and started to cause the layers of the ply to come apart, a process called delamination. This is unsightly and seriously

weakens the boat's structure. Ask the seller if he or she knows what was used in the boat's construction.

Delamination can be seen as swelling and raised edges along joints. Pressing down on suspect areas may show the surface flexing. Tapping surfaces with the handle of a screwdriver should produce a solid resonating sound – if a dull thud is heard there could be a problem. Unfortunately, even top-quality marine plywood can eventually delaminate if damaged or neglected. A seriously delaminating plywood boat is best avoided. Repair can be difficult and the cost uneconomic.

Fibreglass

Most of the sailing boats you'll find for sale will be made of glass-reinforced plastic (GRP), often referred to as fibreglass because the 'glass' is actually a woven matting of glass fibres. The word 'plastic' tends to be avoided, as the materials that bind the fibres are actually sophisticated and strong synthetic resins. You'll find more on GRP in Chapter 11.

Parts of many fibreglass boats are often made of wood or

Plywood delaminating under layers of deck canvas and paint.

Rot along corners and edges of woodwork can mean that substantial replacement is needed.

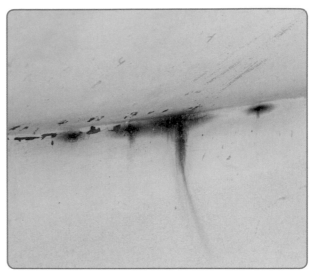

Above left and *right:* Rust where a keel is fixed to the hull indicates problems.

plywood – in some older sail cruisers the whole deck and cabin might be. Consequently the points raised in the preceding section on wood should also be checked carefully.

A particularly difficult type of build to check is 'sandwich construction', where plywood or some other type of wood is sealed between two layers of fibreglass. If this seems spongy it shows that water has penetrated into the plywood core, which can rot and greatly weaken the structure. If you suspect this might have occurred, either avoid the problem by not buying the boat or employ a surveyor – if doing so is really worthwhile.

To check the sides of the hull when the boat is ashore, put your eye close to the hull at the stern and look along its length. It should be smooth and regular apart from points where bulkheads or parts of the internal structure are attached. Any other bumps, ridges or flat spots that interrupt the curve may indicate damage, poorly executed repairs or distortion. This type of inspection can be helped by shining a torch along the surface of the hull to reveal any irregularities. In some circumstances wetting the hull can also reveal such problems.

Also look along the top of the hull from bow to stern. This is easier to do on a dinghy or open day boat than on a cruiser, where the cabin gets in the way. Look for any distortion or twist in the shape of the hull. Such defects could indicate serious structural weakness, damage or poor-quality construction.

Impact damage is often shown by stress cracks, either as a bullseye pattern of cracks or some other regular pattern. Gently tap round the cracked area with the handle of a screwdriver. A dull thud, rather than a sharp report or more resonating ringing sound, may indicate delamination, where the layers of fibreglass and gel coat are parting company and allowing water to penetrate. Check the inside of the boat at the location of the cracks to see how serious any damage is: has it broken the glass fibres?

When a fibreglass boat is hauled out of the water on a dry day, it should dry in a few hours. However, if there's still a damp patch it's likely that water has penetrated through a crack which may be concealed under paint. Checking for this 'weeping' of water is particularly important around the keel and rudder on a sail cruiser. If the keel contains encapsulated iron ballast this could be rusting, expanding and causing serious damage.

In a sailing dinghy or cruiser with a lifting keel, check the hull round the box that contains the keel for any damage or leaking of water. The stresses on this area can be considerable when sailing, and going aground subjects the keel to considerable leverage force.

Keels consisting of steel plates attached to the hull have bolts through the hull and into reinforcing plates on the inside. Check the condition of these both inside and outside. Corrosion of the bolts weakens the structure, loosens the fixing, and can allow water to leak into the hull.

Repairs to the hull that have been done well will be as strong as the boat, but look carefully round the inside as well as the outside to find evidence of any problems. Question the owner about any repairs. How were they carried out and were they done by the owner or by a boatyard?

Bolts securing a keel can be seen inside the hull. Extra reinforcing plates have been bolted through in this case.

A bad case of osmosis, shown as blistering.

Osmosis and blisters in GRP

The word 'osmosis' has caused considerable anxiety to owners of GRP boats. Much contradictory advice has been written on the subject, and this has led to some confusion. However, our intention in this section is to identify any problems a second-hand boat might have with osmosis, without going too deeply into the technicalities. For further information on the subject see Chapter 11.

The gelcoat which forms the plastic surface coating of GRP boats isn't 100 per cent waterproof. On some boats, where there may have been either faults in their construction or damage that wasn't adequately repaired, tiny drops of water are drawn through the gelcoat surface by a process usually called osmosis. This water then combines with chemicals and is unable to escape back through the gelcoat. The build-up of this liquid then exerts pressure which causes blisters in and below the gelcoat.

The more a boat is in the water, the greater the risk of osmosis. Sailing dinghies kept ashore most of the time are unlikely to suffer from it, unless water has been left in them or rainwater has been allowed to accumulate. Sail cruisers kept on moorings are more at risk, but if they're laid up ashore and dry out every winter the risk is minimised.

Osmosis blisters can be as small as a ladybird or bigger than your hand. Generally, the longer a boat has existed without blisters, the less osmosis is likely to become a serious problem in the future. For instance, a boat over 15 years old with a few well-scattered blisters, each no bigger than a ten pence piece, is unlikely to develop a serious osmosis problem during the next ten years of its life.

On the other hand, if large blisters are found this could indicate delamination and weakening of the hull. If a rash of hundreds of blisters covers the hull of a sail cruiser it's often referred to as 'boat pox'. This is expensive to have repaired,

and involves grinding away the gelcoat over the whole of the hull, which then has to be replaced with new gelcoat. This sort of repair isn't a task for the amateur.

It helps to inspect a boat for osmosis blisters as soon as it's been lifted out of the water, since some blisters can shrink and disappear as the hull dries out.

Sometimes blisters may be in a layer of paint rather than in the actual surface of the hull. Repainting could solve this problem.

It's important to wear goggles and gloves if closely inspecting blisters. Sometimes boat owners are advised to burst a blister to see how deep the problem goes. This can cause the acid liquid to spray out under pressure, potentially into your eyes and onto your hands.

If there are no more than a few small blisters a boat may still be worth buying if it's good value in other respects. They can, in fact, provide grounds for negotiating a reduction in the price. The decision will then be whether to leave the blisters to see whether or not they get worse over a number of years, or whether to remove and fill them with marine grade filler. Boat pox and large blisters indicating possible delamination are good reasons to look for another boat free from such worrying problems.

Bear in mind that evidence of osmosis will usually reduce the price of a boat when the time comes for you to sell it on.

Some boatyards carry out osmosis treatment, but check the cost before buying a boat that needs it.

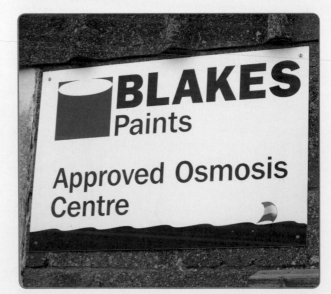

The discolouration on this hull could probably be treated and the original gelcoat colour restored.

Painted GRP

The surface of a GRP boat can stay in good condition for many years and you may be lucky enough to find a second-hand boat that still has its shiny, well-polished, original gelcoat. Sellers often make a point of advertising such a boat as 'unpainted'.

GRP that's had heavy use and not been polished with protective products will show discolouration through oxidation. This can show as yellowing on a white hull and a cloudy, chalky surface discolouration to the gelcoat. It may be possible to bring this surface back to a much more attractive finish as described in Chapter 11, but if not, painting is an option. This route has been followed by many boat owners, and second-hand sailing boats frequently have painted gelcoat.

Painted GPR isn't a problem if the paint has been

Cracked paint on this hull betrays a poor quality repair.

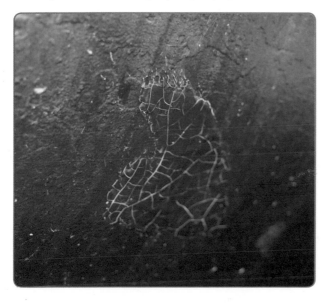

carefully applied to an undamaged or properly repaired surface. But herein lies the problem: paint is sometimes used to cover and disguise damaged or poorly repaired areas of the hull and decks. A coat of paint is, therefore, the cue to be particularly careful when carrying out the inspections described in this chapter.

Of course, once painted the hull will need repainting every few years, and too great a build-up will eventually necessitate removing all the paint and starting again. This task needs to be balanced against the work involved in polishing unpainted gelcoat annually to keep it in good condition.

Antifouling paint will be found on the underside of boats normally kept on a mooring. This, too, can disguise damage and repairs, so once again you need to look carefully at both the exterior and interior surfaces. Many types of antifouling paint can be quite easily rubbed or scraped from areas requiring closer inspection – with the owner's permission.

More recently some sailing dinghies have been manufactured using plastics heated in a rotating mould. Examples are the Topper and the Laser Pico. These are sometimes referred to as 'roto-moulded' boats. This type of hull is very strong and is often described as maintenance free. However, if damaged they're not as easy to repair as GRP hulls because welding of the plastic is usually necessary.

Decks and deck fittings

The interior of a sailing dinghy and the decks of larger boats take a lot of wear. The crew move about vigorously and tread heavily on the decks, while grabbing fittings that they expect to take their weight as the boat heels over. Everything therefore needs to be strongly constructed and secure.

The joint between the hull sides and the decks needs to be checked inside and out. See if the fastenings, such as bolts, rivets and screws, show signs of corrosion or

All deck fittings need to be securely fixed, as these stays and stanchions are.

This wooden rubbing strip can be replaced with a new one screwed into place.

looseness or are actually missing. Any gaps may mean bolts just need tightening and the join needs resealing. Any distortion is more serious.

Inside the cabin, leaks of rainwater from the deck join or other deck problems may show as marks on the hull interior. Inspect the outer surface for cracking that will need repair to make waterproof.

Rubbing strips round the edge of the boat are designed to absorb impact and take some wear. Expect some scuffing and damage on a second-hand boat. A new rubbing strip can usually be screwed on or slotted into place.

Non-slip surfaces moulded into the deck of a sail cruiser or painted into surfaces in a sailing dinghy should still be rough enough to stop you slipping when wet – they can get worn smooth and lose some grip.

Hatch covers made of wood tend to come apart at the corners while the more flimsy fibreglass hatch covers may have split round the edges. Open and shut the hatch to check the hinges or slides, and look for any distortion. Similarly, check the fittings and operation of locker doors, locker lids and the doors or washboards into the cabin on a sail cruiser.

All deck and rigging fittings should be gripped firmly and pressure applied to check for looseness. Cracks in the gelcoat radiating from bolts show stresses have moved a fitting such as a stanchion. Bolts for deck and rigging fittings should go through the deck and into substantial backing plates reinforcing and strengthening the GRP to prevent damage. All fittings, including windows, should be bedded in a thin layer of sealant or suitable gasket. These have a limited life and, once hardened or perished, can allow water penetration. Check inside the hull for any evidence of leaks: a powerful torch will help show up water stains, corrosion, streaks of dirt or rust, and a concentration of mildew stains

These windows have been given new rubber seals to make them watertight.

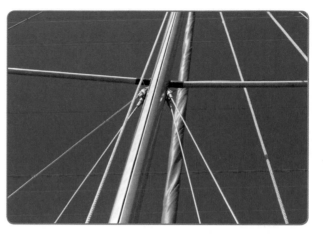

Stanchions and fittings have to be strong enough to take the weight of your body falling on them.

Spotting any wear by looking up at the rigging is impossible, so check the rig with the mast down.

where sealant has failed. The corresponding fitting then needs to be removed and re-bedded in fresh sealant.

A sail cruiser with lifelines or 'guard rails' stretched between supporting posts, called stanchions, provides some safety for crew moving around on deck, but only if the stanchions can take your weight and the lines or rails aren't frayed and about to break.

The rig

Consider all the movement and stresses experienced by the mast, its fittings and the wires and ropes supporting it and the sails. This is not a fixed, static system. All the movement – plus corrosion, even in stainless steel – causes wear and eventual weakness. It's therefore essential to examine the mast and rigging with the mast down, so that you can inspect it at close quarters. Don't rely on squinting up into the sky trying to spot frayed, cracked or dented parts. Those weaknesses can cause the mast to come down. This not only risks immediate injury to the crew but could also have serious further consequences as the mass of rigging and sails drags in the water.

Fortunately, this alarming scenario is rare because most boat owners are aware of the importance of maintaining the rigging. Just have it at the back of your mind when looking for faults.

The stainless steel wire stays that hold up the mast may have broken threads, causing needle-sharp individual wires to protrude. Take care they don't stab your hands when inspecting the rigging. Any such damage or other faults in the rigging make replacement essential, so consider this cost in your price negotiations. Ask when the standing rigging was last replaced. The stainless steel wires should be replaced every ten years even if they look in good condition.

Inside the boat or on the deck, check the mast step – where the mast is secured at the base – and look for any distortion, rot or corrosion.

Sails

Sails in good condition are a valuable asset, being expensive to replace. Overall condition is usually quite obvious. Repairs, tears, frayed edges, stains and broken stitching are easily spotted. However, there are some other points you need to look for. If a mainly clean and unmarked sail has a definite crisp stiffness it's likely to have had little use and been well cared for; old sails are soft and limp. Hoist or hold the sail up so that the light shines through it. If there are many pinholes in the sail panels – ignoring needle holes on the seams – then it's an older sail that may have little life left in it.

Good sails have quite stiff fabric in which no defects are revealed when light shines through them.

Second-hand sailing boats are often advertised as having extra suits of sails. One set may be older and useful for pottering about or teaching children to sail, whilst the best set is used for racing or serious cruising. Usually, the more sails that are included, the better the bargain.

Don't let a smart interior divert your attention from the rest of the boat.

A boat with its own purpose-designed road trailer is ready for a buyer to tow away – after checking the trailer thoroughly.

The interior

In the case of small sail cruisers, the interior is much less important than all the other aspects already covered. Attractive and well furnished bunks, cabinets and lockers with a shiny varnished finish are good to see but can distract you from thoroughly inspecting the boat's structure, rigging and fittings. In fact, some furnishings and woodwork may actually make it difficult to inspect the interior of the hull.

Having said that, a shabby interior is a good bargaining point, whilst bearing in mind that cushions can be replaced and wood can be re-varnished.

Have a good look at how furnishings are attached and whether any fixings are coming adrift. This also applies to the partition walls (called bulkheads in a boat). Sometimes they crack away from the hull or get distorted if the boat's been involved in a collision.

When inspecting the cabin, use your nose as well as your eyes. Boats left locked up for some time without sufficient ventilation will develop musty smells, but after airing out for a while are there still persistent and worrying odours?

Sources of odours include the head, or toilet, and leakage from tanks storing liquids such as sewage and fuel. Tanks, including the holding tanks for sewage, should be vented to the outside to remove methane and other gases. Wiping over any pipes with a damp cloth and then sniffing it may show up leaks not obvious to the naked eye. Check that the toilet operates as intended and that waste is efficiently dealt with.

Lift the floorboards and look into the bilges. Are they free of water, or are they dirty, oily and a source of the odours you discovered earlier?

If a cooker is fitted, ask the owner to demonstrate that it's working safely. Gas appliances should be checked regularly by a qualified person – ask for recent evidence of this, and if it's not available arrange for an inspection by a suitably qualified Corgi-registered specialist.

Electrics

Any battery included should be checked for age and condition. This should be a deep-cycle 'leisure' battery or a heavy-duty marine battery. Check electrical connections for condition and switch on any electrical equipment, such as navigation lights, to test it. For fuller details of the electrical systems on a sailing boat, see Chapter 16.

The motor

Second-hand boats should be viewed afloat as well as on land. This not only helps you check that the hull is sound but also enables the motor to be tried out if there is one. Most small sail cruisers and sailing dinghies intended for cruising and camping afloat will have an outboard motor. If it's not possible to try the outboard with the boat afloat, an alternative solution is to try operating it securely mounted in a tank of water. Running it whilst out of the water is dangerous and damaging as the cooling system relies on a water supply.

If the motor or engine starts easily and runs well with cooling water coming out, it's probably as good as any second-hand one you may come across. For more on outboards and inboard diesel engines, see Chapter 17.

Ask for details of when the motor was last serviced and whether a manual is provided. If you have doubts about the outboard motor or inboard engine, make the purchase subject to a satisfactory check by an engineer.

Equipment included

As previously mentioned, one advantage of buying a second-hand boat is the equipment that's likely to be included with it.

If this includes a road trailer, it needs to be checked carefully before use. Ideally it should be fully galvanised

A launching trolley is needed to launch and recover a sailing dinghy.

A typical tender, with good fendering to avoid damaging other boats when alongside.

and rust-free. Rollers should be free-running and an efficient winch should be mounted to help haul the boat onto the trailer. A problem with trailers used for boats is that they tend to be submerged in salty water while their wheel bearings are still warm from the journey, and as they cool, water is drawn into the bearings, leading to rapid corrosion. Particular attention needs to be paid to bearings. Do the wheels rotate freely? Are there any grinding noises from the bearings? If brakes are fitted, do they operate freely and efficiently? Is a working lighting board included?

A launching trolley should not be confused with a road trailer. The trolley is used only over short distances and to get the boat in and out of the water – definitely not to transport it by road towed behind a vehicle.

A small rowing dinghy called a tender may be included with a sail cruiser. This is used to get to a sail cruiser kept on an offshore mooring. When cruising and anchoring for an overnight stop you may want to tow the dinghy behind the cruiser so that you can use it to get ashore. Children often find that the fun they can have with a dinghy is one of the main attractions of family boat ownership. Obviously it will need oars, and if sails are included for it this is a bonus.

Safety inspection

In the case of boats to be used on inland waterways, see the section in Chapter 6 on the Boat Safety Scheme (BSS). A valid inspection certificate provided by an authorised inspector is needed for sail cruisers on inland waterways. The seller should have this available to show you if the boat is currently used on these waterways. Open boats such as sailing dinghies don't normally need a certificate.

As has been intimated elsewhere, water accumulates inside the hulls of boats, in the bilges. A bilge pump included with your purchase may be either electric or manual. It needs to work efficiently, and it's best to have both types on a sail cruiser.

The condition of other included equipment needs to be checked and a clear list of exactly what's included should be agreed. Later chapters in this book provide information on such things as safety equipment and anchors, etc.

Negotiating price and purchase

Try not to show too much enthusiasm or excitement about a boat, however keen you are to buy it. The seller of a second-hand boat is unlikely to expect the full asking price unless a queue of potential purchasers are keen to thrust cash in his hand.

The above checks are likely to reveal some faults that will provide you with a basis for negotiation. Make the point that defects found will cost particular amounts of money to rectify, and ask for a reduction. The ability to pay cash promptly will also help to achieve a reduction. A compromise price can usually be agreed amicably.

Small boats aren't necessarily registered in any way in the way that cars are. However, there could be useful paperwork available from the seller, such as insurance documents, Recreational Craft Directive paperwork (see the section on 'Minimising risks' above), harbour or waterway registration certificates, or local boat watch scheme documentation. It's worth asking for these. Check the sail number and any boat identification number you can find on the boat against numbers on the paperwork and get these numbers included on the receipt. Outboard motors have serial numbers, which should also be recorded. A receipt can then be provided by the seller after discussion with you about its exact wording. The RYA provides further advice on the paperwork involved in buying boats, particularly for those that cost substantial amounts.

5 New boats

Owning a new boat will make you feel particularly proud.

Buying new

If your boat-buying budget allows, buying a new sailing boat ensures instant pride in ownership through its appearance and up-to-date features. It should also avoid the need for the inspections and surveys that are involved in finding a second-hand boat, and will spare you having to deal with the faults that take time, money and effort to rectify. If any faults do appear, your warranty should cover them.

On the other hand, depreciation in price is rapid in the first few years of ownership compared with second-hand boats. These tend to hold their value, which can even increase if they're well maintained. So it's important to be sure that the new boat is one that you'll want to own for a number of years.

The majority of sailing dinghies and smaller sail cruisers are likely to be available to a standard design, and often from stock already built. However, you may get into a situation where the boat you order needs to be built especially for you. It may seem obvious, but it's important under such circumstances to be sure that you know exactly what you're ordering. Occasionally a salesman will be more inclined to sell you a design and specification he wants to sell rather than one you actually want and can afford.

Be sure you know whether the company you're ordering from is the builder of the boat or an agent/dealer. Also ensure that they're the company providing the warranty and are easily accessible – you don't want any problems if claims need to be made under the warranty. Niggling faults can occur with a new boat and you'll want to deal with a company that's willing and able to respond promptly, and is preferably not too far away from where you'll be keeping the boat.

Avoid paying too much as a deposit in the case of a new build; ideally you should pay less than 25 per cent on a boat that hasn't yet been built. Also, check the contract for reasonable arrangements regarding payment by instalments, and try to arrange for satisfactory sea trials of a sail cruiser before taking delivery and making the final payment. The British Marine Federation has a standard contract approved by the Royal Yachting Association and it's wise to check the contract for your own boat against this, taking appropriate professional advice if there are any uncertainties. The BMF website at http://www.britishmarine.co.uk is helpful and provides many contact details.

The delivery date for the boat needs to be clearly established, and if possible you should take the opportunity to include penalty clauses in case delivery is delayed.

As with any purchase, caution is needed to ensure a smooth transaction. Suggestions in this book do not guarantee or endorse the reliability of particular companies.

Opportunities to try new boats afloat are often available at boat shows.

Boat shows

Boat shows have a magnetic draw for those with even the slightest interest in getting afloat. Whether buying new or second-hand, or simply fascinated by the huge range of boating equipment on display, they provide a great opportunity to learn how to have fun on the water.

As a boy, the annual London Earls Court Boat Show was a highlight of my year. My Uncle Maurice was involved in its organisation and was well known to the exhibitors. He got me in free of charge – along with some friends – and gave us the grand tour. We gazed with awe at the vast and colourful range of magnificent vessels and their equipment, displayed in surroundings that evoked the joys of summer afloat, even in the gloomy depths of winter.

Since 2003 the original London Boat Show has taken

Even at the London Earls Court Boat Show, some boats are exhibited afloat.

place at ExCel in the London Docklands, and in December 2007 an additional London boat show was established at Earls Court. The number of boat shows elsewhere in the UK is also increasing, showing the growth of interest in this sport and leisure activity. The major boat shows currently held in the UK are, in calendar order:

■ The London Boat Show at ExCel in the London Docklands in early January: http://www.londonboatshow.com
■ The National Boat Caravan & Outdoor Show at the NEC, Birmingham, in February: www.boatandcaravan.com
■ The Affordable Boat Show at the SECC in Glasgow in February: www.caravanshows.com/scotoutdoorleisure
■ The RYA Dinghy Sailing Show at Alexandra Palace, London, in March: www.dinghysailingshow.org.uk
■ The South Wales Boat Show at Margam Park, near Port Talbot, in June: www.southwalesboatshow.co.uk
■ The North Wales Boat Show near Bangor in July: http://www.northwalesboatshow.co.uk
■ The Southampton Boat show at Mayflower Park on the waterfront in September: www.southamptonboatshow.com
■ The Earls Court Boat Show, London, in December: http://www.earlscourtboatshow.com

Boat shows provide an ideal opportunity to see and compare the many new sailing boats on display. The price can be established on the spot, along with details of exactly what's included. In particular check that VAT has been included, otherwise this can come as a nasty shock later. You can then determine exactly what additional equipment will be needed, find it on the appropriate exhibitors' stands and price it into your calculations.

Boats out of the water at shows also provide an opportunity to see the type of hull, rudder and keel. Some shows, such as the Southampton event, have plenty of new boats afloat, which will show you how they'll look in the

water. There may also be an opportunity to be taken out for a demonstration.

Because of the large numbers of visitors attending shows, many companies selling the larger sail cruisers have a booking system to view by appointment. This is likely to be essential if a demonstration afloat is offered. Although having to arrange an appointment can be frustrating, it

This page: Boat shows provide plenty of opportunities to establish the additional cost of the equipment needed for a new boat.

Above: Boats out of the water provide a rare opportunity to see the shape of their hulls.

Below: Special offers are often available at boat shows.

should provide you with a guaranteed opportunity to view the boat and discuss it in some detail. Of course, the viewing process is simpler with sailing dinghies and most small sail cruisers: you just turn up and look!

Special offers are often advertised for the boats exhibited, so some research regarding your preferences of boat type and class are recommended before you go to a show. You'll then be in a better position to make a decision on the spot to take advantage of any special show prices.

If you're not ready to actually buy or order a boat at the show, collect the literature for each boat that interests you and get the name and contact details of the salesperson you spoke to. This makes it easier if you want more information later, and you may even have more success in negotiating a discount.

If the cost of a particular boat is beyond reach it could be worthwhile to enquire if any nearly-new display, part-exchange or part-finished boats (for DIY completion) are available at a lower price.

Remember that you won't necessarily find every type of new sailing boat at a boat show, so it's still worth checking advertisements in the boating magazines and on the Internet. Some boatyards still build particular boats to order and may not exhibit them at shows.

Minimum standards for new boats

The Recreational Craft Directive was established by the European Union in June 1998. This introduced minimum standards for all new pleasure boats between hull lengths of 2.5m and 24m. It also divides new boats into four categories according to their seagoing suitability. As has already been mentioned in Chapter 4, these regulations change from time to time: the latest version should be available at http://www.berr.gov.uk. Put 'Recreational Craft Directive' in the search box.

Documents provided by the builder of the boat and the labelling on the boat itself should indicate compliance with the standards laid down for construction and equipment. If in any doubt about this, ask the builder or dealer for full information about compliance.

Self-build

An alternative to buying a new boat is to build it yourself. Numerous plans are available for self-build projects using marine plywood and epoxy resin. Kits of parts are also available for self-assembly. This topic is covered in Chapter 10.

6 Running costs

A secure storage compound for your boat will help you to gain insurance cover.

Keeping a dinghy at home and transporting it on a roof rack or trailer saves on storage costs.

accidents are rare compared with road accidents, but if they happen you'd want the other party to have insurance, and you may need to rely on your own cover if hundreds of thousands of pounds of third party claims are made.

Some organisations, such as boat owners' associations and sailing clubs, have arrangements with particular insurers to provide discounts for their members. A further advantage of this is that in the rare event of a dispute over an insurance claim, the organisation may help you negotiate with the company concerned, since the insurer is unlikely to want to risk damaging its reputation among that organisation's members.

Another tip is to ask your house or car insurer or broker if they do boat insurance. There are sometimes discounts to be had if you arrange your cover with a company with whom you already do business.

No-claims discounts can reduce premiums considerably.

Most insurance companies will want assurances that your boat is in good, safe condition. This can mean a professional survey is required for older boats, such as sail cruisers over 15 or 20 years old. It might be possible to avoid the need for a survey by negotiation – perhaps by getting a reputable boatyard to carry out an inspection or by arranging cheaper third party insurance. The problem with third party only insurance is the eventualities that it doesn't cover, such as the removal and disposal of a wreck if such a disaster should occur, as well as, of course, any damage to your boat.

The insurance premium will also be influenced by the location and security level of the mooring or storage for the boat and exposure to the risk of storms, vandalism, flooding or other damage. Remember to inform your insurance company if you decide to keep the boat in a different location.

Shopping around for insurance has been made much easier by the Internet, and the best way to find out what's available in a rapidly changing market is to use a search engine. Some companies provide online forms to complete and provide an immediate online quote.

Running costs need to be calculated before you buy a boat. Overall totals can range from an annual outlay of a few hundred pounds for a sailing dinghy to a couple of thousand for a sail cruiser kept in a marina.

The expense involved in owning and using a sailing boat tends to be related not only to its size but also to how and where it's sailed. A sailing dinghy kept at home and transported on a trailer or roof rack for occasional use will be the cheapest. If it's transported frequently to slipways, charges for launching and parking for the car and trailer can add up to a significant sum. In this case it may save money and time to arrange and pay for storage beside the water. A similar situation applies to larger boats like sail cruisers, for which a low-cost mooring might be chosen.

Whatever economical arrangements you may make for storage and actually getting afloat, there are some costs that can't be avoided. These include insurance, navigation licences, maintenance, equipment replacement costs and, on inland waterways, the BSS inspection. Motor fuel and servicing and club membership fees may also need to be added in.

Insurance

Everyone who owns a boat should have adequate insurance cover. Unlike car ownership, it's possible – though very unwise – to own a boat and to use it in some locations without insurance. However, there's a strong case for boat insurance to be made a legal requirement, and this could happen at any time.

In many locations byelaws and licensing regulations make insurance compulsory if you want to get afloat there, so always have your insurance documents with you. Sailing clubs invariably require their members to be insured. Obviously this is in everyone's best interests. Boating

Read the policy's requirements for maintenance carefully
In the past insurance companies have used the expression 'due diligence' to explain how boat owners are expected to take reasonable precautions to ensure the boat and its mooring are in a safe, sound and reliable condition. More

Considerable skill in sailing at close quarters is being shown here, but extra insurance is needed when racing.

recently there has been a trend to change this to more specific and exacting requirements, including the requirement for mooring equipment to be professionally laid, inspected and maintained at regular intervals. A further recent development in some companies' insurance conditions has been to specify that the boat, along with equipment and repair materials, be used and serviced in line with the manufacturer's recommendations. Consequently the following chapters on practical tasks include frequent reminders to consult product manufacturers' instructions in order to be able to comply with insurance requirements.

Cover extensions

If you decide at any stage to take part in a race it's essential to contact the insurance company to extend your cover to include racing. Understandably, they'll require a higher premium from you in order to cover the increased risks involved in racing. If you plan to take your boat abroad check that your policy will provide appropriate cover, and if it doesn't arrange for it to be extended.

Navigation licences

Unfortunately there's no overall licence for all waterways. Instead, each area or river is administered by a particular authority. The main ones are British Waterways (http://www.britishwaterways.co.uk), which covers most canals and some rivers including the Severn, Trent and Yorkshire Ouse; and the Environment Agency (http://www.environment-agency.gov.uk), which licences boats on the Thames, the Medway and many East Anglian rivers with the exception of the Norfolk and Suffolk Broads, which are run by The Broads Authority (http://www.broads-authority.gov.uk).

The situation on the coast varies greatly. No licence is needed for the open sea, but many of the sheltered locations where boats are likely to be launched are covered by a harbour authority. Normally a notice will be displayed beside slipways giving instructions on obtaining any necessary licences. This may be available from the harbour master, who'll collect harbour dues and fees for launching, provide keys to access facilities, and give valuable advice on safe boating in the area. Facilities might include such things as parking for boats, trailers and cars, visitors' moorings, short-stay mooring pontoons and toilets.

The charge for a licence is based on the size and type of the boat. Many are annual licences, but if you're visiting an area for a shorter period a cheaper one-week or one-month licence may be available.

It's not worth taking the risk of going afloat without the necessary licence, as the authorities do patrol their areas by boat and by foot along the banks where boats are moored. Fines for not having a licence can be quite substantial.

Mooring costs

Mooring charges for a sail cruiser will depend very much on the location and facilities, and might range from around one or two hundred pounds a year on a swinging half-tide mooring in a remote East Coast creek, to several thousand pounds in a South Coast marina with luxurious facilities.

Boats are usually hauled out for the winter to be laid up on hardstanding. A sailing club may provide this facility cheaper than a boatyard or marina. Such storage charges can, of course, be avoided if the boat can be taken home on a trailer.

In some areas such as the Norfolk Broads the freehold or leasehold of a mooring may come up for sale. Prices

Above and *below:* A licence is needed from the Salcombe harbour master to sail in its extensive sheltered creeks and use the substantial facilities.

Below: A mooring in an estuary is usually much cheaper than in a marina.

A marina may cost more but you also get the use of the shore-based facilities.

for these have gone up in a similar way to house prices, but if sufficient cash becomes available it might be worth considering such an investment if you're sure you want to make the area your base for boating. Although outright purchase avoids the cost of renting a mooring, check whether there are still annual charges to be paid, such as rates, ground rent or mooring equipment maintenance. Bear in mind too that you'll have to pay the cost of repairs to the quay heading or access roads, although this might be covered by any increase in the property value over time.

Boat Safety Scheme inspection charges

The BSS was established in 1997 to improve safety on inland waterways. All boats with engines, and/or lighting,

cooking, heating, refrigerating and other domestic appliances, need to have passed an examination by a BSS examiner before they can be used on inland waterways. Manually propelled open boats and open boats propelled only by outboard motors or sails don't need a BSS certificate.

Basically, then, certification applies mainly to sail cruisers and motor boats with cabins rather than to open boats such as sailing dinghies. Unfortunately the regulations

A BSS certificate is needed for cruisers on inland waterways.

do change quite often. It's therefore best to check the exact rules that apply to your boat, for a particular waterway, to check if it requires a BSS certificate. This is usually made clear in the documentation when you apply for a navigation licence and you'll be asked to produce a current BSS certificate before being issued with the licence.

The actual examination is rather like a vehicle MoT but has to be carried out every four years rather than annually. Another difference is that BSS examiners' fees vary considerably, so it's worth getting several quotes. Typical fees are between £100 and £150.

The examination checks that the risks of fire, explosion and pollution are minimised. A new boat should be built to meet the specifications. It should have the CE mark and documents showing that it complies with the Recreational Craft Directive. Check with the navigation authority for your waterway that this documentation will be sufficient for their regulations without a BSS examination. This should prove to be the case and an examination is unlikely to be needed until the boat is four years old.

If buying a second-hand boat on inland waterways, be sure to check it has a current BSS certificate or that the seller will arrange for a satisfactory BSS examination before purchase. A boat that's passed the examination previously is less likely to fail when re-examined, but faults could have developed in the meantime that may require work to be done, for example on the fuel supply system, gas fittings or the replacement of expired fire extinguishers. Any work on gas fittings must be carried out by a suitably qualified engineer and not by an amateur.

The full up-to-date *BSS Essential Guide* can be downloaded, and a list of examiners accessed, at http://www.boatsafetyscheme.com. A printed version can also be ordered. Additional safety advice is also provided on the website.

DIY or maintenance by professionals?

A major purpose of this book is to offer advice on the DIY jobs that can help you to keep down maintenance and repair costs. Much of such work is quite straightforward, but as with most DIY you need to ensure that safety is a top priority. In the case of boats, this means more than just ensuring you don't injure yourself or others whilst you work: you also need to be sure that your repairs will cope with the stresses of sailing. Having said that, a major advantage of DIY repairs is the fact that you'll save the expense of labour charges, which can vary from around £25 per hour to more than twice that figure.

How you value your own time has to be taken into consideration, of course. The amount of time needed tends to vary according to the materials used in the boat's construction. Any wood on the boat will probably need more time spent on it than GRP. The amount of use a boat gets will inevitably have an influence on wear and damage, but bear in mind that unused boats also deteriorate.

Specialised marine products are available from chandlers.

If you enjoy DIY at home, you'll enjoy the work on your boat away from home, in a different environment, preparing for fun on the water. This can make the money-saving aspect even more rewarding.

Materials used for maintaining boats tend to be more expensive than DIY materials for home maintenance. This is often because a boat exists in a harsh and very wet environment, and the strains put on it by sailing are considerable. Higher quality and tougher paints, fillers and equipment are needed, which cost more to produce. This has been used in some cases to justify unreasonably high prices, but the ability to shop around on the Internet and buy by mail order has recently led to far greater competition, and this has helped to make prices fairer.

It's sometimes suggested that certain household DIY materials such as cleaners, paints and so on could be used to keep costs down. However, though this might work with the best-quality products on a boat not exposed to the worst of conditions, you could still end up having to pay for the true marine products if the experiment should prove unsuccessful.

If a job's too big, affects safety or is too time-consuming for an amateur to learn and use the necessary skills, you'll need to get the professionals involved. As with all situations where work is to be carried out for you, ask for recommendations from people who've used the appropriate specialists, and ask several boatyards for estimates of the costs and/or their hourly charges for labour. Boat owners' association websites and general boating websites have forums where such topics are discussed. An example is the highly informative and entertaining Norfolk Broads discussion forum at http://www.the-norfolk-broads.co.uk

7 Moorings, storage and transport

Left and *right:* A boat trailer provides a choice of storage and launching options.

The availability of moorings and storage spaces varies from location to location. In some areas it's necessary to go on a waiting list before securing one. In others one of the least popular moorings may be available initially, with the possibility of moving to a better one when vacancies occur. Elsewhere, moorings may be available immediately, particularly if new ones have just been laid or constructed in a marina, boatyard or by the local sailing club.

Moorings are often advertised in the same places as boats for sale, *eg* websites such as http://www. boatsandoutboards.co.uk and the classified sections of boating magazines.

A mooring may be available to take over when buying a second-hand boat, providing the owner of the mooring agrees. Check whether there's a hand-over fee and exactly what the regular charges are. If you plan to buy a new sail cruiser or buy one from a boatyard, ask what help they can give with finding a mooring before buying the boat.

The combi trailer arrangement has the boat mounted on a launching trolley on top of a road trailer.

Trailer sailing

Sailing dinghies and most small sail cruisers can be transported on trailers, making them suitable for storage at home, in a club's boat storage compound or in a rented storage facility on land. This assumes, of course, that you have a vehicle that's suitable for towing your boat.

Check the weight of the boat and trailer against the car manufacturer's specified towing weights, and the nose weight, where the trailer attaches to the car. Also bear in mind the cost of having a towing hitch and electrical connections fitted.

Trailers need to be fully roadworthy and need to conform to the regulations. The *Haynes Trailer Manual* covers this very fully. If in any doubt about the trailer or your ability to

make it legal and roadworthy, local trailer specialists or car servicing garages will usually advise you and carry out the necessary work.

The National Trailer and Towing Association provides helpful advice on using trailers and on the current regulations, at http://www.ntta.co.uk/law/index.htm.

Check that your car insurance allows for towing. Your driving licence should also be checked to see if it covers towing the trailer weight involved.

Towing a boat on a trailer needs to be done at a slower speed than normal and care needs to be taken on cornering. Once you get used to it, though, towing a boat is fairly straightforward and somewhat easier than towing a caravan, as you can see the wheels and most of the boat, whereas a caravan blocks much of your rear view.

The most vulnerable parts of a boat trailer are its wheel bearings. If it's necessary to submerge them when launching, allow them to cool completely before you do so. As mentioned earlier, hot wheel bearings submerged in salt water will draw the water into them as they suddenly cool, causing considerable damage. Break-back trailers and combi trailers provide ways of getting a boat in and out of the water without submerging the trailer. The break-back trailer adjusts to lower the boat into its launching position, while the combi trailer includes a launching trolley mounted on top of the road trailer. This launching trolley slides off the trailer, launching the boat into the water.

Above: Check the boat on the roof rack before driving off. In this case a cat has taken up residence – and no, it's not a catamaran…

Above right: Remember to lock your trailer when leaving it after launching your boat.

Left and *below:* Finding space at home may be difficult, but the owners of these boats have managed it.

Roof rack transport

Some of the smaller and lighter dinghies can be carried on a car roof rack, but check carefully the maximum load permissible on the roof of your car and be sure to fasten the boat securely. I'm often accused of overdoing it when fastening a dinghy onto my roof rack, but I've seen the consequences of not doing so. I once only just avoided colliding with a boat that fell from another car's roof rack in front of my car.

I strongly recommend fastening the boat to the front and back of the car as well as side-to-side by careful use of straps or ratchet straps. This should prevent sudden braking causing an unscheduled launch onto the road ahead.

Storage at home

Wherever you keep your boat, remember to secure it against theft. Hitch locks, wheel clamps and chains with padlocks all help deter theft. Remove items such as the outboard motor, oars and sails before a thief does.

Low-cost slipways and boating locations

Trailer sailing is an effective way to minimise boating costs since it avoids mooring fees, although you have to get

Below: The use of this slipway is included in the parking charges for your car and trailer.

Above: Notices beside a slipway usually explain the procedure for using it and the arrangements regarding car parking, etc.

Left and *below:* Most slipways provide access to sheltered waters, but get local advice on tides and currents before launching.

permission and pay to launch at supervised harbours and slipways. The harbour master will provide any necessary keys for barriers and provide valuable advice on sailing safely in local waters.

Some public slipways are available to use without charge and many seaside locations are suitable for carrying a boat over the beach to the sea. Always get local information on tides, navigation and safety before launching.

Although some slipways may be free and easily accessible, you'll still need parking for the car and the trailer. This needs to be checked out in advance, as there may be problems of congestion and overcrowding if you arrive later in the day during warm summer weather at weekends.

Details of many slipways, with location maps, are available at http://www.boatlaunch.co.uk. The book *The Good Launch Guide* can also be purchased from this website. Local tourist information offices and navigation authorities can also help with advice on finding launching sites.

If you're a sailing club member it may be possible to get permission to launch at other sailing clubs. They often welcome visitors from other parts of the country and their facilities may be made available to you.

Below: Sailing clubs may give visitors from other clubs permission to use their slipway.

Harbour moorings and marinas

Keeping a boat afloat when not in use is sometimes described as pouring money into a hole in the water. This is a very negative view from a minority who don't understand the appeal of having a boat afloat, ready to sail away. How much you actually pay is linked to the facilities that go with this watery hole.

Marinas provide plenty of facilities, such as access to your boat via easily accessible walkways and floating pontoons, car parking, toilets, water taps, electricity and

Above: A marina provides plenty of facilities.

Left and *below left:* Jetty and swinging moorings offshore are usually much cheaper than a marina but not as easily accessible.

Below: A tender is needed to reach a mooring such as this.

security. Obviously, however, you have to pay for this luxurious level of boat accommodation. The most expensive marina moorings can run to thousands of pounds a year, depending on the length of your sail cruiser, fees being generally charged per metre per month or year. Also, beware of VAT: is it included? Also, are there any other extras, such as for electricity used?

By comparison, a basic mooring with few facilities on a jetty at a basic boatyard, or on a swinging mooring offshore, may cost no more than a few hundred pounds a year. But bear in mind that a boat on an offshore swinging mooring will need a rowing boat to reach it, and this will also need a storage space on land. An alternative is an inflatable dinghy carried in your car.

The usual practice is to bring a boat ashore at the end of the sailing season and keep it on hardstanding at a boatyard, marina or sailing club during the winter. Depending on the way charges are calculated, this may be included or may involve an extra storage payment. Taking the boat home on a trailer is a cheaper alternative. This process of laying up for the winter provides better protection for the boat from winds and weather damage and provides an opportunity for maintenance, painting and the application of antifouling paint before launching in the spring.

Maintenance of moorings

Insurance companies will want to know exactly where you'll moor or keep your boat, since the level of risk will affect the annual premium. If you keep it on an offshore swinging mooring they'll want to know that the mooring equipment is regularly and professionally maintained. More on this can be found in Chapter 14.

Above: Lifting out for laying up.

Left: This mooring buoy had broken adrift because of chain wear and corrosion, which demonstrates the importance of regular mooring maintenance.

Boat storage on land near the water

Boatyards and marinas have storage areas where boats can be kept for a monthly or yearly fee. A rapidly increasing facility at many locations, helping to overcome shortages of mooring space, involves a park-and-launch area for boats, with the facility for an owner to telephone the boatyard and ask for the boat to be launched when it's needed. After use the boat is taken out of the water by the boatyard or marina staff. Obviously there are charges for this service, but it can work out to be similar to or even cheaper than the cost of keeping the boat afloat in a marina.

Some campsites, caravan sites and caravan storage facilities are also prepared to store sailing dinghies and cruisers on trailers. This can be a cheaper alternative if near to a launching site. It can also be an option if there's no space to store a boat at home. Check that the boat can be kept away from children on the site, who may regard it as playground equipment.

Sometimes a co-operative farmer near the coast or waterway may find room for a boat in a barn for a small fee. Farmers are being encouraged to diversify and vary their business activities…

Top: Lifting and storage on land advertised at a boat show.

Right and *below:* Boat parking and launching on request.

Left: A sailing club is a much cheaper place to keep a boat than a marina.

Below: Returning onto a club's slipway after a race.

Bottom: A neatly organised dinghy park.

Sailing clubs – cheaper than marinas

Sailing clubs provide a much cheaper opportunity to keep a boat near the water. Clubs are generally non-profit-making organisations, mainly organised and run by elected committee members. The ones with the lowest membership and boat storage charges rely on voluntary work by their members to maintain facilities.

If you join a club and use its facilities frequently you need to be prepared to play a part in this – usually by joining working parties or a rota of volunteers for various tasks. This need not be regarded as a chore. Involvement with a club becomes an enjoyable way of life for many. Racing is a major reason for clubs' existence, and watching races and helping in various ways can be as enjoyable as taking part.

As well as community spirit, a sailing club will have the all-important car park and slipway, and may have dinghies or a crewed motor launch to reach moored cruisers. It will also have a sailing dinghy park, where the most active members have been given positions near to the slipway. Low-cost moorings for sail cruisers may be available through the club, although there could be a waiting list.

The membership fees of many clubs provide remarkably good value for money compared with the commercial alternatives.

8 Introduction to sailing

Watching others rig their boats will help you understand how to do it.

Wind-powered boating can be relaxing or exhilarating and exciting – it's your choice. But you first need to know how to sail. The brief introduction provided in this chapter will help you get started if you're new to the activity.

Preparation

Reading a book certainly helps to prepare you for sailing but you'll need practical help too, so try to get some experience as crew in your chosen type of sailing boat. Sailing clubs usually have sessions for beginners who'd like to crew and to learn how to sail. Sailing dinghy owners can't always find someone experienced to crew for them and may be willing to show you how.

Plenty of sailing schools and outdoor activity centres also provide courses where you're strongly advised to put the theory you've read into practice with experts to tutor you. Most run Royal Yachting Association-approved courses.

Unlike many other countries, the UK has the tradition of allowing anyone to go afloat in charge of a boat without qualifications or certificates. This freedom is greatly valued but could be removed if too many people take the risk of going afloat without any idea of what they're doing and get into difficulties. The Royal Yachting Association has established a range of qualifications and approves course providers. A list and full details can be found at http://www.rya.org.uk.

Courses are not run only in coastal locations – sailing club and sailing centre courses are available on many rivers, large lakes and some reservoirs. You could combine learning to sail with a holiday abroad, where the water is warmer for taking a sailing course and learning how to deal with a capsize.

Water sports centres provide sailing courses.

The Cruising Association provides crewing opportunities and courses for members and for non-members who're interested in learning to sail in a cruiser. Their website is at http://www.cruising.org.uk.

The RYA has special opportunities for children to learn to sail. Their 'OnBoard' programme is designed to introduce half a million young people to sailing over ten years, as explained on their special website at http://www.ruob.co.uk.

Many schools organise outdoor pursuits where learning to sail is an option. Youth organisations such as the Scouts also provide opportunities and some areas have a Sea Scout troop.

Sailing instruction on Lake Bala.

Watching and helping other people rig and launch their boats is good preparation for doing the same with your own. The first lesson in a sailing course will be on these aspects of preparation.

Along with the practical skills involved in sailing, you need to know about the effects of tides, currents, wind direction and weather in the area to be sailed. The local harbour master, sailing club, experienced local boat owners and up-to-date marine maps and charts will help with this.

Check the weather forecast – wind direction and particularly wind strength can change quickly or fog can develop. Plenty of forecasts are available through various media such as the Internet, local and national radio stations and television. In particular, the Meteorological Office and the BBC provide detailed forecasts via their websites at http://www.metoffice.gov.uk/weather and http://www.bbc.co.uk/weather/coast. Many other websites also provide forecasts for sailing. The coastguard broadcasts weather forecasts updated every few hours to VHF radios.

Obviously you'll also need to dress appropriately for sailing before preparing the boat. Remember that it's almost always significantly colder out on the water than on land, and that you'll need non-slip footwear. The most important item is your lifejacket or buoyancy aid, which you should first check is in good condition. Equipment and clothing are covered in Chapter 18.

Don't go out on your own until you've learnt to sail with someone competent in sailing skills. Always make sure someone reliable knows where and when you're going out in a boat and what time you expect to return. They can then take appropriate action, including contacting the coastguard, if you haven't returned and may be in difficulties. Obviously, you need to let them know when you've returned. Chapter 18 includes details on communication equipment and distress flares, etc.

A lifejacket or buoyancy aid is essential. Wear suitable warm and waterproof clothes as well, though – unlike the dummies shown here…

Rigging and launching the boat

Right: Push sail battens into the pockets on the outside edge of the mainsail.

Below: Push the battens down in their pockets or secure any ties so that they can't fall out.

Get the sails attached and ready to hoist before actually launching the boat. Some dinghies need the mainsail to be slipped onto the mast like a sleeve before raising and stepping the mast. Most boats, including cruisers, need the sails to be attached to their halyards (hoisting ropes) with shackles. The edge of the sail, called the luff, is inserted into the groove or track on the mast, and sail battens are inserted securely into their pockets before raising the mainsail.

The rudder and centreboard, or dagger board, need to be

Check that any bungs are inserted in drainage holes in the hull, otherwise you'll sink!

Have the rudder mounted on the stern before launching.

Trolleys should be moved clear of the slipway after launching.

positioned ready to put down when in deep enough water. Then, after launching the boat and securing it so that it won't drift away – probably by having someone hold on to it – move the trolley well away from the slipway.

Don't step into a sailing dinghy until it's actually floating, as this could damage the hull. When stepping into any small boat remember to place your foot as near to the centre of the boat as possible, so that your weight won't tip it as you step in. Also, keep low down so that you don't lose your balance if the boat moves, and watch out for the boom swinging at the base of the mainsail – a sailing dinghy facing into the wind when launched, to stop the sails filling and heeling the boat over, will cause the sails to flap and the boom to move unpredictably. Always get the boat pointing into the wind before hoisting the sails.

Getting away from the shore can be difficult; with an onshore wind you may need to use a paddle to get away from the slipway. It helps if someone nearby pushes you

Launching is much easier with the help of crew and sailing club members.

off, or if the crew pushes off before getting in – a tricky manoeuvre that improves with practice.

Then the wind fills your sails, and you're off – a thrilling experience. But at all times you need to watch where you're going and where other boats and hazards are in relation to you.

Don't forget to lower the rudder and the centreboard. The latter helps to keep the boat moving forwards rather than sideways.

Above and *right:* Hazards you need to be aware of can be both large and small.

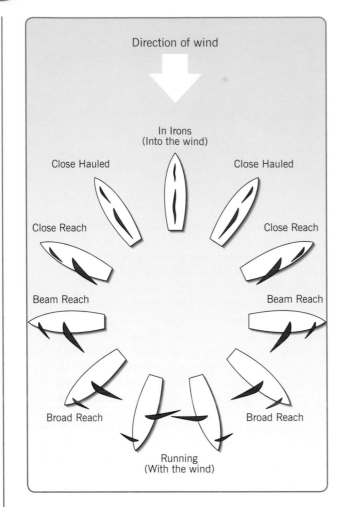

Direction of wind

In Irons
(Into the wind)

Close Hauled

Close Hauled

Close Reach

Close Reach

Beam Reach

Beam Reach

Broad Reach

Broad Reach

Running
(With the wind)

Above: These are the points of sail that depend on the direction of the wind in relation to the boat.

Using the wind

Whole books have been written on sailing skills and techniques. Below are a few basic points to introduce you to this most enjoyable process before you take to the water with someone who can cover everything that you need to learn.

The easiest way to start is by sailing on a 'beam reach': this means the sail is halfway out at an angle of about 45° to the centre-line of the boat. This gives you a chance to get used to the steering and control of the sails whilst moving quite quickly in a good breeze. The boat feels alive with the natural forces of wind and waves, and as you respond to these you develop the skill to make the most of them.

You sit on the windward side of the sails and this helps to balance the boat against the force of the wind. The mainsail can be pulled in – known as 'sheeting in' – and the boat steered to a sailing position called a 'close reach'. Steering closer into the wind will cause the boat to heel and you may need to sit out on the windward side to counterbalance it. Luff up to a 'close hauled' course by pulling the sail right in to where it's almost in line with the centre-line of the dinghy. You can't, of course, sail directly into the wind, but close hauling enables you to sail as close to the wind as is possible. Constantly adjust the sails so that they don't flap. You can then make progress upwind by tacking, as shown in the diagrams below.

When you turn into the wind the boom moves across from one side to the other, and the crew move to the opposite side of the boat. The helmsman calls 'ready about' to warn of this manoeuvre, and it's very important to keep your head down so that the boom misses you as it swings across.

Left: Sailing on a beam reach.

Below: Sailing close hauled.

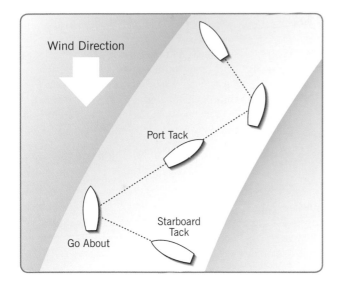

Wind Direction

Port Tack

Starboard Tack

Go About

Tacking involves sailing a zigzag course to make headway against the wind.

Sailing with the wind behind you involves 'bearing away' from the wind and letting the mainsail out almost at right angles to the boat's centre-line. You're now on a 'run', and the jib can be set on the opposite side to the mainsail in a 'goose wing' position (with the mainsail and jib out on opposite sides) to catch the maximum amount of wind and increase your speed. The centreboard can be raised to reduce resistance.

Changing direction with the wind from behind is called 'gybing'. This is best practised in a light wind and with someone experienced aboard, as things happen quickly. The boom can swing across with some force, and the boat needs to be carefully controlled so that damage or a capsize are avoided.

Below: Sailing on a run with the wind from behind and the sails goose winged.
Right: Watch out for other boats as you approach the slipway.

Returning to the shore

When approaching the shore take particular care to watch out for hazards and obstacles, particularly other boats approaching the same slipway.

It's best to plan ahead carefully, bearing in mind the wind direction, wind speed and any current running. When the wind is blowing onshore it's described as a 'lee shore'. If you approach the slipway directly from offshore you may not be fully aware of your true speed until it's too late. Be ready to spill wind from the sails and head up into the wind to slow down in good time before reaching the shallows.

If possible, on a two-sail boat, lowering the mainsail whilst turned into the wind at a safe distance offshore helps to reduce speed and make manoeuvres slower and safer under jib alone. You can let go the jib in the shallows and drift in. With the wind parallel to the shore or offshore (described as a 'weather shore'), the process and speed can be controlled by approaching diagonally and by spilling wind out of the sails as you approach the slipway.

Be ready to raise the centreboard to avoid grounding and causing damage to both the boat and the crew, who can be thrown forward as the boat suddenly stops. As you progress into shallow water, turn the boat into the wind and jump out, hold the boat steady and pull it up onto the slipway. Lower the sails quickly to get the boom under control and to prevent sail deterioration.

Get the crew to hold the dinghy while you collect the trolley and slide it underneath whilst the water is deep enough. Once you're up on the dinghy park, wash down the boat with fresh water and allow it to dry before putting the cover on.

On a sailing course, your instructor is likely to get you to practice leaving and returning to the shore several times to ensure you've mastered these procedures before doing anything else.

Racing

Olympic sailing and rowing events always get the UK a good collection of medals, although our highly skilled experts don't always get the same media coverage and recognition as other sports in which the number of medals is fewer.

Sailing clubs provide the opportunities, preparation and organisation for racing, and for many clubs this is their main activity. They organise the rules, courses, marshals and the safety boat to accompany racers.

Above and *below:* Racing is a major activity for most clubs.

Below: The majority of clubs will have a rescue boat to assist with races.

Racing enthusiasts travel around the country to visit open events and special events. The most successful are selected for 'The Nationals' for their class of boat and may go on to international events including the Olympic Games.

The substantial coverage that would be needed to describe the preparation of a boat and its crew for racing is beyond the scope of this book – the best way to learn racing skills is through involvement with an active sailing club.

Sailing a cruiser

In the case of a sail cruiser on an offshore swinging mooring you'll need to use a tender to reach the boat. This can be the most hazardous part of a boating session. All too often overloaded dinghies can be seen going to and from moored cruisers. It only takes an unexpectedly big wave, wash from a thoughtless passing boat owner, or the sudden movement of an occupant to swamp and sink an overloaded dinghy. It's much safer to load less and make more than one journey to the cruiser.

Stepping into and out of the dinghy – particularly to and from the cruiser – needs to be done slowly and cautiously. This is where many mishaps occur.

As well as tying the dinghy to the cruiser securely, at both ends, someone should hold it steady, and those left in the

Removing the mainsail cover.

Above: The mooring buoy shown here must be attached to the tender dinghy unless you take the dinghy with you, towed behind your sail cruiser.

Below: Keep a good lookout all round – something big may be about to overtake.

dinghy should be prepared for the change in weight distribution – the dinghy can tip up dangerously if all the remaining weight is at one end. Obviously, lifejackets must be worn at all times.

Once on the cruiser, getting started can be more relaxed than with a sailing dinghy. First attach the dinghy to the mooring buoy. Then, when you're ready, remove your sail covers and prepare the sails for hoisting. You have a choice of either sailing off the mooring, or getting away using a motor and then hoisting the sails whilst you're under way. However you do it, take care to look all around for other boats and hazards before leaving the mooring, and at all times whilst sailing. Keeping a good lookout is essential.

Keep your head clear of the boom and watch out for winches or pulleys that might try to trap your fingers. Otherwise, much of what's already been said above about sailing a dinghy applies equally to cruisers. You may have additional aids such as headsail reefing, winches and halyards taken back to the cockpit, as well as the motor, but you'll still need the all-important hands-on sailing tuition already recommended. Sailing as crew on a cruiser, with a helpful and patient skipper, can also help improve your skills before you venture out in your own boat.

Note that even in quite gentle winds the pull on the ropes, called sheets, that control the sails will be much stronger than on a dinghy, and you'll need to get used to using extra equipment safely, including winches.

Picking up the mooring and leaving in a tender.

Returning to the mooring, it's best to start the outboard motor and lower the sails. Those with plenty of experience can sail up to a mooring and drop the sails as the mooring is secured, but this is difficult for a beginner. The best approach under power is against the tide or the wind, depending on which force is the stronger. This will help to slow you to a stop whilst still maintaining your ability to steer the boat.

You could send a crewmember to the bows with a boat hook to catch the mooring buoy's pick-up line and secure the boat, but it can also be done from the safety of the cockpit. Run a rope from the bows back to the cockpit on the outside of all stays, stanchions and other obstacles and secure it before approaching the mooring or before setting off. This rope can then be threaded through the ring on the mooring buoy as you come up to it. Put the motor in neutral, and as the boat drifts backwards the buoy will slide along the rope to the bows. When you're ready it can be secured there. This reduces the problems that can occur if the crew and/or helmsman aren't experienced in picking up a mooring.

Practising boat handling in quiet conditions is worthwhile. If you miss the mooring buoy first time it doesn't matter – just go round and do it again. You can always tell those onlookers ashore that you were just practising your approach!

Safety

It's probably true to say that your road journey to the boating location is more hazardous than the risks involved in going afloat in suitable conditions. For probably 80 per cent of the time spent boating in sheltered inland and coastal waters in suitable weather, there's very little risk of accident. However, you do need to be fully prepared for the unexpected, such as a sudden change in the weather, submerged hazards, mistakes made by others and your own miscalculations.

The Royal National Lifeboat Institute and HM Coastguard are well-known for carrying out rescues, but they're also very active in promoting safety, and the following advice is based on their recommendations. For the RNLI's full range of safety information, visit their website at http://www.rnli.org.uk and select the 'sea and beach safety' link. For HM Coastguard, go to http://www.mcga.gov.uk and select 'safety information' and other relevant topics concerning risks, etc.

Both organisations publish leaflets on safety and the RNLI provides a booklet entitled *Sea Safety – The Complete Guide* with an interactive CD ROM. This information is free of charge, but remember that the RNLI is a charity dependent on contributions and that lifeboat crews are volunteers. Everyone involved with boating should join one of their membership schemes and contribute on a regular basis.

The RNLI offers free 'Sea Check' safety inspection to boat owners. Carried out by trained volunteers, this is a way of providing friendly and helpful advice to improve the safety of your boat.

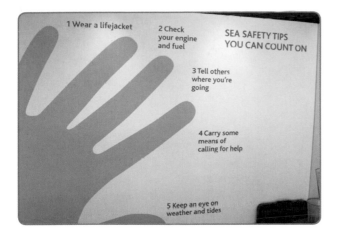
Five fingers safety tips from an RNLI display.

The Boat Safety Scheme, already mentioned several times in earlier chapters, requires a compulsory safety inspection and certification every four years for boats with cabins on inland waters. The BSS website provides excellent safety points for all boats whether for inland or maritime use.

The excellent and very thorough safety advice available from the RNLI and Coastguard could fill much of this book, so it's essential that readers consult their websites and/or their printed publications as part of the learning process before going afloat.

The most important piece of advice from the RNLI is that you should always wear a lifejacket. This isn't a legal requirement like wearing a seat belt in a car is – except under Irish legislation, which does require it, so the decision

Be aware of changes in the weather. A race was finished early to avoid this approaching storm.

whether to wear it in the cabin and cockpit of a cruiser is, of course, one for the individual to make. As can be seen in some of the photos in this book, some people also decide to risk not wearing one when boating in calm conditions, and they have a right to make that choice. But as the RNLI says, a lifejacket can only save you if you're wearing it – and people have been known to fall overboard even in the calmest of conditions.

Detailed information on buoyancy aids and lifejackets is given in Chapter 18.

Rules of the road

Under sail –
- Port tack gives way to starboard tack.
- Windward yacht keeps clear of starboard tack.

Under power –
- A yacht under power gives way to a yacht under sail.
- Vessels under power approaching head-on should turn to starboard.

General rules –
- An overtaking yacht must always keep clear.
- The skipper is responsible for maintaining a good lookout at all times in order to carry out the above and avoid hazards.
- Vessels of less than 20m length should not impede vessels having to keep to a narrow deep-water channel or vessels using a traffic separation scheme.

The Royal Yachting Association publishes *The Complete Regulations for the Prevention of Collisions at Sea*, which covers all eventualities for those carrying out more ambitious cruising.

Of course, common sense must prevail. Some boat owners may not know the above rules, so always be cautious and ready to take avoiding action if necessary.

The Yachting World Day boat can be used for camping afloat.

A Drascombe Lugger renovated by Tim Pettigrew and fitted with a tent.

Dinghy cruising

You don't necessarily need a sail cruiser with a cabin in order to stay on your boat overnight during an extended sailing session in suitable weather. Any large and stable dinghy, such as the Yachting World Day boat, can carry the necessary camping equipment. You then have the choice of finding a remote beach for camping or sleeping in the boat under a boom tent.

Sailing dinghies often have covers that go over the boom, which rests in a crutch at the stern. This is designed to keep the rain out when the boat is stored in a dinghy park, but it can also be adapted to use afloat. However, it may be necessary to improve the floor of the dinghy with boards to provide a flatter surface for airbeds and to protect the hull.

The Dinghy Cruising Association has many members who regularly enjoy this extra dimension to sailing. Plenty of advice can be found on their website at http://www.dca.uk.com.

Here the boat's builder, Chris Somner, demonstrates how a platform fits into it to make a flat base for airbeds.

Small sail cruisers – boats with berths

If the idea of camping in a moored open boat or beside a beached dinghy doesn't appeal for cruising there are two other options. One is to moor near overnight accommodation and the other is to buy a dinghy with a lid on – a 'mini' or 'micro' or 'pocket' cruiser. These small sail cruisers can be quite comfortable for two people. A cruiser with a little extra length can provide a quite surprising amount of additional room in its increased 'beam', or width, sufficient to accommodate a family of four or more for a holiday afloat.

Whether to take small children on a cruising holiday is a difficult decision. Even if well-behaved they can be unpredictable and get bored easily, so take plenty to keep them occupied so that they're not tempted to 'explore' where they shouldn't. Ways of improving their safety are not to allow them on deck and to have safety netting secured all round the boat. Obviously, they should also wear lifejackets at all times, and these must be carefully chosen to fit and support them without slipping off over the head. Again, the RNLI's advice on this is thorough.

Inside the cabin, with limited space, it's vital to have your storage organised and to keep clothing and equipment tidy. The crew need to take care with the limited water supply – remind them that it's not like using the taps at home.

It's wise to keep sleeping bags and clothing in plastic bags, or plastic boxes with clip-on lids, whether in lockers or not. It's surprising how spray, condensation and drips can penetrate the cabin of even the best-designed and maintained boat.

Netting provides additional safety when you plan to take children on board.

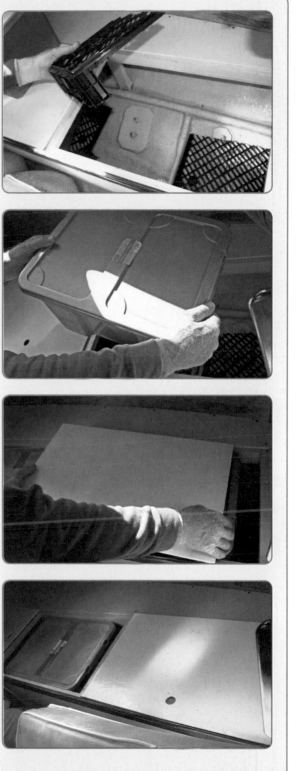

In this Halcyon 23 sail cruiser, refitted by sailing enthusiast Ian Davies, the lockers under the bunks have been equipped with cut-down plastic vegetable crates. These keep items clear of any accumulating bilge water and provide a level surface for waterproof plastic storage boxes with clip-on lids.

9 Basic maintenance and repairs

A new boat can be kept in good condition quite easily with regular maintenance. Older boats will need more effort and it may not be realistic to try for 'as new' condition if you want time for sailing as well.

Anyone capable of basic DIY can do most of the tasks necessary to keep a sailing boat in good condition, and most of the tools you'd use at home can also be used on a boat. As explained at the end of Chapter 1, most of the practical advice in this book is about straightforward maintenance tasks and basic repairs rather than modifications or the installation of extra equipment.

Perfectionist or pragmatist?

Boat owners tend to fall into three categories. The first is the perfectionist, who always has a beautifully clean and superbly maintained boat. After all the time spent keeping their boat in this 'as new' condition, a perfectionist may not actually have much time left over to actually use it. But if pride in having the smartest boat around is his way of getting the most pleasure from the boating experience, that's fair enough – provided he's not critical of those who prefer to shift the balance in favour of actually sailing a boat.

The second category is the pragmatist, who wants his boat to be well maintained, as safe as possible and reasonably smart most of the time. A sailing session will take preference over polishing when the weather is great for enjoying the boat.

The third category includes those who only work on their boat when things start to fall apart. Cleaning is rarely done and safety issues threaten the enjoyment of sailing. Obviously, becoming a member of this third category is to be avoided: neglected boats tend to sink.

The second category may well be the most appealing, and the tasks described later in this book are intended to strike a balance between maintaining your boat to a perfectionist standard and still finding plenty of time to enjoy sailing it.

Safety aspects

The safety rules that apply to the DIY work you do at home also apply to working on boats, but with some additional considerations. Obviously, if you do the work afloat on a sail cruiser you have to take care not to end up getting very wet, either by losing your balance or by damaging the hull below the waterline. The safest situation in which to work is, of course, on land, with the boat securely set up so that it won't tip over or collapse on top of you. Ladders and platforms need to be securely fixed.

All tools, equipment and materials come with instructions on the packaging or in an enclosed leaflet, and can also be found on the manufacturers' website. These instructions should be read carefully, even though the health

A neglected boat may eventually sink.

and safety details often include the irritatingly obvious. In amongst patronising comments such as 'take care not to cut yourself with sharp objects' are less obvious and important cautions you need to know about. This isn't only a matter of safety – some people take the misguided attitude, 'If all else fails read the instructions,' but misusing and wasting expensive repair materials, and incorrectly fitting costly equipment, constitutes a wealth risk as well as a health risk.

As mentioned previously in connection with insurance, the conditions and requirements for insurance cover have been getting stricter concerning the quality of boat maintenance. Policy clauses now place more emphasis on following the manufacturers' instructions provided with

Hazards are indicated on this cleaning product container, but it's also important to read the health and safety instructions often supplied in the small print on labels, leaflets and company websites.

Above: Special chemicals used with marine quality products can be toxic, so instructions should be followed very carefully.

Below: Some boatyards allow DIY work on their premises, where experts may be available to offer advice and provide materials.

boats, equipment and maintenance materials. Reminders of this will therefore be found repeated at times in the following chapters.

Suitable facemasks, overalls, eye protection, gloves and ear protection need to be worn even though they can be irritating and uncomfortable. The chemicals in boat repair materials are often stronger and more harmful than corresponding household DIY products. Toxic fumes and dust from using and sanding epoxy resins are examples, and antifouling paint

obviously has to contain harmful poisons to deal with the organisms that like your boat as much as you do.

In order to protect the environment from the above types of pollutants, place a tarpaulin where it will catch spillage, drips and any other effluent from work on your boat. All such waste should be disposed of carefully and appropriately. Boatyards, marinas and clubs are increasingly installing facilities for this. Plenty of advice on environmental issues for boat owners can be found at http://www.thegreenblue.org.uk.

DIY or not?

All electrical, gas, fuel and safety installations should be carried out or inspected by properly qualified engineers before use. An appropriately qualified Corgi-registered engineer *must* carry out gas installations and should be asked to do regular inspections.

You need to ensure that any other repairs you carry out can cope with the pressures of sailing, wind, waves, currents and the actions of the crew. One way to be sure of this is to arrange for it to be checked by professionals. If you do the work in or near a boatyard with co-operative staff this may be easy to arrange. They'll also be available to take over if you find some tasks are beyond your ability.

Where to do the work

Some boatyards allow DIY work on their premises when you keep your boat on their area of hardstanding. In return for

appropriate charges, they'll make available the necessary electricity, water supply and possibly shelter and heating inside the boatyard buildings. This has the advantage, as mentioned above, of specialists being nearby who can advise and, if necessary, carry out any tasks you may find too difficult. If you can establish this ideal arrangement with a boatyard you'll find it very reassuring, and you can still keep costs down by doing most of the work yourself.

If you have the space, taking the boat home on a trailer means you can work on it whenever it's convenient – although there can be distractions, such as the garden that's been neglected whilst you've been sailing. A garage or workshop can be used, or a tent-type cover can be erected over the boat. This not only provides you with dry working conditions but also the possibility of introducing suitable safe heating.

This is significant, because most paints, resins and fillers need a minimum temperature of 10°C to set or cure, and this can be a problem out in the open during winter. However, heating which involves a naked flame needs to be kept well away from the inflammable fumes given off by many repair products. Suitable containers filled with hot water may be able to sufficiently warm a small, enclosed space round a repair without any risk of fire.

Practice makes perfect

If you're not an expert at working with quite expensive paints, varnish, fillers, resins and other materials used in boat repair, don't start applying the advice in this book without first

practising where a mistake won't matter. For example, try varnishing a piece of scrap wood, painting the inside of a locker, or applying filler, glue, resins and the like in some out of sight spot where a bit of extra strengthening might be a good idea but isn't vital, such as inside the storage compartment of a sailing dinghy or day boat.

Before going into detail on maintenance and repair, the following chapter provides a brief insight into how smaller sailing boats are built using some modern materials.

Above: A cover or tent over the boat provides necessary protection.

Below: Materials and equipment for boat maintenance, repairs and improvement are available from chandlers, along with advice. Many also have websites so that you can order by mail.

10 Construction, self-build and materials

A Secret sailing in at six knots. This
lightweight racing gaffer is designed to be
sailed with a trapeze, and is based on a
planing hull.

Wood was the traditional boat-building material for centuries, and many books have been written on the building, maintenance and restoration of wooden boats. Here, however, we're concerned with the materials and methods that have been used more recently, as well as some of the basic aspects of boat construction using wood and GRP.

Boat kits and plans for self-build with marine ply and epoxy resin

Plenty of designs using these materials have been tried and tested over the years, and the plans, specifications, kits and instructions for building such wooden boats can be purchased from suppliers.

Kits

Building from a kit of parts can save a large amount compared with the cost of buying a newly built boat. One of the best-known sailing dinghies has been built from a kit of parts for decades, since it was designed by Barry Bucknell back in 1963. This is the Mirror dinghy. In fact my first sailing dinghy was a Mirror that I built from a kit in a friend's garage. Very kind and co-operative friends, Roger Kaye and his wife Judy, kindly put up with me drilling, hammering and gluing in their garage every weekend for several months.

The Mirror dinghy as a sailing class is still very much alive and well and over 70,000 have been built, including many in GRP. Kits for building in marine ply and for completing GRP Mirror dinghies are available from Trident UK (http://www.trident-uk.com).

Synthetic resins include the polyester type commonly used for GRP boats or epoxy resins which have greater adhesive and waterproof properties and are often used in building wooden boats, as in the examples below. The basic method of use is to mix the resin and the curing agent or hardener supplied with it, according to the instructions provided by the manufacturer. The speed at which it solidifies usually depends on the temperature, the humidity and the ratio of the quantities mixed together. Various resin products are available, providing a range of glues and fillers.

The following picture sequence demonstrates the construction of kit boats by Simon Tomlinson and Max Campbell of Whisper Boats. A range of boat-building kits, known in Australia as the 'Scruffie', are available from Whisper Boats (http://www.whisperboats.co.uk). This particular boat is the Secret.

These photographs were kindly provided by Simon Tomlinson and Max Campbell.

1 Boat-building kits are supplied with a great many hardwood parts, pre-cut to shape. They're shown here in the shipping crate.

2 The boats are built 'right way up' by adding components to the ready-made keel assembly, seen here on the left.

3 The ply components are supplied pre-cut, with small tabs that the builder has to cut through to separate them. The sheet shown here has two full-width frames, one half-width frame, and one side of the anchor well floor.

4 The ply frames have slots pre-cut in them that correspond with slots cut in the fore-and-aft components.

6 The first fore-and-aft components to be fitted include the anchor well floor. Wherever two-ply components slot together they're bonded with a fillet joint made with epoxy resin.

5 The frames fit into slots pre-cut in the keel, very quickly forming the shape of the boat.

7 Further structural strength and rigidity are added by bonding beams and stringers into the plywood frame.

8 This shows the top of the stem, where the deck stringers and the foredeck support beam meet.

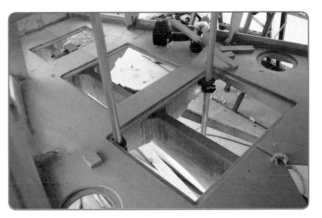

9 Beams are supplied laminated from the customer's choice of trim timber, with cedar for lightness, which ensures the correct radius. This area will be covered with a ply panel forming the transom.

11 The interlocking ply structure forms a number of discrete cells, which can be used for stowage and/or buoyancy. Stowage under the bunks can be accessed through self-made lids. Use of proprietary watertight covers allows the cell to be counted as buoyancy.

12 The ply frame and the stringers are in place, ready for the skin panels to be glued and screwed to it.

10 Epoxy will granulate if its temperature varies frequently, and this box, heated by a single light bulb, keeps it liquid. Granulation can be reversed by gently heating the epoxy, perhaps in a bath of hot water.

13 The cabin has been built and veneered using silky oak, an Australian timber. These veneers are 4 to 5mm thick and add to the structural strength.

14 After the top skin panels are fitted with the boat 'right way up', it's turned over and the bottom panels are fitted. The hull is then faired with epoxy filler.

15 Fibreglass sheathing adds structural strength and abrasion resistance, and the epoxy resin is immune to the problems of osmosis that occur with most resins used in GRP boat production.

16 The boat is painted whilst it's upside-down. The cabin will be built after turning her 'right way up' again.

17 The final stages of the build, such as building and trimming the cabin, are under way. The bowsprit, at 6ft, allows the Secret to fly a big asymmetric gennaker sail to help get her on the plane.

A number of kits use similar construction methods to the original Mirror dinghy. The example illustrated below is a 12ft Northumbrian Coble, under construction by David Pertwee. The kit, one of a number produced by Alec Jordan of Jordan Boats (www.jordanboats.co.uk), is assembled from pre-cut marine plywood parts using the 'stitch and glue' method of construction.

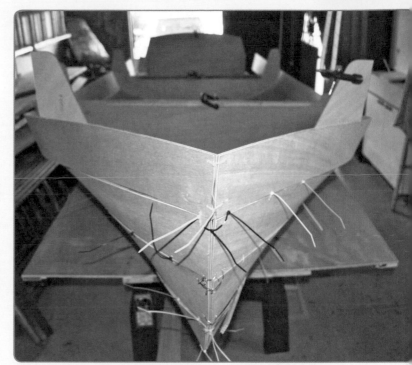

The shape of a Coble built from a kit appears as the planks of plywood are 'stitched' together with copper wire and, in this case, plastic cable ties, which David Pertwee prefers to use on many of the joints.

Epoxy resin is applied to the joints and the supporting ties are gradually removed as fibreglass tape soaked in epoxy is used to seal the joints. Several more layers of resin are applied and the surface is 'faired off', *ie* sanded smooth ready for finishing with paint or varnish. Further work follows to glue and screw additional parts such as the gunwales, seats, centreboard case and the fittings and rig needed on a sailing dinghy.

Opposite: David Williams's sail cruiser.

Completion of partly built sailing boats

Another way to save money on a new boat is to buy one that's been only partly built and then complete it yourself, thus saving on the labour costs involved with a fully completed boat. This provides an alternative for those who lack the time or inclination to build from plans or a kit. It also means that there's the possibility of having a GRP hull rather than the wooden one anticipated in most plans and kits.

Plenty of boat builders can be asked if a partly completed boat can be supplied instead of a fully completed version. There may already be several levels of completion available and priced but not necessarily publicised.

Equipment not included

In calculating the overall cost of kit boats and self-completion projects, remember to allow for the equipment that's not included, such as anchors, ropes, rigging, sails and outboard motor.

The European Recreational Craft Directive and self-build

The European Recreational Craft Directive applies to self-built boats if they're sold within five years of being built. As you can't be sure whether you'll sell the boat in that time, it's important to be familiar with the Directive's rules and requirements.

A future buyer will want to see the necessary documentation and there are heavy fines for anyone convicted of selling a qualifying boat built since June 1998 without the necessary evidence of compliance. As mentioned in earlier chapters, the regulations change from time to time, so be sure to check the latest rules and procedures for compliance. These are available on the Internet at http://www.berr.gov.uk. Put 'Recreational Craft Directive' in the search box. Suppliers of kits and partly-built boats will also give advice on the regulations and may do much of the work towards compliance for you. Be sure to ask about this before you order the kit.

Some very skilled, talented and determined future boat owners actually design and build their own boats from scratch. An example is David Williams, whose superb sail cruiser is pictured below. His boat has been exhibited and admired at the Norfolk Broads Green Boat Show. It was built mainly using wood, uses the wind for its main propulsion and has a silent and clean electric motor for auxiliary propulsion.

Top and *right:* The cabin roof raises to provide more headroom.

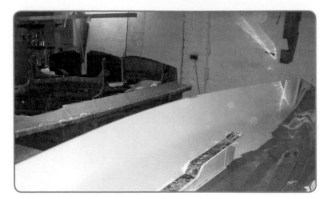

Left and *above:* Mould preparation and application of the gelcoat that forms the smooth surface of the hull of a Contender.

GRP construction

GRP boats can't easily be constructed by amateurs, as special moulds and controlled workshop conditions are required along with substantial knowledge and experience of boat building. The following examples should, however, provide a basic understanding of GRP construction.

The first group of photographs show the hull of a Contender sailing dinghy being moulded at Chris Somner Dinghy Services (http://www.cserve.co.uk).

The second series shows some of the initial stages of construction of a Drascombe sail cruiser being built at Churchouse Boats Ltd (http://www.drascombe.org.uk).

Roto-moulded hulls

As mentioned in Chapter 4, the method of constructing the hulls of some dinghies involves the use of a rotating mould to produce a tough plastic shell. Polymer powder is placed into the mould, which is then heated in an oven and rotated to tumble the powder. The latter melts and sticks to the inside of the mould to build up an even surface. When cool the shell of the dinghy is removed and construction then continues. Buoyancy is provided by means of plastic foam.

Left and *below:* The application of layers of fibreglass saturated with synthetic resin, and a foam core, is followed by the fixing of internal stiffeners.

Right: The deck is bonded to the hull and further construction continues on this Drascombe cruiser.

Below: The finished Drifter 22 in its fully fitted glory on its boat show stand.

Above and *right:* The moulds for the hull and deck are prepared and coated with two layers of gelcoat. Fibreglass lay-up follows.

Below and *bottom*: The deck and cabin mouldings are removed from the mould.

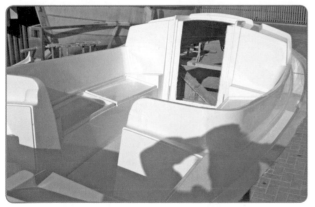

11 The hull and decks

Repairs to wood and plywood

Although wood was overtaken by GRP as the main material for leisure boats in the mid-20th century, there has been a resurgence of boat building using marine ply and other timbers treated with epoxy resins, as described in the previous chapter. These make wooden boats much more waterproof on a long-term basis and can therefore compete, to a certain extent, with the advantages of GRP. An epoxy-treated boat should need much less maintenance than an untreated, traditionally painted and varnished wooden boat. Even so, the epoxy finish has to be protected from sunlight by paint or a suitable protective varnish.

The emphasis here is on boats that have GRP hulls rather than wooden sail cruisers requiring substantial repairs. However, the care and maintenance of plywood and some woodwork is relevant to many dinghies and sail cruisers partly built from or fitted out using these materials.

The most important consideration is to keep all wood covered with a protective film of paint, varnish or other preservative coating. Any damage to this coating therefore needs to be touched-up as soon as it occurs. Full replacement of the protection can then be carried out at the end of the sailing season.

The salt in sea water gives it an antiseptic quality that makes it less likely to cause wood rot than fresh water. In fact it's fresh water from rain that does the most damage, along with weathering – the effects of sunlight and the

Weathering from sunlight and rain attacks unprotected wood. In this instance it has also caused the plywood to delaminate.

Many boats made of synthetic materials also have parts made of wood that need to be maintained.

expansion and contraction caused by heating from the sun and wetting and drying.

Wherever water can accumulate and persist, rot is likely to set in. In the case of unprotected plywood it also causes the resins binding the layers of wood to fail. The resulting delamination is difficult to treat on a boat and will usually mean replacement is necessary in order to maintain a safe level of strength.

Painting wood

Many sailing dinghies are made of plywood and need painting regularly. Some GRP sail cruisers also have woodwork that needs to be painted, and most dinghies and cruisers have some woodwork in need of varnish or woodsealer. The preparation of wood for painting, and the application of traditional paints, or one-part paints, is very similar to that needed for varnishing. This is described below.

Two-part polyurethane paints, requiring the mixing of base paint and hardener before use, are not as flexible as one-part paints. They're good for painting GRP, but one-part paints can cope better with the more flexible surface and varying moisture content of wood. Two-part paints should not be used to overpaint existing areas of one-part paint.

Appropriate primers and undercoats should be used with all paints. The manufacturers' instructions on their tins and leaflets provide appropriate advice for each type.

Painting the gelcoat of a GRP boat is covered on pages 103, 104 and 105 which should be read for additional advice that can also be applied to the painting of wood.

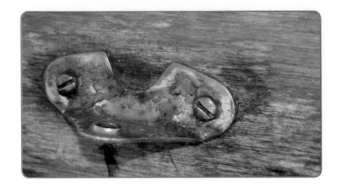

Neglected varnish spoils the appearance of woodwork.

Varnish and alternatives

Shiny varnished wood looks beautiful when in good condition, but the problem with this beauty is its fragility. Even a little varnished woodwork improves the appearance of an otherwise ordinary boat, but neglected varnish has the opposite effect.

However, peeling varnish and discoloured wood can be avoided. The main preventative measure is to touch up every little scratch and scuff before water gets a chance to

enter and lift much more of the varnish. Then you need to give the varnished area a new coat at least once a year. This commitment is required for most types of varnish.

If you don't want to do this, strip the varnish off as described below and either paint the woodwork or apply sealer or an oil-based preservative such as Burgess wood sealer. A new coat of woodsealer can then easily be applied each year. Oily wood, such as the teak in the photographs, is often more successfully treated with sealer than with varnish.

Assuming that you want to persevere with glossy varnished woodwork such as rubbing strips, hatch covers and grab rails, the following description takes you through the process of stripping back to bare wood and applying the necessary coats.

It's important to wear a suitable mask or respirator before any of the following work. Make sure it fits tightly to filter out harmful dust and fumes.

On flat solid wood, varnish can be removed quickly by the careful use of an electric belt sander, detail sander or various types of scraper. Take care not to gouge the wood and always sand along the grain – not across it – to avoid scratches showing up in the varnish later. The rounded shape of wooden masts and spars will need careful scraping

A teak rubbing strip being treated with wood sealer instead of varnish.

Marine wood sealer provides a finish that's not as shiny as varnish but is easier to maintain.

Weathered wood can be sanded carefully by hand with 120-grade paper and then cleaned with white spirit before applying wood sealer.

Varnished horizontal surfaces deteriorate more rapidly because they receive more intense sunlight.

Above: A belt sander can remove old varnish rapidly from the flat surfaces of solid wood.

Right and *below:* Removing varnish from awkward surfaces.

Above: Careful sanding is needed to get a smooth scratch-free surface.

Right: Take care not to remove the top layer of plywood.

Below: A traditional type of varnish.

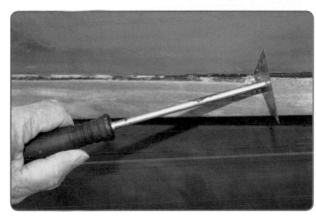

and sanding by hand to preserve their profile. Finish with medium, then fine, abrasive paper to get a smooth surface.

Chemical paint and varnish remover can be used. This helps to reduce the amount of sanding necessary. The gel type reduces the risk of it running onto surrounding areas, where it might damage any GRP gelcoat surfaces. The remover needs to be cleaned off once it's had the necessary effect. This is usually done with white spirit.

On plywood, the process of stripping varnish is more delicate. The top layer of the plywood provides the attractive wood grain. Unfortunately, however, it's usually very thin, and overenthusiastic scraping or sanding can penetrate the top layer to reveal the ugly contrasting layer below.

A confusingly large range of varnishes exists. Some, such as the two-part varnishes, are harder than others and may last longer. Many are intended for the wooden boat enthusiast who knows exactly how he wants his varnish to

perform. The problem with the more sophisticated harder varnishes is the difficulty of touching them up and removing them completely at some time in the future. You may therefore want to choose a straightforward traditional original-style or one-part varnish. This can be touched-up, over-coated and later removed more easily than many harder varnishes. Remember that sunlight damages varnish, so check that the varnish you choose has ultraviolet inhibitors.

Use a cloth or brush to remove dust. A vacuum cleaner is also useful here. The use of a 'tack rag' is often recommended to remove dust before applying coats of varnish or paint. These are cloths impregnated with suitable substances to lift dust. However, if you use them you should only use light strokes, as there's a risk that some of the chemicals in the rag could be spread onto the wood, reducing adhesion of the varnish.

Remove all traces of dust from the surface of the wood using a cloth dampened with white spirit or a tack rag.

If varnishing outside, check the weather forecast: you need dry weather, preferably with little or no wind, which could blow dust onto the wet varnish. Don't varnish when fog or dew might form and ruin the finish as it tries to dry. Unfortunately, bright hot sunlight can also be a problem, since it makes the varnish dry more rapidly than it should, which can cause blistering.

Never shake a tin of varnish, as this can cause vast

Varnish should be gently stirred, not shaken.

Pour some into a container before you start varnishing.

Right and *below:*
Thin the varnish with white spirit and stir gently.

numbers of troublesome bubbles. For the same reason stir it only gently. Don't apply varnish straight from the can: pour a small amount into a clean container and then put the lid back on the varnish tin. This protects the bulk of your varnish from contamination.

The traditional way to seal and prime bare wood is to thin the varnish with about 15 per cent white spirit or according to the instructions on the tin. Alternatively, you can buy special clear wood sealer to use before the varnish, but this can cost three times as much as using thinned varnish and doesn't automatically achieve better results.

Use a good quality brush. With a new brush it's worth checking for loose bristles before you start – even the best brushes seem to lose the odd bristle, dragged out by the sticky varnish. Apply the thinned varnish sparingly and fairly

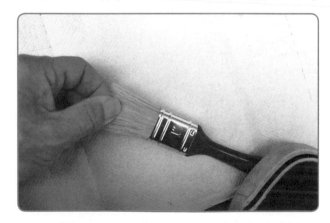

Remove any loose bristles before using the brush.

Brushing a layer of thinned varnish will change the colour of the wood as it soaks in.

quickly. The wood will change colour as most of the thinned varnish soaks into it.

Leave this first coat to dry overnight and then sand lightly with a fine grade of sandpaper to smooth any roughness and to key the next coat. Remove any dust and apply a full coat of unthinned varnish. Take care not to apply too much at once and watch for sags and runs if you overdo it. They need to be brushed out promptly before the varnish gets tacky.

Remove any sags or runs before the varnish starts to set.

After replacing the lid firmly, slowly turn the can upside down to seal the lid and avoid a skin forming on the remaining varnish.

To achieve a gloss finish and good protection for the wood apply at least two more coats, leaving each to dry overnight. For a mirror finish you may need a total of six coats, though this will depend on your enthusiasm and patience.

Epoxy repairs to wood

If you've damaged the wooden decks on a GRP sailing boat or are determined to repair an old wooden boat, modern epoxy products have been produced to make repairing and strengthening your boat much easier. Don't be tempted to use cheaper alternatives such as car body filler; this can't cope with the marine environment and disastrous leaks could ensue if it's used to repair the hull.

Epoxy products come with detailed instructions, and the website of Wessex Resins and Adhesives, one of the manufacturers of epoxy products, at http://www.wessex-resins.com has much helpful information on wooden boat restoration. The company also produces publications such as *Wooden Boat Restoration and Repair*.

Further information on the use of epoxy on wood can be found in Chapters 10 and 13, in connection with boat construction and repairs to a wooden mast.

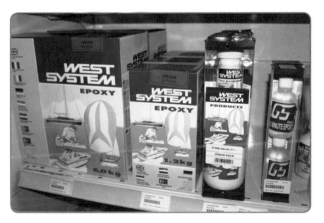

West System Epoxy products, from Wessex Resins and Adhesives.

Cleaning, polishing and preservation

Fibreglass boats are sometimes referred to as 'maintenance free'. However, although they may need less maintenance than a wooden boat they still need cleaning and polishing. Surface dirt can be washed off with water and a mop. A hosepipe or pressure washer can be used on a sailing dinghy, but on a sail cruiser you'll need to take care that water isn't forced into air vents or through other gaps such as joints round hatch covers.

More persistent dirt and stains will require the use of cleaning fluids. Take care with these too and be sure to rinse them off immediately, since there's a risk of some commonly used chemicals etching into the gelcoat surface if left to dry on it.

'Simply Gone' removes algae.

Special products for removing rust stains and yellow waterline stains.

Above and *right:* Brush Y-10 onto the stain.

Below: Leave for a few minutes.

Thick growth on a neglected boat can be dealt with by spraying or brushing it with 'Simply Gone'.

Green algae grow on GRP surfaces quite rapidly in warm and damp conditions. They can be wiped off smooth surfaces but are difficult to remove from non-slip deck surfaces, even with vigorous scrubbing. A product that kills such growths, makes removal much easier and helps prevent re-growth is 'Simply Gone'. This is advertised as harmless when left on boat surfaces. It's sold as a concentrated liquid, which is diluted according to instructions provided, and then sprayed or brushed onto the algae and left for a few days to kill it. The algae turn black. They're then easily removed and may even get washed off by rain without scrubbing. If not available locally it can be ordered from the company's website at http://www.simplygone.com.

Particularly persistent stains occur along and just above the waterline. A product called 'Y10 Stain Absorbent Gel' removes these and will also shift rust stains from the deck. It contains poisonous oxalic acid, so, as when using all chemicals, wear suitable gloves. You simply brush it onto the stains, leave it for a few minutes and the stains fade away before your very eyes, without scrubbing – though a little agitation with the brush might be necessary to spread the gel and remove all signs of staining. You need to rinse it off thoroughly after use. Although it's formulated not to damage GRP or painted surfaces it's not a good idea to leave acid on the gelcoat.

Above: Agitate the gel with the brush.

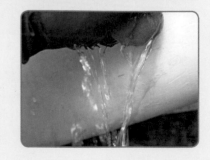

Right: Rinse off thoroughly.

Oxidation

The sides of the hull above the waterline and GRP decks will lose their shiny surface and discolour as the boat ages. Sunlight is the main cause of this, along with abrasion, dirt and salt water.

Rinse a sailing dinghy with fresh water after every use if possible and cover it thoroughly when dry to protect it from the sun. The application of a suitable wax polish helps to protect the gelcoat and gives it a good shine. It also reduces drag and helps increase a sailing dinghy's speed through the water. Obviously, rinsing and covering can't easily be done with a sail cruiser on a mooring, so the boat needs to be polished instead, both to protect it and to restore its shiny surface when it becomes dull.

As the boat ages, oxidation will eventually cause the gelcoat to roughen slightly and coloured surfaces will become cloudy-looking. Mild to moderate oxidation shows as dullness which polish won't remove; there's no reflection in the surface at this stage. Severe oxidation is indicated by a chalky powder that can be wiped off the gelcoat with your fingers.

Above: Cleaning and polishing the hull not only makes a boat look smart but protects its surfaces from oxidation.

Below: Hose down a sailing dinghy after use to rinse off the dirt.

Above: Oxidation and scratches on an old boat.

Right: Oxidation causes a chalky powder to form that comes off on your fingers.

Polish protects
against further
oxidation.

Above and *right:*
Products for
restoring the
surface of gelcoat.

When polishing will no longer bring back the original shine it's possible to restore it with oxidation remover. Various grades of remover are available. As they remove a thin layer of the gelcoat, be sure you don't use an abrasive restorer that's stronger than necessary. The instructions on the remover will indicate how to use it and whether it should be rubbed until it disappears or should be left to dry before being rubbed off. Check the cloth you use for build-up of the surface material being removed and change to a clean cloth frequently in order to prevent scratching.

Removing oxidation can take considerable energy and you may want to do one side of the boat at a time, leaving you the opportunity and remaining energy to polish the newly restored gelcoat. It's quite important to get polish onto the new shiny surface as soon as possible in order to preserve it. Electrically-powered polishers can be used, but be careful to keep the rotating head moving so as to avoid building up heat through friction, as heat could damage the gelcoat.

Although hard work, the process of removing oxidation is more rewarding than many, as you're likely to see your boat return to its former shiny self.

When polishing, avoid getting polish on the non-slip surfaces where you tread. These are best kept clean by scrubbing with water and a little cleaning fluid. Polish on these surfaces will cause your feet to slide around the boat faster than the rest of you, with unfortunate consequences…

Boat polishes should delay or even prevent the build-up of oxidation again. This is quite important because each time an abrasive product is used to remove oxidation, another thin layer of gelcoat is removed. Obviously, therefore, as the gelcoat is quite thin to start with it's best if the process isn't repeated too often.

Application of rubbing compound with a circular motion to remove oxidation.

Buffing with a cloth to remove the whitened surface.

Finish with wax polish to restore a good protective shine.

To paint or not to paint?

Instead of restoring and polishing, the gelcoat can be painted. On an old boat, however, you should first try the process described above on a small area to see if it will work, before you decide to cover the hull with paint. But eventually an old boat's gelcoat will no longer respond to this process. There may be too many scuffmarks, scratches and gelcoat repairs to get a worthwhile finish. This is when painting the gelcoat becomes necessary in order to improve the appearance of and provide protection to the ageing GRP.

Painting GRP

As with all painting jobs, careful preparation and priming/ undercoating of the surface is the key to success. This may well take up 80 per cent of the overall time involved. Before commencing work, read the health and safety data sheets which all paint manufacturers publish and which can also usually be found on their websites.

Choice of paint

A two-part polyurethane paint is usually recommended for the best results on the area of the hull above the waterline, referred to as the 'topsides'. When choosing the colour you can, of course opt for one that appeals to you and matches or complements other colours on the boat, such as the sails. However, a practical point to consider is the possibility of the paint getting scratched. Although this type of paint is tough, the layer is thin and can get worn with time. Touching-up will help, but if you apply a colour that contrasts with the underlying gelcoat finish scratches and worn areas will become very obvious.

The following websites provide plenty of help on choosing paints and varnishes:

http://www.blakespaints.com
http://www.yachtpaint.com
http://www.boatpaint.co.uk

Wash and rinse the surface thoroughly.

White spirit helps to remove grease and dirt.

Preparation

Mask all fittings and remove nameplates and lettering, the latter by sanding or peeling it off. Remove any remaining adhesive.

Bare gelcoat needs careful cleaning and preparation to remove all dirt and traces of wax and silicone polish. Use a product such as International Super Cleaner. Wash the whole hull with a sponge, rinse with fresh water and allow to dry.

Scratches and any other blemishes can be filled at this stage, or after the first coat of paint, using a filler such as epoxy. Wear suitable gloves when handling the filler.

It's important to wear eye protection and a suitable mask or respirator before doing any sanding work. Make sure the

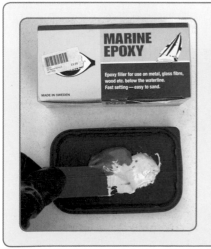

Left: Mix the filler with the appropriate amount of hardener.
Above: With this make of filler the colour changes to an even grey when it's completely mixed.

After scraping the filler into scratches, sand off the excess.

Sanding the whole area before painting is best done gently by hand to avoid penetrating the gelcoat.

Start to apply paint at an edge where the join with a later application won't notice.

mask fits tightly in order to filter out all the toxic dust and fumes.

Using 240 grade sandpaper, sand the areas to be filled. Clean away all dust. Mix the filler according to the instructions on the product and apply it with a spreader or pallet knife. When it's set hard sand it back to a smooth finish.

Overall sanding is next. Although an electric random orbital sander could be used, sanding gelcoat isn't like sanding solid wood, where going a little too deep doesn't matter. You could go through the gelcoat into the fibreglass underneath if too much pressure is applied. It's therefore safer to sand lightly by hand over the whole area.

Remove all dust with a brush or vacuum cleaner and wash and dry the surface again as before. Check for any remaining scratches and fill them, repeating the process already described.

Mask the waterline with tape, ready for applying the undercoat. Note that masking tape needs to be chosen carefully. The cheaper types need to be removed promptly, otherwise the adhesive clings too firmly to the surface and becomes difficult to remove smoothly and neatly. Look for tapes like 3M 'Long Mask' that can be left on until the job is finished. Details of a tape's suitability for different types of painting job are usually given on the packaging.

The undercoat
The ideal temperature for most paints is 10 to 20°C, with little or no wind, relative humidity below 70 per cent, and no risk of rain, mist, frost or dew whilst it's drying. You may want to wet the ground around the boat to settle any dust that could get blown onto the paint.

It's possible to paint the topcoat straight onto the prepared gelcoat, but a perfectionist requiring the best finish will want to apply an appropriate undercoat first. Two coats of undercoat will prevent patchiness and ensure a good depth of colour. More filling and sanding could be necessary if scratches are still visible.

In the case of a two-part polyurethane paint system, which gives the most durable finish, the corresponding two-part undercoat needs to be mixed according to the instructions. Stir and then measure out the appropriate amount of each of the two liquids – base and curing agent – and mix them in a clean metal paint kettle or bucket. Allow any bubbles to disperse by leaving the paint for ten minutes, placed away from the boat. During this time you should give the hull surface a final wipe to remove any dust.

Disasters have been known to happen when a helper has grabbed the base paint and brushed it on without first adding the curing liquid. To avoid this, make sure that any helpers know the procedure to be followed with the paints that you're using.

Start with a paint roller to apply the undercoat in places where a join with later applications won't notice – at the edge of the transom, or at the point of the bows. Cover a section of the hull and then use the tip of a wide brush to remove any roller stipple and spread the paint evenly with downward stokes of the brush. Runs in the paint should be avoided by taking care with the amount

When using a brush, diagonal criss-cross strokes followed by downward strokes will help to ensure thorough coverage.

Suspend the brush in a container of cleaning fluid appropriate to the type of paint.

Light downward strokes with the brush at 45° to the surface will help to achieve an even and smooth finish.

applied, but check for any runs that have occurred and brush them out now, before they set.

Move on to the next section of the hull and repeat the above procedure. Where the inevitable roller overlap occurs, use your brush to smooth the paint with light downward strokes. Repeat the process along the whole of the hull and leave it to dry overnight. Actual drying times depend on the temperature, and are usually shown on the paint can or an accompanying leaflet. Remember that it gets colder at night and that this could slow the process.

Clean the brush and suspend it in a container of the cleaning fluid recommended for the type of paint you're using. It's best to discard the roller, as they can be difficult to clean properly and it will probably set hard.

A second coat of undercoat is recommended, using the same procedure as described above. When set, this provides sufficient thickness to sand lightly, dust down and get a really smooth surface for the topcoat.

The topcoat

Now for the final 20 per cent of the job. Stir the base paint tin first and then mix the appropriate quantities of base and curing agent liquids, stirring them together thoroughly. Take care to read the instructions regarding the amount of each to be used – don't assume the proportions are the same as for the undercoat. Leave the mixture in a covered metal bucket for ten minutes for bubbles to disperse.

Have the appropriate thinner to hand in case you need to add a little of it to the mixture or to clean up any spills. Give the hull a final dusting.

Apply the paint with roller and brush in the same way as the undercoat. When using the brush, hold it at an angle of 45° to the surface in order to minimise brush marks.

This type of paint dries quickly, and delays can result in a hard dry edge forming. It therefore helps if two people are involved, the first to apply the paint with the roller and the second to follow on quickly with the brush while the paint is still wet.

If the brush feels like it's dragging on the surface the paint needs a little thinning, but no more than 10 per cent. This can happen when the air is dry and warm.

Leave the paint to dry overnight. Sand it with 400-grade paper to remove any sags or dirt and then lightly sand over the whole area. Dust it thoroughly.

Prepare and apply the final coat as previously. When it's set, pull off the masking tape carefully and replace any lettering that you previously removed. It's best to leave the paint for a week to harden fully before you move the boat.

The superb shiny finish will need occasional washing and polishing at the start of the sailing season as described earlier in this chapter.

Painting other surfaces

The principles of painting with most paints on most surfaces are similar to those outlined above for painting gelcoat. Consequently they aren't repeated here.

If repainting a previously painted GRP hull don't use the two-part paint described in the preceding section, as there will be adhesion problems. Instead you should use a conventional one-part system, but otherwise follow the same procedure – omitting, obviously, the paint mixing process. The existing paint needs to be sound and thoroughly prepared by careful cleaning and sanding. If it isn't sound it will have to be removed, otherwise painting over it will be a waste of time.

One-part paints are normally used on wood, as they cope better with flexing. On bare wood a suitable primer should be applied before the undercoats.

Inside the boat, the harder varnishes can be used if preferred, to resist the inevitable knocks and scrapes.

Steel keels may be galvanised and require no treatment. However, they may need to have rust removed and be treated with appropriate rust curing paint.

Left: Painting the bilges isn't a pleasant job but suitable paint will help protect the hull from accumulating dirt, oil and other liquids.

Right: Special paints are available for the bilges.

Painting the bilges

The bilges, down in the lowest part of the hull, will inevitably accumulate some water. Although it's best to keep them as dry as possible to minimise the risk of rot in a wooden boat and osmosis in a GRP boat, you won't achieve permanent dryness. Painting will help to keep any water and less pleasant liquids away from the wood and plastic.

First the bilges need to be thoroughly cleaned and old flaking paint removed, along with all traces of oil and grease – not a pleasant job, but it will help to get rid of any odours that rise from below, and once they're painted bilges are much easier to clean.

Before painting, dry out the bilges completely. The use of absorbent materials will help. Some expensive products are available for this, but disposable nappies can be almost as effective. Old leftover paint is often used to paint bilges, but because the liquids and oils that leak into this area can be quite damaging special paints are available for the purpose, such as Danboline.

Antifouling paint

Sailing dinghies and cruisers kept ashore or taken out of the water on a trailer after each use can either have the underwater area of the hull painted as described above or their unpainted gelcoat polished and then hosed down.

Slime, weed and barnacles accumulate on the hull.

However, sail cruisers kept in the water on moorings will need antifouling paint applied to the underwater area to prevent the build-up of weed slime and barnacles. These would otherwise consider the hull an ideal home. Antifouling paint is designed to deter them, since fouling of the hull roughens its surface and causes drag, which slows the boat.

Wooden boats also benefit from antifouling protection against attack from wood-boring marine creatures. An alternative is to scrub the hull regularly, but how many owners want to spend good sailing time on this chore every month or two?

A neglected boat that's been left to accumulate marine growth is likely to have a covering of slime, weed and barnacles. However, even with antifouling paint on the hull, some growth will take hold in places. The amount will depend on the water conditions, including temperature, light penetration and the speed of the water flowing past the hull.

When working with antifouling paint you need to bear in mind that it contains poisons. It's therefore particularly important to avoid contact with it and with any paint removed by any method. Read the instructions on the tin for a guide to the full precautions to be taken, which should include wearing protective clothing, goggles, mask and gloves. Inadequate protection leads to permanent health damage.

Any growth revealed when the boat is hauled out of the water should be cleaned off immediately while it's still wet.

Growths should be washed and scraped off whilst still wet.

contact with the water, within times specified by the manufacturer, in order to be effective.

Mask the waterline with masking tape. If there are 'sacrificial anodes' attached to the hull (see page 118), mask them with tape, as painting them will negate their effectiveness.

If you keep the tin of paint indoors before use, it will be easier to apply than if it's below room temperature. This type of paint is different from others in some ways as it contains heavy ingredients. A little thinning – by 10 per cent or less – helps when spreading the paint. Use the thinner recommended on the tin.

Stir the paint very thoroughly and frequently during use, since otherwise its heavy substances will settle to the bottom. A roller is normally used to apply it, as this covers the large area involved quickly. Alternatively a large and wide brush could be used. Two coats of paint are usually recommended, with an extra coat where turbulence wears the paint and growth tends to accumulate, such as on angular edges of the hull, along the waterline and on the keel and rudder.

Leaving it to dry results in some types of fouling setting as hard as concrete. Removing it with a hose and scrubbing brush or pressure washer is preferable to laborious scraping later. If a boatyard is arranging the lifting out of your boat when you're not there it's best to ask them to wash the hull too.

The choice of antifouling paint depends on where the boat is used. Fresh water contains different species wanting to attach themselves to your hull compared with sea water. The paint also needs to perform appropriately. Poisons in the paint are designed to deter growths. Softer antifoulings also gradually dissolve, shedding thin layers of paint so that any growths leave with them as they erode in the flowing water.

Harder antifouling paint is used for boats that are raced frequently. The harder versions last longer and include some that can be polished clean. On small cruisers likely to be hauled out every winter, the softer eroding paints are more commonly used. This type is cheaper and easier to apply each spring before launching.

Usually the paint should be applied no more than a week or two before launching the boat. Obviously it needs to have dried before launching but many types also need to have

Overpainting with antifouling

Most of these paints can be applied over existing antifouling but it pays to check with the paint companies' websites and publications for specific details. If you've just bought a boat try to find out what was used by the previous owner. If you don't know, a coat of the appropriate primer paint should be applied first. Obviously the existing surface needs to be sound to be able to accept a new coat, otherwise removal of the old paint will be necessary. When removing antifouling paint, take the precautions described earlier. *Never* dry sand antifouling – the dust is highly toxic.

A combination of hosing or pressure washing and

Left: A range of antifouling paints is available to suit different conditions and uses of boat.

Right: If there's a thick build-up of old antifouling paint it may all have to be removed.

A New coat of antifouling paint ready to repel growths on the hull.

scraping can be used to remove old antifouling, although use of an appropriate paint stripper suitable for GRP makes the job much easier. A thick layer of stripper may need to be left on the paint for some time before being washed off, taking the paint with it. Disposal of the poisonous slurry resulting from antifouling removal needs to be done carefully. Many marinas and boatyards have settling tanks to collect such waste in their DIY areas, along with suitable disposal procedures.

Non-slip deck paint

A wet shiny paint surface is dangerous to walk on even with proper deck shoes. Non-slip surfaces are needed on deck if you want to stay upright when moving about, and these will need to be cleaned and maintained to preserve their effectiveness. Cleaning non-slip surfaces is actually the hardest part of boat cleaning, as they have to be scrubbed to extract dirt from the rough surface. It's worth doing, though, to ensure that the surface remains non-slip.

Where it's desirable to improve or extend the areas of non-slip surface, additives are available that can be mixed

Non-slip deck surfaces need to be scrubbed in order to stay non-slip.

with paint of whatever colour you wish for use on the decks. Alternatively you can buy one-part paints that already contain a slip-resistant additive.

Various grits are also available to add to paint, or you can sprinkle fine sand onto a fresh coat of paint. When it's dry, paint another coat on top of the sand. This provides an effective rough surface, although it can be damaging if your skin comes into contact with it.

A less abrasive surface can be achieved by sprinkling salt or sugar onto a coat of paint. After the paint has dried, dissolve the sugar or salt by washing over it with water. This leaves a slightly rough surface.

Non-slip material is also available that can be stuck on the deck in patches or strips. Unfortunately it's rather expensive, and may tend to come unstuck after a few years.

GRP damage repair

GRP is able to take wear and use quite well, depending on the quality of the original build. Inevitably, of course, with normal use there will also be the occasional bump and scrape, however careful you are.

Decisions on damage

Scrapes and small holes can be suitable for DIY repair. More substantial damage above the waterline could also be tackled, providing you include sufficient reinforcing to achieve the necessary strength. Repairs to holes below the waterline are another matter and you need to be absolutely sure the repair won't let you down – below the waves. Either get this type of repair checked by someone suitably qualified before going afloat, or have it done professionally.

Repair materials

Scratches in the gelcoat can be filled with a colour-matched two-part filler, often sold as a gelcoat pigment kit. Car body filler has often been used on GRP boats in error: for repairs to boats, a *marine-grade* product has to be used. Marine fillers are easy to use and are sold in chandlers.

Deep scratches, cracks, gouges and holes need building

Slip-resistant paint.

In the interests of safety, larger scale damage – particularly damage below the waterline – is best repaired by the professionals. In this case, a repair to a J24 sailing boat by Chris Somner Dinghy Services involved making a temporary mould from another J24 to re-laminate the bow onto the damaged boat – a job for skilled boat builders.

Be sure to use marine-grade fillers in repairs.

up with something stronger such as epoxy filler or polyester resin reinforced with fibreglass, as in the original construction.

The basic method of use is to mix the resin and the hardener in the proportions indicated in the instructions supplied with the product. This is then applied and allowed to dry before sanding smooth.

Salt and dirt should be removed before any repairs are attempted, and all working areas and surfaces must be completely dry and clean before application. Wear protective gloves and a suitable mask to prevent the inhalation of dust. Good ventilation is also necessary, as toxic fumes are given off. The temperature should ideally be about 15 to 20°C.

Cellophane, cling film, Mylar tape or other similar types of smooth sheet plastic that won't stick to it can be used to cover the applied filler in order to achieve a reasonably smooth finish which will need less sanding.

Try removing superficial scratches as described previously rather than going straight for the filling option. If this isn't successful use the following technique.

Scratches and minor blemishes

Matching gelcoat filler should be mixed and a thin layer applied, ensuring it enters all scratches and irregularities. Add more filler as necessary to achieve the required thickness and leave it to harden.

Sand the repair until it's smooth, using wet and dry abrasive paper with plenty of water to avoid clogging. Use

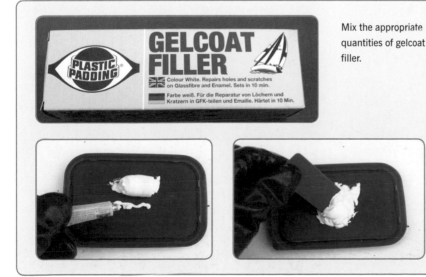

Mix the appropriate quantities of gelcoat filler.

After working a small amount of filler into the scratches, spread more on and smooth it off.

Chopped strand fibreglass mat is the most commonly used material for reinforcing repairs, thoroughly 'wetted out' with synthetic resins. Woven tape and matting are also available.

coarse paper first followed by a fine abrasive paper. If any irregularities remain, fill them with a further application of filler and sand it smooth once it's set hard. When you're satisfied, apply rubbing compound and then wax polish the repair.

Wherever possible, with most repairs, the inside of the hull should be reinforced with a layer or two of fibreglass matting impregnated with resin. Larger repairs to holes have to be bridged and reinforced with such matting on both sides.

Repairs to holes in the deck

The opposite page describes how GRP repairs can be carried out to holes in a deck such as might result when a deck fitting is removed. The repair illustrated was carried out by Essex Boatyards Ltd.

Osmosis again

Osmosis and blistering have already been mentioned in Chapter 4, so hopefully you'll have avoided buying a boat with serious blisters in its gelcoat.

The best way to avoid blistering is to keep a GRP boat away from water! More realistically, you need to give the hull a chance to dry out from time to time. Most sailing dinghies spend most of their time out of the water anyway, so providing rainwater isn't allowed to accumulate in the hull they shouldn't suffer from blistering.

Sail cruisers and day boats kept on moorings are another matter, and may develop blisters as water penetrates the gelcoat, which isn't completely waterproof. Special paints have been developed to protect the hull from osmosis but even they won't necessarily provide total protection for the lifetime of the boat. One precaution that can be taken is to keep the bilges as dry as possible, since wet bilges increase the risk of water penetration.

As explained earlier, blistering occurs when water penetrates the top layer of the gelcoat and combines with chemicals that prevent it from getting out again. The resulting pressure build-up results in blisters.

It's essential to wear eye and skin protection if you

decide to investigate a blister. If penetrated, the acid inside the blister is likely to spurt out into your eyes with harmful consequences.

The advice of apparent experts on osmosis varies greatly. Taking a rather cynical view, those who profit from the costly treatment of a hull with osmosis sometimes emphasise the urgent need to have the gelcoat stripped away and replaced. Others involved with selling boats that betray signs of osmosis may tend to give the impression that all boats suffer from the problem to some degree, and it's just a minor cosmetic problem that can be ignored.

If a boat develops a rash of dozens of blisters the drastic treatment of complete gelcoat removal and replacement with appropriate coatings may be the necessary course of action. On a small second-hand sail cruiser, however, this could cost more than the boat's worth. The blisters may affect the resale value of the boat, but if they're few and only superficial they may not necessarily affect the strength of the hull. Seek independent expert opinion from a surveyor on the best course of action, depending on whether the structural integrity and strength of the hull really is being affected.

In the case of a few small blisters, each no bigger than a ten-pence piece, there are several courses of action you can take. One would be to do nothing, but not to ignore it: check whether the blisters get bigger or more numerous over time or stay the same. An older, well-built, solid boat may not develop more or larger blisters during your ownership of it.

Another option is to cut or grind open each blister, remove the chemicals by washing them out repeatedly with hot water and dry the area very thoroughly. With all work on GRP it's important to remove all moisture before applying any filler, but in this case it's even more important in order to prevent new blisters forming. Leaving the area to dry thoroughly under cover for several months is recommended. The blister can then be filled with an appropriate filler. Epoxy fillers are often recommended for this purpose, followed by paint that provides further protection against water penetration. The filling procedure is the same as that for repairs described earlier.

Hugo du Plessis, author of *Fibreglass Boats*, now in its fourth edition, is a recognised expert on fibreglass boat construction. He recommends filling for most mild cases of blistering, rather than costly complete gelcoat replacement, which should be a last resort. His book goes into great detail and is an excellent source of further information on all matters concerning GRP construction and maintenance.

Roto-moulded hulls

Roto-moulded plastic hulls are very strong, but if they do get damaged they can be more difficult to fix than a GRP hull. Repairing them involves hot air welding with a heat gun and a special weld rod that provides the molten material to fill the crack or hole. This calls for considerable skill in order to avoid melting the boat or causing a fire, so amateur DIY repairs are not recommended.

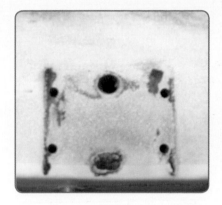

The holes were in the non-slip area of the deck.

Clean the area very thoroughly using acetone. Wear suitable gloves and be aware that acetone is highly inflammable.

Lightly grind the area using a 40-grade grit soft-backed pad grinding disc to expose clean GRP to work up from.

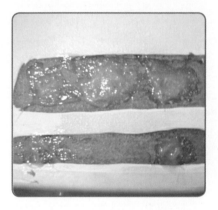

Fill the holes with a reinforced polyester resin. Chopped strand fibreglass mat can be cut into very small pieces and added to resin to reinforce it.

Once dry, grind back the filler until faired off.

Cover with one or preferably two layers of chopped strand mat saturated with resin. This stops circular cracking, which can later appear in the gelcoat around old repairs. Once dry, the matting can be faired off so that it's smooth and flat.

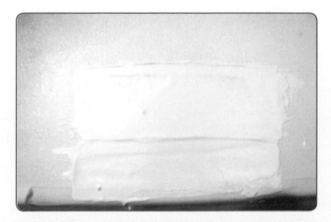

Apply two coats of matching gelcoat with a brush or spatula. A match can be obtained by mixing coloured gel pastes or ordering the correct colour gel from the manufacturer.

A non-slip surface can be achieved by stippling with a stiff brush. If the non-slip deck pattern is repetitive a mould could be made from another area of deck to create a former to press into the wet gelcoat.

12 Fittings and their maintenance

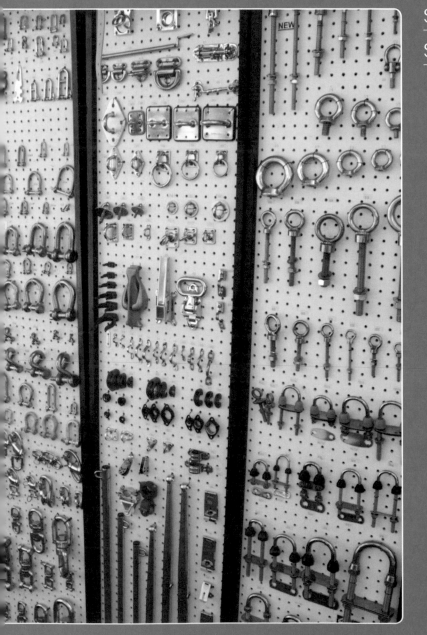

Self-bailers can be opened to drain water from the hull when moving forwards fast enough.

A chute on the self-bailer opens below the hull to allow water out of the boat.

Sailing dinghies

Drainage

Spray, rain and wave splashes inevitably result in some water accumulating in the hull of a sailing dinghy. Most dinghies have some way of draining water from the hull when ashore. This may be a simple drain plug at the stern, which is unscrewed when ashore. The plug should be attached with a short cord so that it doesn't get lost. To avoid embarrassing flooding of the boat, don't forget to replace it before relaunching! A rubber washer or O ring helps seal the plug. Eventually this will need to be replaced, as it deteriorates over time. In order to avoid leaks the fitting itself should also be checked to ensure it's securely attached and sealed to the hull.

Self-bailers are devices that drain water out of a boat during sailing as it moves forward. They usually consist of a rear-facing metal chute that can clip open or shut. If there's water in the hull, the bailer is opened by the crew when sailing forward at a reasonable speed and the boat's forward momentum sucks the water out. Some bailers have a non-return valve, but in many cases the bailer needs to be shut when the boat isn't moving in order to stop it leaking. In order to avoid damage they also need to be retracted when beaching and taking the boat out of the water.

Self-bailers can get blocked with weed and grit so clean them regularly. An old toothbrush and water pressure from a hose can be used for this. If the bailer is leaking it may have to be unbolted and re-seated in sealing compound or a new rubber gasket. It's best to have some new bolts ready in case the old ones need to be replaced. Service kits for self-bailers, which include seals, washers and screws or bolts, can be purchased at chandlers. Identify the type and make to be sure of buying the right kit.

Transom flaps are fitted over drainage holes low down in the transom on many sailing dinghies. A combination of water pressure and, usually, a length of elastic inside the boat hold the flaps closed. As the boat moves forward at a good speed, water inside the hull moves towards the stern and pushes open the flaps to drain out. It may be necessary

Above: A self-bailer seated in sealing compound.

Right: Transom flaps allow water to escape from the hull.

Below: Inside the hull the flaps are held shut by elastic, which will need to be replaced when it weakens.

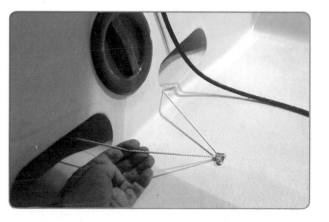

Left and *right:* A scoop bailer and bucket should be tied securely in the boat ready for bailing.

to slacken the elastic to facilitate this. Check nothing presses against the flaps, causing them to open when they shouldn't, and replace the elastic if it shows signs of not holding the flaps shut when the boat is stationary.

A capsize, or water entering during a near capsize, may be drained by self-bailers or transom flaps if you can get the heavily flooded boat sailing fast enough for them to work, but don't rely on them. Have a good-sized bucket, scoop bailer and hand-pump secured somewhere accessible inside the boat to deal with large volumes of water quickly. A sponge can deal with the remaining drops.

Buoyancy

Buoyancy chambers are built into a boat so that it doesn't sink if it gets swamped with water. Hatch covers can be removed to access the chambers. These are usually of the screw-in type. After sailing, remove the covers and any bungs from drainage holes and sponge out any water remaining in the buoyancy chambers. A small amount may be caused by condensation but if they contain a substantial depth of water you need to investigate the cause. It could be a poor seal round the hatch cover fitting, in which case the fitting should be removed and resealed. The thread on the covers and bungs can be lubricated with a little Teflon-based lubricant so that they're easier to unscrew.

Buoyancy chambers can be used for storage – for

example when using the dinghy for cruising – but remember that this will reduce the effectiveness of the buoyancy to some extent, so don't overdo it.

Inflated buoyancy bags are used on some sailing dinghies. Every time you wash the boat remember to get dirt out from behind the inflated bags to prevent chafing. Also check for cracking of the material, which is most likely to occur around the inflation tube. Obviously the bags must remain fully inflated. A bag that leaks air shouldn't be ignored – you might have to rely on its buoyancy in a capsize. If it is leaking it's probably time to replace it rather than attempt a repair.

Check the straps and fittings that hold the bags in place. They have to be strongly fixed because a dinghy swamped with water is held up and prevented from sinking by these fittings. At the end of the sailing season remove the bags, deflate them, and wash and dry the bags and straps. Always take care to avoid sharp items, oil and grease coming into contact with them. When inflating buoyancy bags in hot weather allow for expansion as the air in the bags gets warmer.

Centreboard

Centreboards, dagger boards and rudders on sailing dinghies are often called 'foils'.

The centreboard case needs to be checked for any weakness. Damage and cracks in the gelcoat should be

Lubricate the thread on the screw-in covers on buoyancy chambers.

Buoyancy bags and their straps should be checked regularly.

Check the centreboard case and any bolts holding the board in place.

Wooden centreboards get scratched and need to be touched-up with varnish.

filled and reinforced as described in Chapter 11. If the centreboard swivels on a bolt, check it to see if it's loose, and if necessary tighten it a little – but don't over-tighten it, as this could jam the centreboard or distort the case. Where fittings pivot, washers perform important tasks including the prevention of leaks, so they may need to be replaced if worn or missing.

With the boat raised and supported safely, check that the centreboard or dagger board moves freely and remove any stones or other objects that may be jammed between the centreboard and the side of the centreboard case. Any pebbles left in there could cause damage and even wear a hole through the side of the case. If there's a slot closure at the bottom of the case, this will wear and will eventually need replacement to stop stones entering.

Wooden centreboards, dagger boards and rudders need to have chips and scratches touched-up with paint or varnish promptly in order to stop water soaking into the wood and to keep the surface smooth, minimising friction.

Right: The pintles and gudgeons that secure the rudder may need to be re-fixed with new screws or bolts.

Below: Considerable leverage forces are exerted on the rudder fittings and they can become loose.

Rudder

The transom, across the stern of the boat, receives considerable pressure from the rudder, and the screws or bolts holding the rudder fittings may eventually become loose and worn. The 'pintle' is the pin on the rudder that slots into the hole in the 'gudgeon', which is screwed to the transom at the stern of the boat. These fittings can twist sideways if they become loose. If the screw holes have become enlarged, the screws could be replaced with larger gauge stainless steel screws or stronger bolts. Alternatively, you could fill the hole with epoxy filler and, when set, drill new holes to take the screws. The

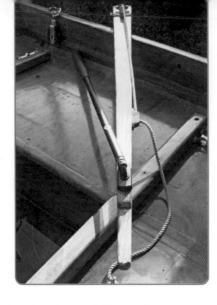

The joints on the tiller may need replacement.

appropriate Loctite thread sealant could be used to ensure that bolts on the rudder fittings don't work loose again.

The tiller is the arm attached to the rudder. A tiller extension is usually fitted to the end of the tiller with a swivelling universal joint, its extended reach helping the helmsman to control the boat whilst moving around and sitting out. The joint can become loose and may need replacement if worn. Tiller extensions of various lengths with tough and smooth-running urethane universal joints are available as replacements. As these are quite costly they're likely to be chosen by racing enthusiasts, who put much wear on such joints.

Outboard motor mount

If an outboard motor is used this can cause additional stress and the transom may need reinforcement by means of a strong back fitted to its inside. Check the condition of the plywood pad where the motor clamp is bolted onto the transom and replace it if it shows signs of disintegration.

Wooden rubbing strips get worn and need to be replaced using screws and waterproof glue.

Rubbing strips

Rubbing strips and bands on the keel and on the gunwales are there to take the scrapes that would otherwise damage the hull. Consequently they may themselves need to be repaired from time to time so they can continue to protect the hull. It may be possible to cut out and replace part of a rubbing strip without replacing the whole length, although complete replacement is likely to be necessary eventually on a well-used sailing dinghy.

Deck hardware

Most good quality fittings will take plenty of wear and use providing they're designed for the strains put on them. The majority are made of stainless steel, which resists rust because a protective layer forms on its surface encouraged by oxygen. However, if air can't reach a sealed part of a stainless steel fitting it can still rust, particularly in crevices, where salt water accelerates any deterioration. So don't expect stainless steel fittings to last indefinitely. They'll also wear, and will need to be replaced eventually. The main weak point, though, is where equipment is attached to the hull or deck.

Attachment points for rigging include fairleads, which guide the sail control ropes, or sheets; cleats to secure the ropes; block mountings where the pulleys (or 'blocks') are

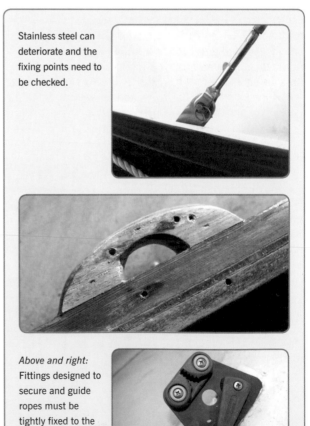

Stainless steel can deteriorate and the fixing points need to be checked.

Above and right: Fittings designed to secure and guide ropes must be tightly fixed to the deck, with no movement.

attached to the deck or other surfaces; and chainplates, which are the fixing points for the shrouds and forestay (the cables that help to support the mast in an upright position). All of these fittings should be checked for looseness by gripping with your hand and twisting. There should be no movement sideways. If there is, tighten the screws or bolts. If this doesn't work, unscrew them and either fill the holes, re-drill them and screw the fitting back, or use thicker screws or bolts.

On sailing dinghies the mounting points should already be strengthened sufficiently to take the load put on the fitting, but if there are any signs of stress or cracking, extra reinforcement with backing plates may be necessary.

Rowlocks are fitted into the gunwales of many dinghies, and considerable pressure is inevitably applied by the oars when rowing. Some reinforcement with epoxy resin may be necessary if cracking has started in this area.

Cleaning and lubrication

All moving parts should, from time to time, be washed with fresh water and a little detergent to remove salt and dirt. They should then be dried and lubricated.

Oil-based lubricants can damage sails and rigging and stain clothing. Use a Teflon-based lubricant or a quick-drying lubricant such as McLube, which, though comparatively expensive, is claimed to last approximately ten times longer than any other type. Such lubricants should be used for the sailing boat's moving parts, including the various types of pulleys or blocks. They resist being washed out by water and help to prevent water penetration. Dry types of lubricant are also preferable as they're less likely to attract and accumulate dirt.

Toe-straps

A dinghy sails at its best when kept upright or nearly so, and in order to keep it upright the crew sit on the gunwales. This is known as 'sitting out' or 'hiking out'. To make this easier and safer, toe-straps are fitted to the floor

Special water-resistant and long-lasting lubricants are available.

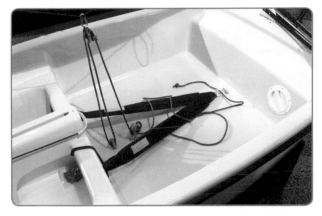

Above: Toe-straps should be secured and tensioned adequately.

Right: Cam cleats have two pivots, which tend to become stiff with salt and dirt. They need to be washed clean of grit and lubricated.

of many dinghies to hold their feet down. The tension on these straps needs to be adjusted from time to time and the fittings need to be safe and secure, otherwise the crew could suffer a sudden severe let down.

Sail cruisers

Open day boats will have much in common with sailing dinghies and the first half of this chapter should be read in conjunction with the following. Small sail cruisers vary in the way they've been equipped with various fittings and, again, the information relating to dinghies may apply to some designs.

Hull fittings

We're mainly concerned in this book with small sail cruisers, most of which are small enough to be easily taken out of the water on a trailer. Fortunately, these boats have few metal fittings to cause concern below the waterline. However, the bigger and more luxuriously equipped the sail cruiser, the more fittings will be attached to the hull, including through-hull fittings for toilet intake and discharge, shower and galley sump pumps and possibly engine-cooling water.

These holes in the hull need to be checked and maintained frequently, as faults will lead to leaks and are a major cause of boats sinking. This is emphasised by the fact

New anodes to replace the worn one in the previous photograph.

Leaking through-hull fittings will need to be unscrewed and re-bedded in a sealant suitable for underwater use, using new screws or bolts.

below the waterline. Zinc is a base metal lower on the galvanic table than these other metals, so lumps of zinc called 'sacrificial anodes' are attached to the hull near the metal fittings, beside propeller shafts and to the underwater casing of outboard motors. Because the zinc gets attacked by electrolysis before the other more 'noble' metals, it protects them from corrosion.

Zinc anodes should be replaced when half of their original bulk has been eaten away. They should never be painted over, as this would stop the protective process.

Checking hull fittings

Even when anodes are regularly replaced, the hull screws or bolts holding the hull fittings should still be checked for looseness and replaced if necessary. Leakage into the boat shows the sealant or gasket between the fitting and the hull has disintegrated, and the fitting will need to be removed and re-bedded in sealant. As usual with all work on the underwater area of the hull, seek the expertise or advice of professionals if you have the slightest doubt about doing this safely enough to prevent leaks.

As indicated above, inside the hull the pipes need to be very securely attached to the through-hull fittings. Any leaks

that many insurance companies insist that all inlet pipes below the water line are fastened to the hull fitting with at least two stainless steel worm-drive jubilee clips.

Electrolysis

Through-hull fittings and all metal fittings below the waterline are often damaged by a process called electrolysis. When different metals are near each other and immersed in water – particularly in sea water – they form an electric cell. As an electric current flows, the baser of the metals, as listed on the galvanic series table, is gradually eaten away.

Some boats have fittings made from a variety of metals

A zinc anode half worn away and ready for replacement.

Valves controlling water flow can be replaced – with the boat out of the water.

Corrosion and leaks from keel fittings indicate that removal and refitting with new bolts is necessary.

here may just require the two jubilee clips to be tightened a little, renewed one at a time, or have an extra clip attached to stop the leak.

Seacocks are the taps or valves used to turn off water from the hull fittings. Open and close them regularly to prevent them from becoming seized up. They also benefit from lubrication.

Keels

The keel or keels suspended under a cruiser provide the necessary weight to keep the boat as upright as possible. Their structure varies: many GRP sail cruisers have lead or iron keels encased in the GRP, while wooden cruisers and some made of GRP have their keels bolted on.

Corrosion and leaks from the vicinity of the keel indicate problems with the bolts and the seal between the keel and the hull. The bolts can corrode over time. Removing them will be difficult if they're badly corroded, and this isn't a simple repair task. As they're below the waterline, removing them and refitting the heavy keel is best left to professionals who have the necessary tools and equipment to do the job safely. They'll take the keel off and re-bed it in sealant, refastening it with new bolts.

Rudder bearings eventually wear and need replacing if looseness is detected.

Rudders

Rudder bearings inevitably wear and eventually need replacement. They should be checked every year by holding the bottom of the rudder and attempting to move it backwards and forwards and from side to side. If looseness is revealed, remove the bearings by undoing the appropriate screws or bolts and replace them.

Deck fittings

The points raised in the 'Deck hardware' section earlier in this chapter also apply to sail cruisers. Fittings will loosen over time and sealant will harden, lose its adhesion and crack. All fittings should be checked regularly. Make sure that fastenings aren't loose – they will need tightening from time to time. Failed sealant usually makes replacement or refitting necessary, with new fastenings – usually bolts rather than screws – and fresh sealant.

On a sail cruiser there must always be substantial backing plates to spread the load, which can be very great and has been known to rip out an insecure fitting and send it flying dangerously across the deck. Obviously, further harm is then caused by the loss of the securing point, which may have held heavy rigging or vital mooring lines in place. Where stanchions and their lifelines take the force of stopping someone from falling overboard, secure attachment is vital.

Bolts go through the fitting, the deck and the thick, preferably metal, backing plate, before sealant, washers and nuts are attached and tightened inside the boat. On some boats plywood backing plates have been installed. Leaks through the boltholes can cause these to rot and the whole fitting to become dangerously loose. Streaks on the inside of the hull, caused by leaks from the deck running down through tiny gaps around loose fittings, help to show when refitting is needed. Stress cracks in the gelcoat may also develop, showing where refitting and reinforcement is needed to ensure the fitting is safely secured.

Sealants

The range of sealants available can be rather confusing. Polyurethane sealant has strong adhesive properties, so it

Sikaflex 291 is a widely used adhesive sealant.

Silicone rubber sealant forms a flexible gasket.

you want to stick and seal a joint this is a good choice. Sikaflex 291 is a particularly popular general-purpose sealant of this type. Its disadvantage is that it sticks quite firmly and it may be difficult to remove the fitting in the future and to eliminate all traces of it.

Silicone-type sealants can be removed more readily and are good at forming a flexible gasket, but they're not strongly adhesive in the way that polyurethane sealants are. Silicone should not be used below the waterline or where it's expected to provide a strong bond. However, it does make a good insulating barrier between different metals and strongly resists most chemicals.

'Captain Tolley's Creeping Crack Cure' – a sealant for stopping leaks through hairline cracks – is useful for sealing leaking decks and windows, as will be explained in more detail in Chapter 15, which includes work on window frames.

Replacing a deck or hull fitting

The procedure described below applies to most deck fittings such as fairleads, cleats, stanchions and attachments for rigging. Obviously it's easier to do this work ashore but it may have to be done afloat. With all work on a boat afloat on a mooring, there's an amazing tendency for loose items to find a way to fall overboard, so take care to hold on to the fitting as you undo its fastenings – ideally you should tie it to something in order to stop it taking a dive over the side.

Penetrating and releasing fluid can be used to help release the nuts and bolts holding fittings. Have someone hold one end of each bolt firmly with a spanner or pliers while you undo the other end if it's below the deck, otherwise the loose bolt may simply swivel as you try to undo the nuts.

Once the fitting is removed, scrape and clean all adhering sealant thoroughly from the base, the thread of the bolts, and the deck. Both surfaces have to be completely clean and dry. This can be a difficult part of the process, as the remaining sealant can cling on amazingly firmly, despite the fact that some of it has failed. Acetone or a thinner appropriate to the sealant can be used to remove remaining traces. Wear gloves when using such chemicals in order to avoid removing skin as well as old sealant. Also bear in mind that they and other such chemicals are highly flammable.

If the bolts aren't permanently attached to the fitting, it's best to buy new bolts and nuts of the correct size.

Replacing a fitting such as a fairlead or mooring cleat on the deck requires a backing plate of thick aluminium. This should be cut larger than the base of the cleat – as large as will fit in the space available under the deck. File the sharp edges and corners off the plate.

Place the fitting on the plate and mark the position of the holes. With a punch and hammer, make an indentation in the centre of one of the marked holes, and with the plate held in a vice drill a small pilot hole in the dent. Next, drill a hole of an appropriate size to take the bolt.

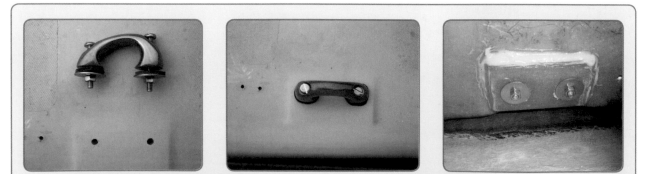

These pictures show the replacement of a fairlead on a Drascombe Lugger. Below the deck the bolts pass through a backing plate. Sealant is added to surfaces before it's all assembled and before washers and nuts are screwed onto the bolts.

Place the fitting on the deck and push a bolt through the hole. Get a helper to hold the plate up onto the bolt under the deck and screw the nut on from below. The positions of the remaining holes can then be marked and drilled.

Before bolting down the fitting, remove it and apply a substantial amount of sealant to the base of the cleat, the holes, and the upper surface of the plate. Enough has to be applied for it to squeeze out from under the base as you screw it down. The fitting can now be bolted in place, lightly bedding it down in the sealant until it begins to squeeze out. Don't over-tighten at this stage, otherwise all the sealant could be squeezed out. Let the sealant partially set and then tighten the bolts fully. Remove the excess sealant from the fitting above and below the deck.

Winches

Where a sail cruiser is fitted with winches, the main regular task involves keeping them free of dirt and grit by flushing them with fresh water. Lubrication is also necessary according to the manufacturer's recommendations for the particular type of winch. Unfortunately there are a great many different makes and models, so it's not possible to give a worthwhile full servicing guide here.

Boat owners tend to put off servicing winches. However, a winch has to deal with heavy loads and it will eventually seize up if neglected. A replacement is expensive.

All winches should be washed regularly with fresh water and dried with a cloth. Persistent dirt on chromed and stainless steel winches can be removed with non-abrasive chrome cleaner. Don't use polishes or abrasives on alloy winches.

The frequency of servicing depends partly on the amount of use. Winches on a boat used several times a week during the main sailing season will need to be cleaned and lubricated two or three times. At the end of the season the winches should certainly be stripped, cleaned, checked for damage and lubricated thoroughly.

Winches should be kept free of dirt and grit.

Service kits, including spare parts, are available for many winches, and following the instructions will involve you dismantling the winch. Taking digital photographs of each stage will make it easier to put it back together later. Take care to note, sketch or photograph how the pawls are positioned before removing them. The spring-loaded pawls engage with notches or teeth in a drum to stop the winch rotating the wrong way and it's important to replace them the right way round.

With the simplest designs of winches it is necessary only to unscrew a cap and remove the drum to access the interior. However, it's important to consult the appropriate manual for your type of winch. Many manuals are available via the websites provided below.

A problem of disassembling a winch is that pawls and tiny springs can fly off and disappear or a bearing can fall out of the drum when it's lifted. One solution is to place a large transparent plastic bag over the winch and your hands whilst you dismantle it, in order to catch the parts that attempt to escape. Check and block any holes, such as cockpit drainage holes, into which parts might vanish, never to be seen again. Lay the dismantled parts on an old towel or similar non-slip surface for cleaning and lubrication. An old toothbrush can be used along with white spirit or paraffin for degreasing the metal components, but don't use these with any plastic components in case they cause damage.

Lubrication of winches varies according to the make and model. The pawls of the winch tend to stick in their pockets when grease is used so it's better to use light oil on them. A light smear of grease is recommended for the gear teeth, ratchets and bearings. There's a risk that overdoing the application of grease can attract dirt and grit. Excess grease can also collect in areas such as pawl pockets, causing the winch to malfunction dangerously just when you need to rely on it. Exact lubrication procedure depends on which of the many types of winch you have and the likelihood of dirt entering the mechanism. Manufacturers usually recommend the best course of action. Some websites offering such advice, and access to full servicing manuals for particular winches, are:

http://en.lewmar.com/support/PDF/
   Winch_Service_Manual.zip
http://www.harken.com/winches/winch.php
http://www.ybw.com/ybw/harken/winch_service.html

Winches are reassembled in the reverse sequence to that used for dismantling. It's particularly important to make sure that pawls are engaged the right way round for your particular winch in order to avoid causing damage and dangerous malfunctions. Make sure water drain holes are not obstructed. Always carefully and slowly test the winch immediately after reassembly.

See Chapters 13 and 15 regarding work on masts, spars and windows.

13 The rig

The mast and rigging have to deal with constant movement, which results in wear.

Mast and spars

Aluminium, stainless steel and synthetic materials used for rigging are hard-wearing. However, it's surprising how many sailing boat owners rely on this, and leave the mast up through winter, allowing rigging flogging in the wind and movement caused by winter gales to cause unnecessary wear and future expense.

The mast and spars take the strain from the sails and deal with forces from all directions. Inevitably all this movement will cause wear, which needs to be investigated regularly. All fittings should be inspected and the fixings checked for movement and tightened or replaced. The main ones are covered below, but the exact types of fixings and fittings will vary according to the type of boat.

Mast lowering

Sailing dinghies

In the case of a sailing dinghy, lowering the mast is best done by two or more people. A falling mast will easily damage people and boats alike, so involve someone with experience in the process if necessary.

Remove the boom from the mast. Check that there are no obstructions overhead or on the ground. On a sailing dinghy, the mast may be 'stepped', with its lower end fastened into a 'gate' down on the keel. The mast pivots on this and can be lowered with one person holding the detached forestay and the other holding and guiding the mast as it lowers. If the dinghy has a deck-stepped mast, with the end resting in a step on top of the deck, one person needs to hold the mast whilst the other slackens the shrouds. The mast is then lifted up a little out of the step and then sideways to lower it. Place your hands some distance apart when lifting and lowering the mast to ensure a good hold and better control.

Sail cruisers

Masts on sail cruisers are obviously bigger and heavier than on a dinghy and need several people to control their safe descent. A sailing club should have plenty of people available to help with this. No doubt they'll be happy to provide advice on how to lower the mast of your particular type of cruiser.

Many boats designed for trailer sailing have equipment provided and simple procedures to follow for the necessarily frequent lowering and raising of the mast. This might, for example, involve using one of the boat's winches to make the process easier.

If in doubt about safety issues with mast raising and lowering, particularly with larger and heavier masts, involve the local boatyard in the process. Masts over 8m (26ft) are particularly heavy and you'll need such help to lower these.

Before starting, remove spars attached to the mast and prepare all fastenings such as bottle screws, clevis pins, shackles and so on, removing any tape from them and

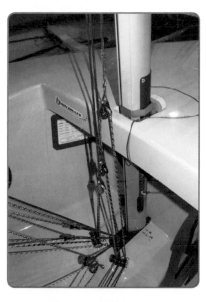

The mast may be secured in a number of different ways requiring lifting or lowering gradually.

A tabernacle secures the foot of the mast and provides a pivot for mast lowering.

Supports for the mast are provided on this boat's road trailer.

ensuring they're free to be undone quickly as and when necessary. The stages at which mast supports need to be slackened or undone will depend on the rig used on the particular boat. This varies greatly from one cruiser to another and the sequence needs to be carefully planned.

The mast step may be in the form of a 'tabernacle' on the deck, with a bolt or bolts through the mast. This holds the foot of the mast and provides a pivot for raising and lowering it. In some cases one of two bolts is removed before lowering.

Work out how and exactly where the mast will go as it comes down. It may need to be supported part of the way down while adjustments are made, depending on the shape of the decks and any obstructions. A mast crutch is needed to support the mast at the stern. Larger masts may need A-frames to help support them, to stop them from moving sideways and to control lowering more efficiently.

The usual way to control the mast is with the forestay. Attach a rope to the lower end of the forestay before undoing the fastening at deck level. This can then be used to control

the gradual lowering of the mast as it pivots on the mast step fastenings.

After lowering, it's worth labelling where stays and other fittings should be replaced, using matching strips of coloured plastic tape. This will make it easier to match each fitting to its correct home and save much puzzled head-scratching when it comes to re-rigging later. Taking photographs of the rig before you lower the mast will provide similar help when you want to raise and re-rig the mast at a later date.

The mast can be removed completely to go into a purpose-built mast store, where it's supported at frequent intervals along its entire length. Alternatively it can be laid along the length of the boat, with mast crutches helping to support the ends. Leather or other cushioning material can be used on the crutches to avoid scratches and abrasions. Likewise, ensure both the mast and the boat are sufficiently protected from each other where the mast rests. A cover is often arranged over the mast in the manner of a tent, with the mast forming the ridgepole.

Left: A crutch supports the lowered mast at the stern of this boat.

Right: A well-supported mast can form a ridge-pole for a tent-shaped cover.

Mast repair

This wooden mast had chafed against the teak thwart that supports it. The damaged and rotted wood was sanded away and the bare wood coated with West Epoxy Resin 105 using standard 205 hardener and immediately built up with a stiff mixture of resin 105 plus high-density filler 404. This was then left to cure for 24 hours before sanding smooth and coating with Resin 105. The high-density filler gave a tough repair that will resist further abrasion where the stepped mast rests against the thwart.

Wooden masts and spars

Wooden spars need to be checked for any chips in the varnish. Touch them up as soon as possible in order to prevent water absorption and discolouration. Varnish the spars before storing them away for the winter, but make sure that the varnish doesn't run into the 'sheaves' (pulleys embedded in the mast).

As indicated previously, epoxy resins are effective in repairing the parts of boats that are made of wood, including spars. For example, screw holes may have enlarged and need to be treated with epoxy filler. Alternatively, if possible without causing other problems with fittings, fill the old holes and drill new holes in fresh timber.

The following examples of repairs to wooden spars were carried out by Tim Pettigrew during renovation of his Drascombe Lugger. The procedures show how epoxy resin can be used to repair the wooden parts of a boat.

Gaff repair

1 The split in the gaff was caused by a screw being driven into the wood without an adequate pilot hole being drilled first.

2 This end-view shows the deep split.

3 A wood saw was used to widen the split before filling it.

Gaff repair (continued)

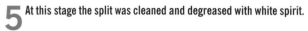

4 The saw 'polished' the sides of the cut, so coarse abrasive paper was folded in half and used to roughen the sides so that the filler-adhesive would stick to it.

5 At this stage the split was cleaned and degreased with white spirit.

6 Unthickened epoxy resin was mixed with the correct amount of hardener and painted into the split so that the wood was thoroughly wetted out.

7 Epoxy resin was thickened with West 404 filler powder and injected into the split. The central thickened epoxy was enclosed between wood soaked with unthickened epoxy, producing a strong bond.

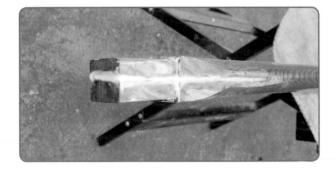

8 After the epoxy had cured it was sanded smooth and varnished.

9 The gaff jaws were refitted to the end of the spar ready for use.

A luff groove is a groove where the reinforced luff edge of a sail slides into the mast as the sail is hoisted. On a wooden mast this groove needs to be smooth, otherwise the sail will catch on it. Glue back any split shreds of wood and sand along the groove, taking care not to widen it to the point where it won't grip the luff of the sail.

If the luff groove is badly damaged it may be better to screw on a new aluminium mast track and sew matching slides to the luff of the mainsail. Compare the price of the track, slides and screws with the price of a new mast, or a good second-hand mast, before buying the equipment. Take care when you decide exactly where to position the track, and ensure that the screws will have a good grip on solid timber.

Glue joins in old wooden spars need to be watched in case they split open, particularly at the ends. If this happens, cut a 'V' into the join and fill it with epoxy glue. Bind it tightly with strong polyester waxed thread. The spar could also be bolted through to strengthen the repair.

The luff groove or track needs to be clean, smooth and lubricated so that the sail slides up the mast easily.

Luff tracks can get dented quite easily and need to be eased open carefully in order to prevent the sail luff jamming on its way up the mast.

Aluminium masts and spars

Aluminium masts and spars usually have an anodised finish that resists corrosion. Polishing with wax helps to keep the surface smooth but avoid using anything containing abrasive cleaners. Surface scratches and abrasion may be polished out. If the anodising has been badly worn the mast can be painted with an appropriate type of paint. Clean, degrease and remove any polish with methylated spirit and wire wool, prime with a self-etch primer, and paint.

Aluminium rivets eventually corrode. The rivet indicated here has come apart and needs urgent replacement.

Check that fastenings aren't pulling away from the mast.

It may be possible to gently bend back a mast that's slightly bent, but if any deep dents, kinks, cracks or corrosion holes have occurred the mast is unsafe and should be replaced.

The luff groove where the edge of the sail runs up the mast can develop very irritating faults which make it hard to hoist the mainsail. If the groove has closed a little, gently prise it open. If the groove is too wide, allowing the sail to pull out, lay a piece of wood along the side of the track and using a mallet hammer gently on the wood – not directly on the aluminium – to close the track a little at a time until it's the right size. Applying a suitable lubricant will help the sail slide up as it should.

Check the fixing points of fittings for corrosion. A white powder on the aluminium may show where this is a problem. Refitting with larger screws and polishing or painting can cure this before it becomes a serious problem.

Take care not to weaken the aluminium mast and spars when drilling new holes for fittings. Holes need to be at least 20mm apart vertically and preferably not in a horizontal line round the mast.

For attaching fittings to aluminium, always use short stainless steel self-tapping screws so that they won't penetrate the interior of the mast. Alternatively, you could use monel rivets, which are made of nickel copper. Ordinary aluminium rivets will corrode.

The sheaves, where the halyard goes over pulleys embedded in the mast, need regular checking and lubrication using an appropriate lubricant. A jammed wheel can damage or break a halyard, so it should be replaced.

Where shrouds that hold up the mast attach to it at the 'hounds' there's a risk that they might pull away, elongating

Spreaders should be checked when the mast is down.

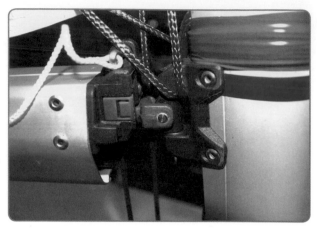

The gooseneck at the end of the boom fits into the mast, and needs to be checked for looseness.

the holes where fastenings penetrate. Replacement with more substantial fittings may be necessary. This also applies to any trapeze wires that may be fitted to the mast of a sailing dinghy.

Many masts on dinghies, and most masts on sail cruisers, have aluminium spreaders, which jut out at an angle to the mast and have shrouds attached to them. If they or the brackets are bent or damaged in any way they should be replaced, as they will have been weakened.

A few boats still have wooden spreaders. These can get neglected, up there out of reach for much of the time. Rot may have set in on the top of the spreader where it can't easily be seen from below, so probe with a screwdriver to check whether replacement is necessary. You should give wooden spreaders some coats of preservative and varnish or paint them on a regular basis. Alternatively you can replace with aluminium ones.

Mast step

Where the mast rests on the deck or hull there will be a strengthened receptacle to take its end. If it's made of wood, water can collect in the step or tabernacle and cause it to rot. This can be prevented by drying the step and adding some extra protection in the form of a layer of epoxy resin. Alternatively, if possible – and if it can be done without weakening the mast step – you could drill a small drainage hole through the step leading out to the side.

As the mast step obviously supports the mast and has to cope with considerable strains in various directions, check that it's completely secure. Its fastenings need to be tight and in good condition. The area around the step should be reinforced and strong enough, but on a wooden boat you should look for any signs of cracking or rot that could affect the support of the mast.

Usually there's a binding or some form of cushioning or 'boot' on each end of the spreaders, to protect the mainsail from chafing. This should be removed to check the spreader's condition. Corrosion could have occurred where the stainless steel shrouds meet the ends of aluminium spreaders. Remember to replace or renew the chafe protection that goes on the ends of the spreaders. Maintaining this protection in good condition is much cheaper than replacing a damaged mainsail.

The boom

The 'gooseneck' is a thick pivoting pin that's inserted into the end of the boom where it attaches to the mast. This clearly takes considerable pressure and is another area to check for looseness and wear. The level of the gooseneck is usually adjustable, but this means that it can slip. If this does happen, screw a stop into the luff groove on the mast so that the gooseneck can slide no further down the mast than required.

Where the boom rubs on the shrouds, thin plastic tubing can be attached to the latter to prevent chafing.

Standing rigging

The wires that hold up the mast are referred to as 'standing rigging'. Multiple strands of stainless steel are nowadays used to make these wires, although in the past they were made of galvanised steel. If a boat still has galvanised rigging it's likely to be old and in need of urgent replacement.

The stainless steel wires called shrouds and stays that support the mast may seem solid and secure at first glance. However, they do deteriorate over time. Metal fatigue is the problem, caused mainly by frequent repeated loads being put on the wires. As well as happening when sailing this can also occur when a boat is stationary with its mast raised, as the wind and movements of the boat put varying loads on the rigging.

Multiple strands of stainless steel are used to make the standing rigging wires.

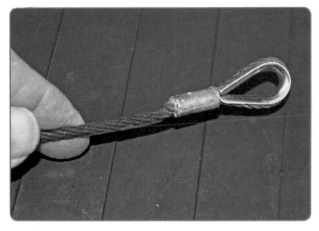

A corroded galvanised steel stay in need of immediate replacement. This stay has a swaged terminal.

When strands break they can be difficult to spot but it's important to check for them, as they show that the wires are seriously weakened and that all the standing rigging should be replaced immediately.

Ten years is often quoted as the maximum life expectancy of undamaged stainless steel shrouds and stays. Collision, kinking, chafing or other damage drastically shortens this and necessitates replacement. A voyage in stormy conditions also shortens their life expectancy.

Regular inspection of the rig should be carried out. The following faults are some of those that indicate replacement to be necessary. Bear in mind that damaged wires have lost the necessary strength and can break very suddenly, causing accidents.

Check for loose strands of wire. They tend to break away at the terminals and fixings. Where this happens, the strand of wire usually forms a small curl with a sharp point – rather like a fishhook, and just as damaging to hands that come into contact with it, so beware. Loose strands may not be clearly visible, so slide a thick handful of rag along the wire to see if it gets caught on any. A broken strand of wire is an indication that all the other rigging wires of the same age also need to be replaced.

Irregular twists, kinks, misalignment or sharp bends also indicate damage to rigging wires. Crazing or cracking around the deck fitting bases or the mast plates show that damaging loads have been put on the whole rig.

Check fittings that attach to the wires for any damage, cracking or distortion, to swaged terminals (see below), the rigging screws used to adjust tension on the wires holding up the mast, toggles and turnbuckles.

Much discussion about exact rig tension takes place amongst racing types, and it can get complicated. The boat owners' associations and sailing dinghy class associations can advise on rig tension for particular boats. However, in simple terms the rig should be reasonably tight but not so tight that it forces the mast down so much that it distorts the deck and strains the rig fittings. Obviously, if it's loose and looks baggy it needs tightening, but look for any signs of strain that may have caused stretching and subsequent sagging.

All fittings should be checked for damage and corrosion, ensuring at the same time that adjustable screw fittings operate adequately.

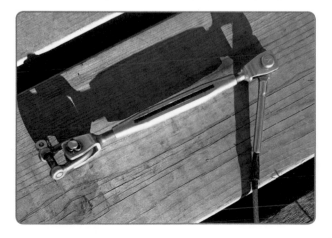

Left: A dismantled swageless terminal ready to receive the end of the rigging wire.

Right: The swageless terminal fastened and fitted in position.

If in doubt about exactly what the right tension is for your rig, buy or borrow a tension gauge of the right size for the diameter of your shrouds and forestay. Various types of gauge are available and the instructions with each type need to be followed carefully. The readings taken with the Loos Tension Gauge are often used by sail and rig makers to provide the rig tuning data for racing yachts.

Replacement and swaging

Replacement of rigging wires requires the ends to be formed into loops or fixed to a stainless steel terminal so that they can be attached to the rigging screws or other fastenings. This 'swaging' isn't something you can do yourself and it's necessary to have traditional types of swaging done professionally. A special machine is used to compress a fitting onto the wire, gripping it.

Stainless steel 'swageless' terminals are available for DIY fitting. These are also known as 'cone' terminals. They rely on compression of a cone within the fitting to grip the rigging wire. It's important to follow the instructions provided with each type of DIY swageless terminal carefully, in order to attach them securely and safely. If considering this alternative, first calculate the cost of buying all the wire and swageless terminals and then compare that with the total cost of having all the work done by a specialist.

When you come to order replacement wires, take the old ones to the local chandler or rigger to ensure that the right lengths are provided. If this isn't possible, measure the length of the wire from the load bearing points on the inside of the eyes at each end of the wire, and explain how you've taken the measurements when ordering the replacements in order to avoid any misunderstandings. If there's a problem obtaining new rigging locally, you can get it by mail order, for example from Jimmy Green Marine at http://www.jimmygreen.co.uk.

When storing wire rigging, wash off salt water and dirt and always coil it carefully so as to avoid kinking it.

Halyards

Halyards are the ropes used to hoist the sails. They pass through pulleys called blocks or sheaves at the top of the mast. Take care not to lose the end of a halyard up the mast when it's not attached to a sail, and remember to fasten it to a cleat when detaching the sail.

Halyards left slack can slap against the mast, the resulting irritating noise being often referred to as 'frapping halyards' – although other words have also been used… The solution is to tie them back away from the mast, securing them to one of the stays with a cord or bungee elastic. This also prevents the inevitable wear they sustain by flapping against the mast.

On many sailing boats the halyards go through the pulleys called sheaves embedded in 'cages' in the mast, and into the hollow mast. The lower end of the halyard then comes out of the mast down near the deck, to be fastened to a cleat. Ideally, the halyard should be checked for wear frequently and replaced before it breaks and the end slips down into the mast. If this does happen, re-threading can be difficult.

Re-threading a halyard

To do this the mast has to be removed from the boat unless it can be reached from the upstairs window or balcony of a sailing club house. Remove the sheave cages that hold them into the mast by unscrewing them. On some masts it's also possible to detach the mast heel to access the interior.

With at least one helper, carefully stand the mast up against the wall of a building where an upstairs window will

Tying back the halyards.

A variety of types and sizes of ropes are available from chandlers.

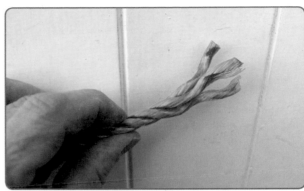

Three-strand rope.

provide access to the top of the mast. Using a fishing line with a lead weight attached, thread it through the detached upper sheave and then into the mast. Lower the weight down the inside of the hollow mast.

Using a bent piece of wire, whoever is at the bottom of the mast needs to hook the fishing line out of its lower end and pass it through the detached lower sheave cage. Next, tie the new halyard to the fishing line at the top of the mast and use the line coming out of the bottom to pull the new halyard through both the mast and the sheave cages. The sheave cages can now be screwed back into the mast. Be sure to secure both ends of the halyard before either of them disappear into the mast!

Ropes

Although it might seem strange to some people, handling ropes of different types can provide a pleasant sensation, which conjures up memories of seafaring traditions and visions of being in control of a beautiful vessel slicing through the waves. The variety of ropes is quite fascinating, and each has its particular uses.

Types and uses

Ropes made of natural fibres are unlikely to be used unless chosen to maintain the appearance and appeal of an old wooden boat. Natural fibres don't have the durability or strength of the synthetic fibres that are most commonly used on modern sailing dinghies and cruisers.

Three-strand rope is twisted together, which this makes it fairly easy to splice. However, it's not as comfortable to handle frequently as the smoother and softer braided and plaited ropes. Consequently the latter types are preferable for ropes that have to be handled a lot.

Ropes are usually available in different colours. Using a colour for a particular purpose – such as to identify each of the sheets controlling sails – makes life easier when there isn't the time to work out which rope to grab.

Some types of polyester rope, such as Dacron, are braided and in addition, have an inner core of braided rope. These are consequently referred to as 'braid-on-braid'.

They combine uniform flexibility with great strength and are used for sheets to control sails, halyards, and similar purposes. They are low stretch, have good UV light resistance and sink in water.

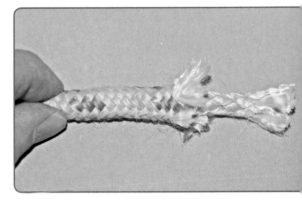

Braid-on-braid with the inner core exposed.

Nylon rope is particularly strong but stretches considerably. It's usually available as a three-strand rope with each strand containing many twisted filaments. The consequent stretch characteristic makes it suitable for mooring lines and anchor warps, where it can absorb the shock of a sudden pull. It also has good UV resistance and sinks in water.

Polypropylene rope is quite cheap but has poor UV resistance, meaning that it deteriorates more rapidly than other types. It's often used for mooring lines, but nylon is a much better and more reliable choice. The main advantage

Polypropylene rope is cheap but deteriorates in sunlight.

Nylon guard-rail netting.

Ropes should be coiled carefully when not in use.

of polypropylene is that it floats and can therefore be effective for rescue lines, which need to be visible on the surface.

Nylon guard-rail netting is easily fitted to the stanchions and guard rails or wires on a sail cruiser. This helps to prevent loose items and people – particularly children – from disappearing overboard. It also keeps sails from dipping down into the water when lowered.

Rope maintenance

As with most parts of a sailing dinghy or cruiser, looking after your ropes prolongs their life, reducing the rate at which their fibres break down and helping to stop them from breaking.

The ultraviolet light in sunlight gradually degrades many types of rope. This is unavoidable in most cases, but if possible you should try to keep them out of direct sunlight when they're not being used.

Ropes should be washed occasionally using lukewarm soapy water. This removes salt deposits and grit, which can cause wear. A pressure washer can be used carefully, but don't apply maximum pressure to the rope: particularly powerful pressure washers can take the surface off a concrete driveway so there's a risk that maximum pressure might force grit inside a rope, where it will cause damage.

Using a washing machine on a cool setting is effective, but an almighty tangle will ensue unless you first place the coiled rope in a suitable cloth bag, such as a pillowcase. Bear in mind, though, that a large, wet rope could be too heavy for the washing machine, damaging it and your relationship with other members of the household.

Ropes stiff with dirt and salt will need soaking for a day or two in soapy water, which should be agitated occasionally. Thorough rinsing may have to be followed by another soaking. Scrubbing with a plastic scrubbing pad helps to remove stubborn dirt. Halyards that remain inflexible even after this treatment may have to be replaced.

Ropes that have become stiff with salt can also benefit from being soaked in a bucket of water with a cup of fabric

conditioner added. After rinsing and drying the rope should be much more flexible, and more pleasant to hold – and to smell!

You should stop ropes fraying by securing the ends as described below, and you should carefully coil all ropes when not in use. This helps to stop kinks forming, which can weaken a rope.

Check rope regularly for wear and abrasion damage. Try to alter the position of contact with fittings from time to time in order to spread the wear on the rope. To stop wear and fraying, you can thread plastic hose onto a rope at the points where it passes through or over fittings such as a roller.

Safety aspects

The safe use of ropes requires care and commonsense:

- In order to avoid entanglement and injury, don't stand in a coil of rope.
- Avoid standing in the line of recoil where a rope or cable might backlash if it breaks.
- Always check and test that knots and splices are secure.
- A rope with a heavy load should not be controlled directly by your bare hands. Take two or more turns round a cleat, winch or post to reduce the strain on your body.
- Don't wind a rope round your hand where there's a risk that your hand could be suddenly pulled into a winch or other fitting. Along with head injuries from collisions with the boom, this is one of the most common types of injury to occur on a sailing boat.
- Be aware that knots weaken a rope, reducing its strength, depending on the type of knot, by between 20 and 50 per cent, or even as much as 70 per cent if the knot is poorly tied.

Sealing rope ends

The traditional way to stop ropes unravelling and fraying at the ends is to use twine binding or 'whipping'. Whether you want to spend a lot of time winding thread round and round rope ends depends on your dexterity and determination, but there are alternatives.

Synthetic rope ends can be fused by using a heated knife blade or the flame from a gas lighter, after first taking the necessary safety precautions to avoid a conflagration. Obviously, you shouldn't touch the rope with your fingers until it's had plenty of time to cool, but you'll need to smooth the melted edges with something non-flammable. Otherwise a nasty sharp edge could form as the solidifying end cools. Heat-shrink sleeving, available from some marine equipment suppliers, can also be used.

A safer method is to use a liquid called 'Dip-it Whip-it'. You simply dip the end of the rope into the glue-like liquid and let it dry.

An even simpler method only really suitable for the temporary securing of a rope end is to bind it with plastic tape of the insulating variety.

Knots and splices

Wherever possible, it's best to use spices to make loops for attaching fastenings. Splices reduce the strength of the rope much less than knots. Ropes can be purchased with eye splices already provided at one or both ends.

Whole books have been written on tying knots. However, with ropes provided with eye splices being widely used in rigging, only a few knots need to be learned.

The website at http://www.animatedknots.com provides animated stage by stage demonstrations of how to tie the knots and splices mentioned overleaf, along with a huge range of other knots. It also offers much advice on the use of each knot.

'Dip-it Whip-it' seals rope ends.

Plastic adhesive tape can be used temporarily to stop a rope fraying.

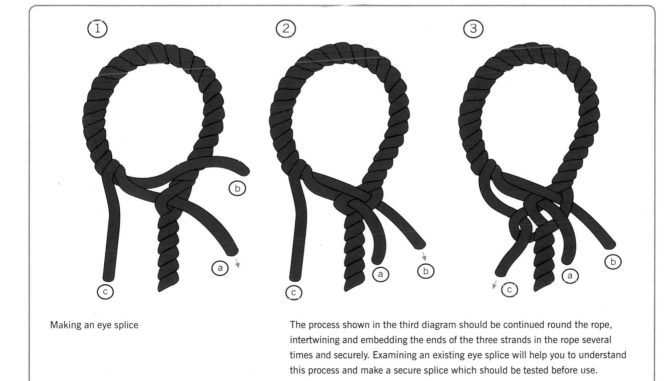

Making an eye splice

The process shown in the third diagram should be continued round the rope, intertwining and embedding the ends of the three strands in the rope several times and securely. Examining an existing eye splice will help you to understand this process and make a secure splice which should be tested before use.

Types of knot

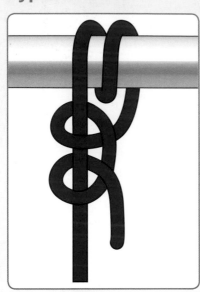

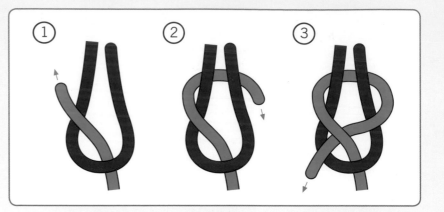

Left: A round turn and two half hitches is very good for tying mooring lines to posts and for many other purposes. Though a clove hitch is sometimes suggested for this it isn't actually suitable, as it can slip in response to a sudden pull.

Above: The sheet bend is used for joining two ropes, particularly where they're of different thicknesses. It's considered by knot experts to be more secure than the reef knot.

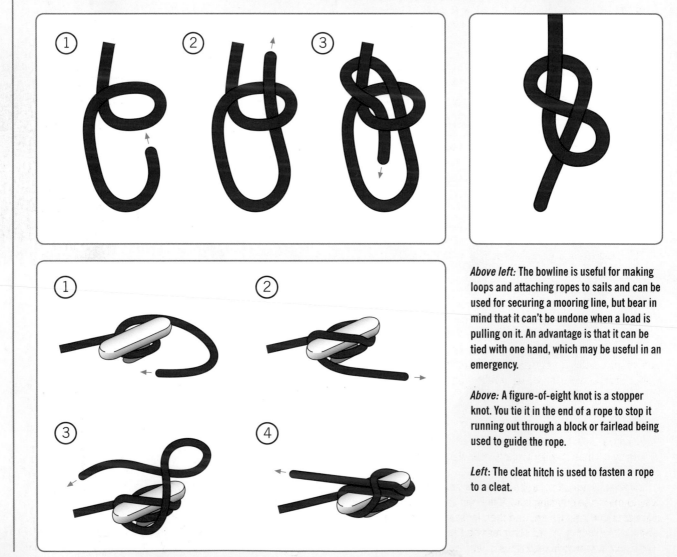

Above left: The bowline is useful for making loops and attaching ropes to sails and can be used for securing a mooring line, but bear in mind that it can't be undone when a load is pulling on it. An advantage is that it can be tied with one hand, which may be useful in an emergency.

Above: A figure-of-eight knot is a stopper knot. You tie it in the end of a rope to stop it running out through a block or fairlead being used to guide the rope.

Left: The cleat hitch is used to fasten a rope to a cleat.

Care and maintenance of sails

Sails are usually made of strong and durable materials including nylon, Dacron and polyester fibres coated or interwoven with Kevlar. Although tough, they need to be looked after in order to maintain their efficient performance and extend their life. When they're in use, take care not to over-tighten the halyards as this puts unnecessary strain on them.

A spinnaker is a lightweight, very full sail attached forward of the mast when the boat is running with the wind coming from behind. It's made of nylon and is quite strong considering that the material used is so thin and lightweight. However, it can get snagged and tear quite easily so care needs to be taken when handling either a spinnaker or the similar sail called a gennaker that's often used in racing.

Storage

When a sailing dinghy is brought ashore, rinse off salt deposits and dirt from the sails. If left on, the abrasive dried salt crystals will damage the coating that gives a sail its stiffness and shape: the salt attracts moisture from water vapour in the air, so the sails stay damp and mildew can form on them. Don't use a pressure washer or strong jet of water, as this could stretch and distort the sailcloth.

It's also important to dry sails before storing them, but don't leave them to flap and flog in the wind – this can cause rapid deterioration and can be particularly damaging to Kevlar sails. Sails are much less likely to get spotted with mould if they're dry before they go into storage. Once stored, it's a good idea to bring them out and air them occasionally.

Rinsing and drying is more of a problem for sail cruisers. Try to bring the sails ashore to rinse and dry them when possible.

Sails will inevitably get creased to a certain extent but you should try to minimise this, as it can reduce the stiffness of the sail and spoil its shape and efficiency. The best way to store a sail is to roll it rather than fold it. Small sails, as on sailing dinghies, can be rolled round the boom. Check that sail battens have been removed from their pockets as these can cause distortion if they're kept in a stored sail. On many sail cruisers roller reefing on the boom and on the forestay neatly rolls the sail away without creasing. Some dinghies also have roller reefing on the forestay for headsails.

The 'jib' is the smaller sized headsail, but the larger headsail called a 'genoa' can be reduced in size whilst sailing by the use of roller reefing, as well as being rolled up for storage.

Large sails may have to be folded for storage. The best way to minimise creasing is to 'flake' the sail down in a zigzag concertina-fashion, and then loosely roll it before placing it in its bag. Avoid compressing the bagged sail – make sure no one sits on it or uses it as a cushion. Ideally

Use a fine spray to clean salt and dirt from the sails.

Sails can be left up for a short time to dry, but don't let excessive flapping cause unnecessary wear.

The sail from a small sailing dinghy rolled round its wooden mast and gaff.

14 Anchoring and mooring equipment

Anchors, chain and rope

The size and weight of an anchor depends on the size of the boat and where it's to be used. The actual choice will depend on how you use your boat. For day sailing in sheltered creeks or inland waterways a simple system using a folding grapnel anchor may be sufficient. But if you intend at any time to venture out of very sheltered waters, and particularly if you plan to anchor in a tidal harbour or estuary overnight, it's most important to have equipment that matches the boat and conditions; otherwise you could drift onto the shore or rocks and be wrecked whilst asleep.

The 'rode' is the chain and rope used with an anchor. A length of chain should always be shackled to the anchor and attached to the rope. The shackle should be 'moused', *ie* bound with wire to stop it coming unscrewed. The chain's weight is vital in holding the anchor down so that it gains and keeps a firm grip on the seabed. It also resists abrasion far better than rope. Recommendations for the length of chain vary from two to a very cautious five times the length of the boat. It may depend on the total weight that you can cope with when lifting the combined chain and anchor.

The rope rode should be of a type that stretches to absorb the sudden shocks and pulls of a boat riding the waves. Nylon is ideal for this. The length of rope, referred to as the 'warp' or 'scope', attached to the chain should be a minimum of three times the depth of the water in calm sheltered conditions. The longer the length, the more secure the anchor is. Length should be increased to at least five times the water depth in windy conditions, and a strong wind will require eight times the depth – although the proximity of other boats and obstacles needs to be taken into consideration, of course. The actual length carried on the boat should, therefore, be much more than the length you anticipate using according to the depths in which you expect to anchor. Remember to include the rise of the tide in your calculations.

The chandler who sells the equipment will provide advice on its selection relevant to the area where you'll be sailing and anchoring.

Chain is sold by the metre.

A 'belt and braces' approach is to have two anchors and a rode for each. The second one can be used at an angle to the other if there are ground-holding problems or the possibility of a sudden increase in wind or waves. An anchor sometimes referred to as a 'lunch hook' is a small folding grapnel type to use for an hour or two in a sheltered creek while you stop for lunch, or any other reason.

Recommendations for the weight of anchor for a particular length of boat vary considerably. A traditional non-metric expression has been one pound (0.45kg) in weight for each one foot (0.3m) of boat length, though recommendations for more recently developed types of anchor may be for a little less weight – as, for example, for a Bruce anchor used in firm sand.

However, carrying an anchor heavier than the minimum recommended – providing you can lift it off the seabed – provides a reassuring safety margin. Chain diameter (the

Folding grapnel anchors suitable for use as a 'lunch hook'.

The Bruce anchor.

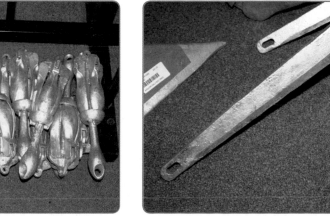

The shackle being 'moused' to stop it unscrewing.

thickness of the steel used in making each link) is normally 6mm for a dinghy and 8mm for a small sail cruiser of up to 7.5m overall length. Match this with nylon rope with a diameter of 10 and 14mm respectively. Shackles slightly larger than the chain size should be used and they should be 'moused', meaning the shackle should be bound with wire to stop it coming unscrewed.

The local harbour master should be consulted about anchoring and about suitable locations where it's permitted and safe to do so. It's always preferable to anchor in sand or firm mud. The anchor can then dig well in.

Anchoring technique is one of the subjects covered in sailing school courses. If you're in any doubt at all about anchoring for an overnight stay, particularly if increasing winds or waves are likely, plan in advance to arrive at a marina or harbour well before dark.

Anchors used on rocky or weed-covered seabed can get stuck and become difficult to retrieve. On many types of anchor, a suitable length of 'trip line' can be attached to the crown of the anchor and a float on the surface. If the anchor gets stuck, this trip line can then be used to lift it clear of the obstruction.

Moorings

Warps

Warps are the ropes used to tie a boat to mooring points. Ideally you should have two for the bow and two for the stern so that two of them can be used as 'springs', as shown in the diagram, to stop the boat swinging and moving excessively when tied up. They need to be long enough to allow for the rise and fall of the tide, the range of which is indicated on tide tables. Some inexperienced boat owners have returned to their boat to find it suspended from the harbour wall by ropes that were too short for the fall of the tide.

Various rope types can be used for mooring warps but nylon has the advantage of being particularly strong and more likely to absorb shocks by stretching.

On inland waterways, L-shaped anchors called 'rond' anchors are used. These are tied to the end of the warps and pushed into the ground on the bank. It can be difficult to hold the boat and get a rond anchor into the ground at the same time, and it's much easier if someone on the bank holds the boat by the ropes until you're sure you have the anchors firmly in place.

Never throw any type of anchor. Rond anchors thrown onto the bank have a nasty tendency to bounce back and hit the boat or you.

Mooring tackle maintenance

In the case of permanently fixed mooring equipment – such as swinging moorings out in an estuary – regular maintenance is essential, as they sustain wear through use, abrasion with the seabed and corrosion. Insurance companies usually specify that such equipment is regularly checked and maintained by qualified and experienced specialists. This should not be ignored. If a boat breaks free from a mooring, the insurer's first questions will be about mooring maintenance before a claim will even be considered.

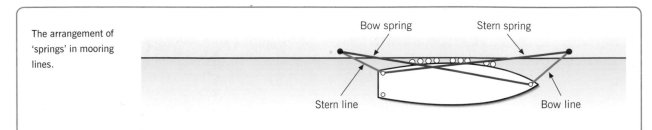

The arrangement of 'springs' in mooring lines.

Bow spring   Stern spring

Stern line   Bow line

Types of anchor

Many new and quite expensive types of anchor have been developed claiming all kinds of advantages for those who cruise far and wide in larger sail cruisers. However, the ones described below are a few of the tried and tested traditional types.

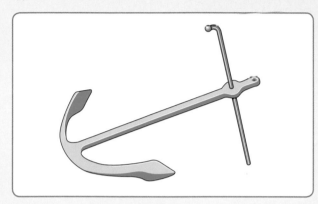

CQR or plough

This type 'ploughs' into the seabed and also holds well. It can be kept conveniently in a stem head roller over the bow of the boat.

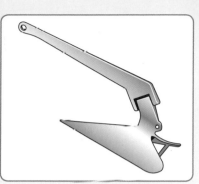

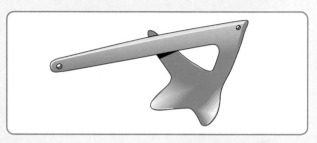

Fisherman

The fisherman anchor has been used for centuries and is still to be found on some boats. It can be effective on rocks or in seaweed but is cumbersome; can become entangled with its chain; the uppermost of its sharp points (called 'flukes') can damage a boat as the tide goes out; and its folding stock has to be pegged in place so that the flukes dig into the seabed. If you get one with a second-hand boat, consider replacing it with one of the following.

Danforth

This anchor has good holding power and folds flat when stored. You need to take care when handling it, as fingers can get trapped when the flukes swivel.

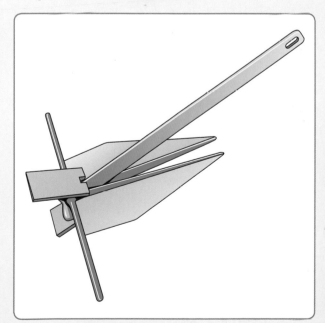

Bruce

The Bruce anchor has particularly good holding power in relation to its weight and stores well on a stem head roller.

Grapnel

The folding grapnel anchor is cheap and convenient for use as a 'lunch hook' on a day boat or dinghy but doesn't hold as well as the above types. It can be reasonably effective in rocky areas but may then get wedged and become difficult to remove.

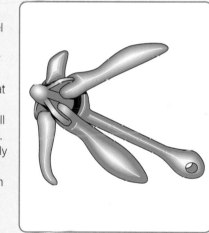

A selection of anchors for sale, some with chain and warp attached.

This mooring shackle has seriously worn and corroded to the point of failure.

On some drying moorings it may be possible to inspect the mooring tackle at low tide unless the soft mud is hazardous.

Where a mooring is rented, get confirmation that regular professional maintenance is carried out. If you purchase the right to moor or gain a mooring through a sailing club, maintenance issues should be agreed in writing and accepted by your insurance company. In the past many moorings were laid by amateurs using all kinds of weights, but greater awareness of safety issues and stricter insurance requirements have emphasised the risks involved with this.

The above should not prevent you from checking aspects of the mooring tackle yourself, in addition to its professional maintenance, if you can reach it safely. Using a boat hook from a secure position on your boat, the chain and shackles that are fixed to the mooring buoy can be lifted. Although they may be substantial, the friction caused by waves, wind and boat movement will gradually wear the shackles and chain links, reducing their diameter and strength.

Check that the screw-in pins on the shackles are tight and 'moused' over (bound with wire to stop them unscrewing). If you replace a shackle you must use one of

A protective sleeve of plastic pipe helps prevent the chafing of mooring ropes.

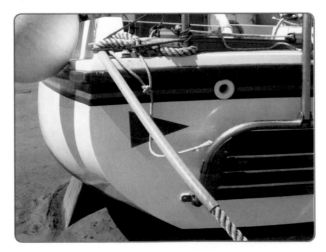

the same size and type, or stronger, and of the same metal as the original. Using a different type of metal, such as stainless steel, enables electrolytic processes to cause a reaction between them, which will weaken the fittings.

In the case of a mooring exposed at low tide on firm sand or gravel, it may be possible to inspect the ground tackle for wear. Take great care to check that soft sand or deep mud won't trap you if you attempt to do this. One unfortunate boat owner attempting to check his mooring became stuck up to his waist in sticky mud, and a helicopter, lifeboat and fire appliances were involved in rescuing him in front of a hundred onlookers out for a Sunday stroll. They were greatly entertained when he was dragged ashore and hosed down. Although his pride was hurt more than his body, he was lucky. In a more remote situation he could have faced a rising tide with no one around to raise the alarm.

Chafing is the main enemy of mooring ropes. Where they rub against a stem head roller, or any other surface, fit a protective sleeve of flexible plastic pipe, a leather covering or something similar.

Picking up a vacant mooring for anything more than a brief stop instead of anchoring may be risky, if it hasn't been adequately maintained. It's best to seek confirmation of its dependability from the harbour master or some other reliable authority. Permission is likely to be necessary in any case, as the mooring owner could return and want to use the mooring you're attached to.

Picking up the mooring
This has already been covered in Chapter 8, but you might want to consider the following tips to make it easier. Firstly you could try using a 'Moorfast' mooring hook in place of the more usual boat hook. And secondly you could attach a small pickup buoy to the mooring rope, with a good-sized loop forming a grab handle. This small buoy is then fixed to the base of the main mooring buoy, and becomes the target for your boat hook. It can be brought aboard and a loop on the rope slipped over the cleat, or samson post, in the bow.

The Moorfast mooring hook threads a rope through a ring or round a cleat and brings it back aboard with a simple push and pull action.

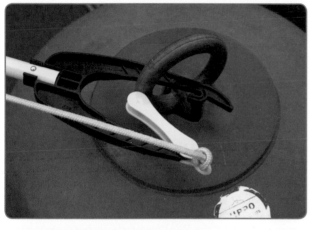

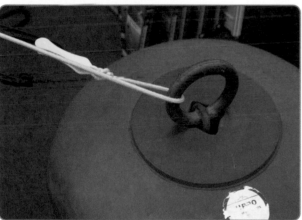

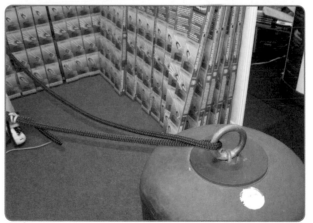

Winter precautions

In the winter, when the sail cruiser has been brought ashore, the common precaution where ice may form or other processes may damage the mooring is to replace the main mooring buoy with a small float and line, which provides a marker. You should certainly avoid dropping the mooring chain to the seabed without some sort of marker, as it will be very difficult to find the mooring next season. A

precaution against this possibility is to use GPS equipment to get an exact fix on the position of the mooring ground tackle and to establish its position with reference to several permanent landmarks.

If the mooring buoy is lost and not exposed at low tide, professional help from a diver will be needed to find the ground tackle and reconnect the buoy. If it's exposed at low tide, be wary of sinking into soft mud and sand when looking for it.

15 The cabin and covers

Leaking window seals

Window seals are a common source of leaks into the cabin of a sail cruiser. The sealant has to cope with the different rates of expansion of the various materials used in the window, the frame and the surrounding cabin sides. It starts off flexible enough to cope but over several years will lose this flexibility, become brittle and start to crack away from the surfaces to which it was originally stuck.

Water from rain and spray enters the cracks, and freeze-and-thaw action in winter can then cause more damage to the sealant. The remedy most often recommended is to remove the window and replace the sealant. This is a messy and time-consuming job, and during the sailing season you may not want to spend valuable sailing time removing and resealing windows. It may have to be done eventually, but there is a way to delay this whilst still solving the problem of drips coming through onto bunks and bedding: 'Captain Tolley's Creeping Crack Cure'.

Though it may sound a bit like an old-fashioned medicine-show remedy, this is, in fact, an ingenious liquid invented to cure leaks into the cabin on the Captain's own boat. The product was launched at the Southampton Boat Show in 1986. Captain Tolley's website at http://www.captaintolley.com is very informative.

Crack Cure is applied to the joints around a window where there are cracks less than 1mm wide. Although it can work in damp conditions, it should, ideally, be used when the joint is as dry as possible, in order to avoid water diluting it and reducing its effectiveness. It should also be applied when the temperature is between 5 and 27°C. It's a very runny, penetrating fluid and you have to be careful to control the rate of flow. Because it's so good at flowing it penetrates even the thinnest of cracks, often invisible to the naked eye. As the fluid disappears down any cracks, it actually helps to find the source of a leak.

After the first application, let it dry, and then apply more fluid to the point of the leak. Repeat this process every 30 minutes until the fluid no longer drains away into the crack. In this way the sealant will have built up layers inside the crack, progressively sealing it against leakage. Wipe away any excess with a damp cloth before it dries.

Although it's recommended for cracks up to 1mm wide, Crack Cure can actually glue together debris in leaking cracks and produce a surprisingly long-lasting waterproof repair.

Since some of the fluid might leak through and out the other side of the crack with the first applications you need to be ready to mop it up. It therefore helps to have someone on the other side of the leak. A further application after allowing it to dry fully for 24 hours ensures that the crack is completely sealed. Although the liquid is white when wet, it dries transparent and can be painted if required.

It's best to use Crack Cure on the window seals and other joints as part of your annual boat maintenance, providing prevention rather than cure. Bear in mind, though, that leaks from fittings that take considerable strains or bear a load indicate possible corrosion of bolts and fittings, which could be weakening them. In this situation, replacement would be better and safer than just sealing the leaks.

Window damage repair

Cast acrylic Perspex is most commonly used for boat windows, although other makes and materials are sometimes used.

Although the Creeping Crack Cure solution described above is worth trying first, severe cracking and failure of window seals will eventually make replacement necessary. Unless it's just superficial scratching, damage to the actual windows will also render replacement essential.

If light scratches to the Perspex are the problem, you could try to remove the scratches before you resort to replacing the window. Liquid car polish that contains no abrasives can be applied using a soft cloth, a little at a time. After the polish has dried, remove it with another clean soft cloth. Repeating this process several times may be sufficient to remove the scratches. However, if they're deep it's unlikely to prove effective.

Toughened glass has a very hard surface and any

Captain Tolley's Creeping Crack Cure bottle is gently squeezed so that the liquid flows into cracks around the window frame.

Any excess should be wiped away with a damp cloth.

The Crack Cure can also be used where deck fittings are leaking water into the cabin.

Above: Crazing of Perspex can't be cured and replacement of the windowpane will be necessary.

Below: Part of a boat show display by Eagle Windows showing how a company such as this can help with window repairs and supply parts for DIY work on windows.

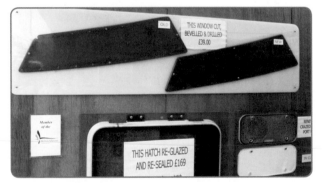

scratches will be very difficult or impossible to remove without causing abrasion marks around the scratch.

Crazing of Perspex occurs over time through the action of ultraviolet sunlight. It can go deep into the Perspex and can't be cured. Replacement is the only solution.

Window replacement

Window replacement can be a fairly straightforward job but if it seems difficult – perhaps because a window is glazed or its aluminium frames are very firmly stuck to the Perspex or glass – you may need to find a local boat window specialist to help. If you can't, a company known as Eagle Boat Windows provides a mail order service to cope with the complications. Windows in their frames can be sent to them for professional repair or they can supply the necessary materials, replacement parts and advice for you to carry out your own repairs. There is much helpful information on their website at http://www.eagleboatwindows.co.uk.

Before removing window frames, label the inside and top of each frame with its location in order to make it easier to replace them correctly. These labels can be written on pieces of masking tape attached to the frame.

On some boats the windows help to strengthen the cabin sides, so don't walk on the roof of the cabin when any part of a window has been removed. It may also be best to remove and replace only one window at a time so as to avoid the risk of distortion.

Make sure you can work reasonably comfortably and safely outside and inside the boat without cutting yourself on sharp edges. Have someone available on the other side of the window, to undo the fastenings and help remove the windowpane or frame. Both of you need to wear suitable leather gloves to protect your hands against sharp edges and broken fragments.

Removing and replacing a windowpane and frame

Windows made of Perspex or similar plastic are often bolted through the cabin sides with stainless steel bolts. These can be undone, perhaps with the help of some easing oil.

Screws or bolts should be loosened by selecting pairs that are opposite each other.

The following series of photos shows the repair of a window in which cracked Perspex needs to be replaced. The same principles can be applied to many types of windows with aluminium frames.

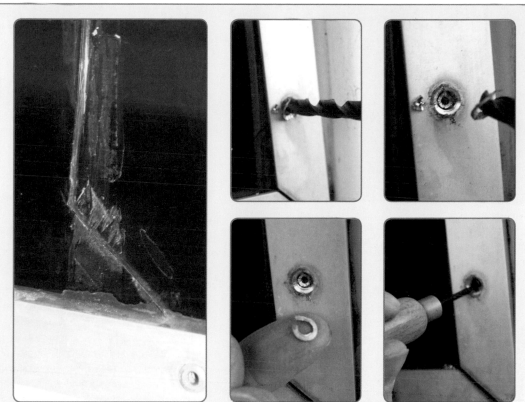

Drill out the flange of each rivet and push it through.

Loosen and remove screws or bolts in a sequence, selecting pairs that are diagonally opposite each other. If any other items are likely to make it difficult to remove the window, carefully remove or unstick them. This may involve detaching lining on the inside walls of the cabin. Be ready to hold the windowpane if it slips down at any stage.

The accompanying series of photographs illustrates the replacement of one type of window in which the cracked Perspex needs to be replaced. The same principles can be applied to many different types of windows with aluminium frames.

Rivets will have to be drilled out. Start from the outside and drill out the flange of each rivet. Next, try gently pushing the rivet out through the hole. If this doesn't work, perhaps because the rivet is corroded, carefully drill it out completely.

A thin knife may have to be inserted between the windowpane and the fibreglass or wooden sides of the cabin to break any sealant away from the frame. Do this a little at a time all round the window. Don't try to lever the windowpane out with the knife, though, as this could crack it or damage the side of the cabin. Aluminium frames may have become brittle with age so the frame must be taken off gently in order to avoid breaking or bending it.

Use a knife to break the hold of the sealant.

Gently remove the frame. In this case it came away in sections.

It may not be possible to remove the windowpane without it breaking into pieces, so suitable leather gloves are needed.

Drilling screw holes in Perspex should be done slowly, gently and carefully to avoid cracking it.

If the windowpane still won't come away readily, a helper can push gently from inside the cabin while you hold it on the outside. If the Perspex or glass isn't damaged it should be possible to remove the whole sheet intact, but if it's broken you need to wear suitable gloves when removing it.

When dealing with an aluminium frame, place it on a level bed of soft cloth to support it and prevent it from distorting. Remove all traces of sealant and dirt from the frame and its surround. If the windowpane is to be reused,

Left and *below:* White spirit should soften old sealant making it easier to scrape off.

all sealant should be cleaned off that too. This can be a time-consuming task, but white spirit should help. Acetone can also be used on metal frames, but keep it well away from transparent plastic windowpanes as it can turn them permanently cloudy. Take care not to scratch the outside surface of the aluminium frame and the Perspex.

Screw holes can be cleaned by drilling through them. Any sharp edges around the drilled holes should be removed gently with a countersink bit.

It's important to save all the pieces of plastic from a broken windowpane. These should then be placed on a sheet of cardboard and fitted together. Draw round the shape of the window to make a template, and use this to mark out the shape and screw holes on a new sheet of Perspex. Support the Perspex carefully and securely and cut it to shape using a fine-toothed blade in either a fretsaw, a hacksaw or a jigsaw. If you're using toughened glass rather than Perspex it can usually be provided ready-cut to size by a local supplier.

With the pane fully supported, mark the positions of any screw holes needed and use a sharp new drill bit to make the holes in the exact positions required. To avoid causing sudden stress to the Perspex, drill at a slow speed to start with and then increase the speed gradually.

With a helper, do a 'dry run' with the windowpane and fittings held in place. Make sure the screws or bolts fit well into the window, the frame and the cabin side, ensuring that they don't exert any sideways pressure or distortion to the Perspex, which could crack it.

Silicone or a similar non-setting sealant such as butyl should be used when refitting the windowpane – strongly adhesive polyurethane sealants aren't suitable, as they could render the windowpane difficult to remove in the future. Run a substantial bead of sealant round the edge of the pane in line with the screw holes. Sufficient should be applied to result in an excess being squeezed out as the window is screwed or bolted into place.

Press the windowpane and frame – with more sealant on the frame where necessary – into its hole in the cabin side.

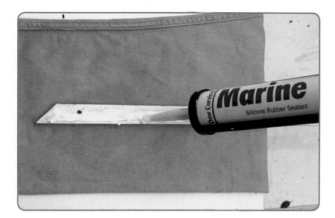

Apply a substantial bead of sealant to the frame and the surfaces to which it's to be bonded.

Screws should be tightened a little each, one at a time, to spread the pressure evenly.

Some sealant will appear in the bolt holes. Check that the screws or bolts can get through the sealant and remove any of the excess that might cause a problem when tightening the fastenings.

Don't use a powered screwdriver, which could damage Perspex by tightening screws too quickly and aggressively. Instead you should use a hand screwdriver or your fingers to lightly tighten the screws or bolts a little at a time. Alternate the tightening across the window, starting with the screws in the middle at top and bottom, and go round them all several times. This beds the window down evenly without putting too much pressure on any one part.

The final tightening should squeeze out a little of the sealant. Bear in mind that you're not intending to glue the window to the boat. The idea is to have a flexible gasket of sealant between the surfaces. Leave this to cure and then carefully cut and peel the excess off, preferably with a plastic scraper. Be sure to avoid scratching the windowpane or the frame. White spirit could be used to remove any residue that's difficult to shift.

If screwing Perspex straight onto the side of the boat without a frame, watch out for any bowing or distortion that could crack the plastic pane or the gelcoat. If the plastic has to bend to fit, it would be best to order preformed Perspex shaped to the curvature required. Thinner Perspex *might* bend enough but there's a risk of cracking. Don't use countersunk screws straight onto Perspex as the wedge shape puts stress on it and cracks will eventually develop.

Rubber Claytonrite window seals

The black rubber window frames on some sail cruisers can be removed by finding the end of the central filler strip and hooking it out. Pull it out all the way round. This should loosen the windowpane so that it can be carefully pushed out without breaking it. The pane should be kept as a template for cutting the replacement, as described above.

Likewise, you need to keep the rubber seal in order to identify exactly the size and type that's needed to replace it. The new seal should be ordered a little longer than actually

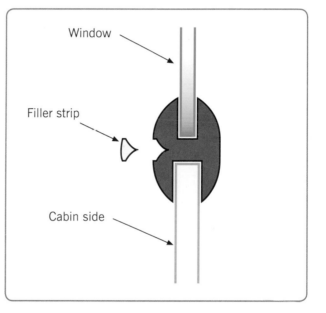

Cross-section of the Claytonrite rubber window seal. The glass or plastic pane slots into the groove on one side and the cabin side slots into the groove on the other. A filler strip is pushed in to hold them in place.

The end of the filler strip is pulled out to loosen the window.

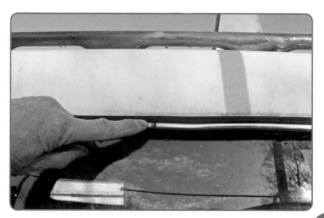

needed. New Claytonrite seals, other types of rubber seals, advice on using them and the special glazing tools required to fit them can be obtained from a number of suppliers, including http://www.sealsdirect.co.uk and http://www.wilks.co.uk.

Clean the surfaces where the seal has been removed. The new rubber seal should be fitted round the aperture first to establish the exact length needed. Push it well into the bends and corners, and cut it around 25mm longer than needed, with square ends to make a butt joint. This joint should go at the top of the window.

Remove the rubber seal and run a thin bead of silicone sealant into the groove before fitting it back and trimming to make a tight butt joint. Apply a thin bead of sealant into the groove that takes the windowpane. Insert the pane into the bottom of the seal. Use the glazing tool to fit the lip of the rubber over the edge of the pane.

Feed the filler strip that tightens the seal, through the eye of the glazing tool and work it into the channel in the rubber seal without stretching the filler strip. Lubricant can be used at this stage to help the process. Cut the end of the filler strip allowing a slight overlap. Push this overlap in to make a tight joint.

Cleaning Perspex

Windows should be kept clean but you should never wipe them when dry, as grains of dirt can cause scratches. Use warm soapy water and a soft cloth.

Damp, mould and smell reduction

A problem with boat cabins is that condensation can cause mould and bad smells. Wooden boats have an advantage here because the wood provides some insulation, although any condensation that does occur can cause rot in the wood. GRP, on the other hand, has a colder surface, which attracts condensation unless it's insulated from temperature changes. Although some degree of cabin insulation is

provided by many boat builders it may not be adequate, and any bare surfaces in the cabin and inside lockers will benefit from the following advice.

A special thick paint called 'International Anti-condensation Paint' is advertised as being able to provide some insulation in order to reduce or prevent condensation, and it's possible that several coats of this may solve your problems. This would certainly be a much simpler solution than cutting and sticking new headlining material to the ceiling.

However, the main method of reducing condensation is to provide adequate ventilation, particularly when our own bodies and cooking processes are generating plenty of moisture. Complications can arise with this, though, as you also need to keep rainwater, spray, nesting birds, rodents and intruders out of the cabin.

Vents are available that have been specifically designed to permit the circulation of air and the removal of water vapour without allowing rainwater and unwanted visitors to get in. You need the type that can be closed when there's a risk of spray entering the cabin.

The main problem occurs during the long periods when a boat is shut up and not used. Anti-condensation units that rely on moisture-absorbing granules may help, but the fact that water remains stored in their reservoir means that it can evaporate again and perhaps condense elsewhere in the cabin.

If your boat is kept in a marina, boatyard or anywhere else that mains electricity is available, a dehumidifier can be used. Small ones have now become available quite cheaply, and they can be adjusted to come on only when humidity increases to a certain level. In this case cabin vents should be closed, otherwise you'll be trying to dehumidify the Earth's atmosphere!

Trying the above should remove the condensation problem. If not, increasing the insulation is the next method. Securely sticking a layer of insulating material on the curved and awkwardly shaped surfaces of a cabin's interior isn't easy, and takes careful planning. Purpose-designed and quite costly headlining materials are available, usually involving foam-backed vinyl or similar. Order more than you need, as you'll need some to practice with before you get it right.

Alternatives to commercial materials that have been used

Below and *right:* Vents are needed to provide air circulation but must be of a type that can be closed when sailing, to prevent spray from entering.

Materials similar to thin carpet are used to line cabin interiors.

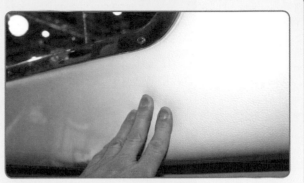

Foam-backed vinyl provides insulation and a soft surface.

Left and *right:* Sticking headlining to the awkward shapes inside a cabin takes some practice but looks good once complete.

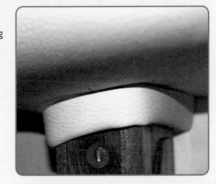

successfully on many boats include thin carpet, carpet tiles, cork tiles and spray-on foam behind thin plywood panels.

When sticking up any type of insulation, keep the cabin doorway open and ensure there's plenty of ventilation, as harmful fumes will accumulate in the confined space. Read the instructions on adhesive products carefully. Accidental glue sniffing can lead to other accidents as you attempt to leave the boat in an intoxicated state!

Mould

An inevitable by-product of condensation is mould. Many paints, including the anti-condensation paint mentioned above, contain mould-killing chemicals, but don't expect them to last forever.

Plenty of anti-mould liquids are also available and can be applied to surfaces, but take care to check whether they're safe to use in the confined space of a cabin, and ensure that you have plenty of ventilation. Strong bleach-containing preparations can give off choking fumes.

One product that's effective in removing mould inside a cabin is 'Simply Gone', which has already been mentioned in Chapter 11. After treatment the mould turns black and is easy to remove with a wet sponge.

Smells

A locked-up cabin is very likely to accumulate musty odours – or worse. Really bad smells need to be investigated fully: they could be caused by leaks from a diesel engine, toilet or

Right: 'Simply Gone' can be used to clean off mould and algae, and is advertised as being suitable to leave on GRP surfaces in order to prevent re-growth.

Below: The diluted liquid is brushed or sprayed onto the mould or algae.

Adsorbex powder and sachets help to remove odours, as does adequate ventilation.

them. After a few months you place the bag outside in the sun to discharge the trapped smell, and it can then be reused. Loose Adsorbex powder can be used in the bilges, where there may be persistent smells.

Water and waste

Water can be carried and supplied on a cruising dinghy using containers obtained from camping shops. These are often equipped with a tap, so the container can be mounted on a seat with a bowl underneath. Make sure that the container is made from 'food quality' material, otherwise it could contaminate drinking water.

Water can be provided in a small sail cruiser in the same way, though a pumped supply is more usual. Manually-operated pumps have an advantage over electric pumps in that they don't drain the battery. It's wise to have either spare parts or a spare pump on the boat.

Water tanks, containers, pumps and pipes can become contaminated with bacteria and various mould growths, and should be sterilised at least annually with a suitable product such as Milton sterilising fluid or Puriclean powder. Remember to flush away the sterilising fluid thoroughly before refilling with fresh water.

Sterilising tablets or water filters can be used to improve the quality of stored water, but if you have any doubts about the quality of the water from your tank, have a separate container of drinking water that you can trust or drink the cheaper varieties of bottled mineral water.

The simplest way to dispose of washing water is to use a bowl and empty it over the side. However, many sail cruisers have sinks and washbasins that are drained by a waste pipe discharging through the hull.

The main points to check regarding your water supply are that there are no leaks allowing dirty water – and smells – to accumulate in the bilges, and that the waste pipes stay firmly attached to the fitting that goes through the hull. This is a point where water can leak into the boat and is a cause of boats sinking.

Before the winter lay-up period, disinfect the drain pipe from the sink and place plugs in sink drain holes to prevent any odours.

sink accumulating and festering in the bilges. Decaying food and dead birds or rodents can also cause an appalling stink. Having removed and disinfected such horrors, any remaining smells are likely to be caused by the mould described in the preceding section. Improvements to ventilation and treatment of the mould should remove such odours.

However, even in the cleanest of cabins an infuriatingly persistent musty smell may still have to be dealt with. Household 'odour killers' usually just replace one smell with another that some people find more acceptable. A product that actually removes smells is Adsorbex (http://www. adsorbex.co.uk), which is made from Zeolite, a granulated mineral formed by volcanic activity. An 'Adsorbex Multi Sachet' hung in a cabin can remove odours by trapping

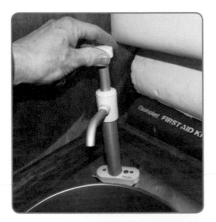

Left: A hand-operated pump supplying water to the wash basin.

Below: Food-grade containers for water storage.

Below right: Electric pumps for the water supply are installed on some sail cruisers.

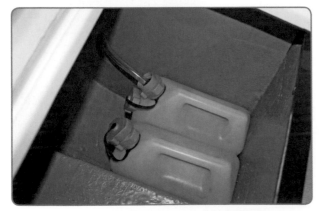

Cooking equipment

The most common fuel used for cooking aboard boats is bottled gas. However, there are alternatives. When dinghy cruising and camping ashore, driftwood can be collected for a genuine, original-style barbecue on the beach. Of course, portable barbecue kits can also be used ashore.

Some barbecue devices are available for use on the boat itself, such as a pushpit rail overhanging the stern, but great care needs to be taken in order to avoid burning more than just the food. Also consider where the smell and the smoke is going, since other people may not enjoy the aroma and will prefer to breathe fresh sea air.

Portable gas stoves using disposable canisters have become available very cheaply and are fine when used ashore camping-style, and in accordance with the instructions provided with the cooker. However, they aren't designed specifically for use on a boat and don't have clamps to hold pans in place if the boat moves. Consequently their use aboard a boat is very risky, and they certainly shouldn't be used on a moving boat. Even on an apparently calm mooring an inconsiderate boat owner may pass too fast, creating a hazardous wash that might dislodge a portable cooker or its unsecured pans of boiling water.

Disposable gas canisters shouldn't be stored in the cabin, but should be stored in the same way as large gas cylinders: in a flame-proof container ventilated to the outside of the boat. Even when apparently empty, the canisters leak heavier-than-air gas that must be vented overboard and not allowed to get into the cabin or bilges.

You have to be sure that any cooking equipment is securely fixed in place on the cooker, to allow for unpredictable movements of the boat. Cookers installed on cruisers normally have pan clamps or a framework of 'fiddles' (also called 'sea rails') round the burners to hold pans in place or gimbals to keep the cooker level. These fittings can usually be purchased as extras from cooker manufacturers and dealers, and are fairly straightforward to clip or screw in place.

Ensure that curtains and other inflammable materials are kept well away from the cooker and won't fall onto it with the movement of the boat.

Filling a large stainless steel vacuum flask with hot water before setting off is one way of avoiding having to use a cooker whilst sailing or mooring, by providing the hot water needed to make soup or a cup of tea.

Gas installations

Bottled LPG (liquefied petroleum gas) installations should always be installed and repaired by a Corgi-registered fitter experienced in working on boats. Doing such work yourself involves considerable and unacceptable risks of gas leakage, fire and explosion, and not involving a Corgi-

A rail-mounted barbeque device.

Various types of clamps are available to hold kettles and pans in place on a cooker.

The drain to the outside of the boat for any leaking gas can be seen at the bottom of this purpose-made gas storage unit, which is sealed off from the rest of the boat.

Turn off the gas supply at the cylinder when not in use.

registered engineer will probably invalidate your boat insurance. Fire in the confined space of a boat is particularly dangerous and frightening, so every precaution should be taken to avoid the risk of gas explosions.

Burning gas gives off harmful fumes including carbon monoxide. Sadly, every year there are cases of deaths where people have died from inhaling these fumes on boats. Adequate ventilation is therefore vital when using gas. Permanent adequate ventilation is a requirement of the BSS certification for inland waterways and this sets the standard for all boats. A carbon monoxide alarm can be purchased and installed in the cabin.

LPG bottles should be stored and secured in an upright position somewhere that any heavier-than-air gas leakages can escape rather than accumulating in the bilges. For this you'll need a storage unit sealed off from the rest of the boat and with ventilation from the base of the storage space to the outside. Make sure that such vents are always clear and unobstructed. The storage unit mustn't contain any electrical equipment because of the risk of a spark igniting the gas.

Always turn off the gas supply at the cylinder when it's not in use. This normally involves either screwing closed a valve by means of a turn-wheel on the cylinder or turning off a switch on the regulator. The regulator connected to the pipework may have a sealing washer that should be replaced regularly.

The flexible hose that connects metal gas pipes to the regulator attached to the gas cylinder deteriorates with use and exposure to sunlight. Such hoses should be replaced at five-year intervals, or sooner if there are signs of deterioration (such as loss of flexibility or cracking where the hose joins metal pipes). A date on the side of the hose should show when it left the factory.

Although amateurs shouldn't carry out any work on a gas system, it's obviously important to check for leaks. LPG has a smell added to it, so warning of leaks should reach your nose. A leak detection liquid can be applied to the equipment with a brush to investigate where the leak is coming from, but the problem here is that gas will be seeping down to be trapped in the bilges even while you're looking for the leak. It's therefore best to turn off the gas as soon as you suspect a leak and get a Corgi-registered engineer in to do the necessary work. A properly installed system will have a testing point where the engineer can use a tester to check for leaks.

At the risk of stating the very obvious, don't light a naked flame or turn on any electrical equipment that might cause a spark if a gas leak is suspected.

The use of washing-up liquid is sometimes recommended to find a leak, as the escaping gas will blow bubbles in a smear of it. Unfortunately, however, washing up liquid contains salt, which can cause corrosion of the metal components in the gas system. If proper leak-detection liquid isn't available and you decide to use washing-up liquid, it's essential to wash it off thoroughly and promptly with clean water. And remember: leaking gas could be gathering in the bilges while you do all of this.

A gas cooker on a boat should have a 'flame failure device' to turn the gas off if the flame goes out, thus preventing leakage of gas. When you want to light this type of cooker you have to hold in a knob for a time to disengage the device.

If the gas flame on a cooker's burner flickers yellow and soot can be seen deposited on pans, it shows that the gas isn't burning fully. The cooker must be turned off and corrected by a qualified gas engineer before being used again.

Alcohol/methylated spirit cookers

An alternative to gas is the Origo cooker, which uses unpressurised denatured alcohol or methylated spirits. Origo cookers are safer than the old pressurised alcohol/paraffin stoves still found on older boats, and many people consider them to be safer than gas. They're certainly much less complicated to install safely than gas cookers. Even though they're quite expensive, you should compare their price to the total cost of getting a Corgi-qualified engineer in to install or repair and refit a gas installation.

Origo cookers.

Having no gas installed and using an Origo cooker should also make it much easier to get a BSS safety certificate, which is essential if you want to use your cruiser on inland waterways. Adequate ventilation is still important with this and any type of cooker in the confined space of a cabin.

Fire precautions

Suitable fire extinguishers and a fire blanket should be easily accessible in the cabin. Extinguishers must be in date and inspected regularly according to manufacturers' recommendations. A smoke alarm should also be installed.

A fire blanket and fire extinguishers should be mounted within easy reach.

Sanitary equipment

The lack of floating public toilets on our inland and coastal waterways is inconvenient! Consequently there's no escaping the fact that if any length of time is to be spent afloat, a suitable receptacle is needed.

It's tempting to empty this overboard in the style of 'bucket and chuck it'. Stop and think, though, of the consequences of everyone doing this. The Victorians may have thought the solution to pollution was dilution but they were wrong. Pollutants, harmful bacteria, parasites and viruses can accumulate and persist to poison us – and wildlife. This was discovered on the Norfolk Broads many years ago, and the hundreds of hire boats had to be fitted with toilets that have holding tanks, to be pumped out into sewage disposal systems at boatyards.

On a cruising dinghy, day boat or small sail cruiser the simplest arrangement is the chemical toilet. This can be a bucket-type container with a suitable detachable seat. You need to ensure, though, that the seat doesn't detach as the boat heels over when sailing… It's also important to refit the watertight clip-on cover after use in order to prevent spillage, which inevitably reaches the bilges to haunt you for months.

A more advanced version less likely to leak is the flushing cassette toilet. This has a water tank incorporated in the top half, under the seat, and a handle is operated to flush the contents of the bowl into the holding tank in the bottom half, where a diluted chemical treats the waste and its smell. The servicing of cassette toilets mainly involves cleaning and the frequent lubrication of its moving parts, which have a tendency to stick shut if neglected.

Chemical fluids for toilets have improved in recent years and many are much more environmentally friendly. Even so, the contents of the holding tank must still not be emptied into waterways and should be deposited in the disposal

Left: A compact portable flushing chemical toilet with its own holding tank.

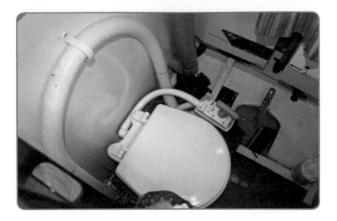

Right: A fixed flushing toilet with a separate holding tank.

points available at some boatyards. If this is a problem, they can be emptied into a domestic sewage drain at home, a little at a time, and flushed with plenty of water from a hose to prevent blocking the drain.

Some larger sail cruisers may have fixed toilets with storage tanks that need to be pumped out at a boatyard. Similar toilets that still get away with discharging into the sea may be found on some boats but these really should only be discharged well out to sea.

Fixed sea toilets are usually found in offshore cruisers beyond the size of the boats covered by this book, and their servicing is more complicated. If you do have a toilet of this type, maintenance tasks will include maintaining pipes that go through holes in the hull, and ensuring that sea water can't leak into the boat. Instructions appropriate to this type of toilet should be followed carefully and professional help should be sought when there's any risk of leakage – either of sewage or the sea water used for flushing, which could end up flushing the whole boat if not properly maintained.

Much useful information on environmentally friendly boating can be found at http://www.thegreenblue.org.uk.

Bunks and cushion care

Hardy backpacking camping types would probably have no problem sleeping on their thin closed-cell foam mats on boards arranged in a cruising dinghy. However, cruising is meant for pleasure rather than endurance, and a sleeping bag on an inflatable airbed is far more likely to provide a good night's sleep. Whatever bedding is carried on an open boat, it should be kept in a strong waterproof bag to protect it from the inevitable spray and rain.

In the cabin of a sail cruiser, bunk cushions are more usual. There are likely to be problems with foam cushions on a boat – it can be difficult to keep them dry, so waterproof covers or even thick polythene bags should be used to protect them from damp clothing, dirt and the spray that always seems to find its way into the cabin somehow.

The long periods when sail cruisers aren't in use, such as during the winter lay-up, mean condensation and mould can contaminate foam cushions. To avoid this, ensure good ventilation and remove the cushions when the boat is going

to be left unoccupied for any length of time. Ideally they should be kept in dry, reasonably warm storage at home.

On a well-used cruiser, cushion covers will eventually need to be replaced. Cautious owners of older cruisers may choose to replace the cushions with fire-resistant covers and what's sometimes called 'combustion modified' foam, to reduce fire risk. If the cushions have become compressed, an alternative to complete replacement is to add an extra top-up layer of foam inside the cover.

The covers can usually be removed from cushions by

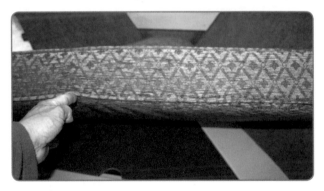

Above: Cushions usually rest on the lids of storage compartments. Condensation can accumulate here so it's wise to lift and ventilate them occasionally.

Below: Cushion covers can usually be unzipped for cleaning.

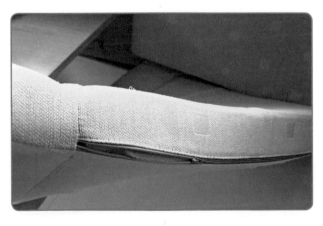

unzipping or by untying tapes. They can then be washed at a suitable temperature that will avoid damage or shrinkage. Stretch-covers can be ordered as replacements. Companies supplying these can sometimes provide quite cheap ready-made covers for standard-sized rectangular cushions. Unfortunately, however, on a boat the cushions are more likely to have a tapering shape, which requires covers to be made to measure – a more expensive course of action, though adequate expertise with a sewing machine can keep the cost down. That way the covers could be made from suitable material, but it may be worth considering the purchase of ready-made rectangular covers and then altering them to the necessary shape, with the excess material being hidden under the cushion. Not the most elegant solution, but one that could keep costs down. Alternatively, cushion cover companies will provide instructions that will enable you to measure your cushions and order covers to fit.

Curtains

Some crewmembers may have strong feelings about the degree of privacy available in a cabin. Being aware of this problem and reacting to it will help you to persuade the

The bottoms of curtains need to be secured back against the window.

Blinds are rarely found on small sail cruisers but could improve privacy.

Floor coverings

The cabin floorboards may be painted or varnished with a non-slip surface. Adding a floor covering may make the cabin more comfortable and homely, but will it provide a suitable surface to walk on when the boat is moving and heeling over? If you're satisfied it will be non-slip, a clean and attractively coloured floor covering is the first thing you see as you climb down into the cabin and it certainly makes a difference.

more reluctant members to cruise with you.

The problem with curtains on windows is the fact that the boat moves and tends to open gaps between and under them. A few well-placed pegs from the washing line can help close the gaps, but more effective is a line, rail or expandable curtain wire fixed to hold the bottom of each curtain against the window.

Lights in the cabin can throw shadows on the curtains and provide an entertaining shadow performance for onlookers. Thicker, lined curtains or the installation of blinds may help here.

Larger sail cruisers may have a toilet compartment with a door but if this luxury isn't available a curtain may provide some privacy for those moments when modesty demands it.

Covers

Sailing dinghies and day boats have two main types of cover: the flat cover, for use when the mast and rigging is removed, and the boom-up cover. The latter type can be adapted to make a 'tent' that can be used for shelter when dinghy cruising and camping overnight on the boat. Well-fitting and secure covers are necessary protection when laying up the boat for winter.

On a cruiser, an over-boom cockpit cover can extend the cabin accommodation substantially. This is usually secured

Sailing dinghies with flat covers and boom-up covers.

An over-boom cover increases accommodation on a sail cruiser.

attract condensation. Traditional cotton canvas is still used and is particularly breathable but tends to deteriorate quite rapidly. Plenty of companies provide made-to-measure covers but the material can also be purchased for DIY. Tools are available for punching holes and fitting metal eyes to the edges.

Sails kept on the boom of a sail cruiser also need a cover in order to protect them from deterioration in sunlight (see Chapter 13).

The cockpit of a sail cruiser can be made more comfortable with 'dodgers', which are rectangular lengths of material fixed to stanchions and guard-rails each side of the cockpit. These provide significant protection from cold winds and spray. As they're simple shapes, someone with minimal needlework skills could make them. The tough material may be a challenge for some sewing machines, though, so in the interests of domestic harmony you should consult other users of the machine first.

Even more luxurious on a sail cruiser would be a spray hood, although it could look incongruous and get in the way on some very small cruisers. Spray hoods provide considerable protection from the elements. A similar canopy rather like a pram hood can be attached to a cruising dinghy as illustrated in Chapter 3. This will certainly help keep off rain and spray but has the disadvantage that it can catch

in place by eyes in the cover and turnbuckles screwed to the boat, or by rubber or elastic loops on its edges that fit over hooks.

Covers are usually made of polyester and cotton fabric or reinforced PVC fabric. Breathable materials are less likely to

Dodgers provide some shelter in the cockpit and a sail cover provides protection from sunlight for the mainsail.

A spray hood reduces the amount of rain and spray entering the boat.

Preparation for the winter

Remove the mast and spars and tie the boat down to reduce the possibility of autumn gales blowing it over. The supports for sail cruisers on land will need to be strong and stable enough not only to cope with the weight of the boat but also to resist the pressure of violent gusts of wind.

Remove canopies, dodgers, sails and any other items that could be damaged by wind or stolen.

The start of winter is also a good time to identify tasks that need to be done before the next sailing season. Either carry these out yourself or arrange in good time for the boatyard to do the work. On a sailing dinghy, remove rigging, any buoyancy bags, drainage plugs and inspection or locker covers. Wash and dry the boat thoroughly to remove dirt and salt, which can attract moisture. If left outside, dinghies can be kept turned upside down and supported clear of the ground.

The cabin of a sail cruiser should be emptied of removable equipment such as GPS and VHF radio if possible. Drain water tanks and containers, as they could get damaged by frost. Tie labels in prominent places to remind you to replace equipment and what needs to be done to re-commission any engine or outboard that you've winterised.

If covers are put on any size of boat, ensure that they're really tight and firmly tied down – flapping covers can do considerable damage. If possible, leave a gap at each end to allow some circulation of air. This helps to stop condensation and is particularly important with a cabin on a sail cruiser, where damp, mould and rot can affect wood and soft furnishings. Ideally bunk cushions and bedding should be taken home and kept indoors if storage space allows.

It's difficult getting the balance right between providing adequate ventilation and keeping out rain, insects and intruders. A flow of air is the best protection from condensation leading to mould and smells. Where other ventilation is provided, some fine-meshed netting can keep out the birds, wasps, bees and flies that find boat cabins, lockers and engine compartments ideal homes for the winter.

Water left in the bilges can evaporate and cause condensation. Try to check regularly for rainwater accumulation and pump out any that appears.

Store mast and spars supported at frequent intervals along their entire length to prevent bending.

unexpectedly strong gusts of wind, rather like an umbrella on a windy day. For the same reason, a spray hood needs to be quickly removable if it seems to be competing with the sails.

Laying up and winterisation

Apart from a few determined, hardy and suitably equipped enthusiasts, most boat owners in the UK lay-up their boats for the winter. Many of the measures necessary to protect a stored boat have been covered above in connection with the cabin, and in earlier chapters, but the following additional points should also be noted.

Insurance

Ensure your cover continues throughout the winter and that your insurance company is aware of and approves of the boat's storage location and security. The darker nights of winter, along with severe winter weather, mean that there are still risks that need to be covered. Insurance companies usually indicate their requirements in their policy documents and tend to expect that a boat will be laid up in a reasonably secure and safe location. They may require that a sail cruiser is ashore by a certain date and for certain months of the year. If this isn't possible, consult the company about it and get an extension, otherwise the insurance cover may cease to apply.

If the boat is kept away from home, the insurance company is likely to require that you or someone reliable checks it regularly, such as every month.

If taking a boat of any size home on a trailer, check that the insurance covers road transport and ensure that the trailer, which may have been neglected for months, is fully roadworthy.

16 Electrical equipment

A push-switch LED light.

Batteries last longer with LED torches.

Electricity on small boats

Sailing dinghies used for racing or day sailing have no need for electricity, but once other uses for a sailing boat are taken into account electricity can become desirable.

Covering any distance and staying overnight on a mooring makes lighting necessary. Torches and other battery-powered lights can provide simple cabin illumination so long as sufficient spare batteries are carried, and may be an adequate source of illumination on inland waterways and in very sheltered coastal creeks and estuaries.

Light-emitting diodes (LEDs) have, in recent years, greatly improved torches and other lights suitable for small boats, and use very little electricity compared with other lights. They also last much longer, and prices have fallen to the point where a number of alkaline battery powered LED lights can provide plenty of cheap and reliable illumination for dinghy cruising and camping afloat.

Neat dome-shaped, push-switch-operated LED lights powered by three 1.5v alkaline batteries can be bought and stuck around the inside of a small cabin. They can also provide back-up lighting in situations where 12V lighting is otherwise used. Plenty of 12V LED lights are also available and have the advantage of saving battery power.

Navigation lights

Sailing at night is only for the experienced boat owner who has learned all about it on a suitable sailing course. You do, though, need to be prepared for an occasion where you may find yourself delayed and still cruising after dark unexpectedly. The main consideration is to avoid a collision by being seen by other vessels.

On a sailing dinghy or day boat, a powerful and reliable torch and white lantern are needed, along with a set of three emergency navigation lights in red, green and white, using

A rechargeable hand-held spotlight may also have a 12V connection.

A set of emergency navigation lights with internal batteries.

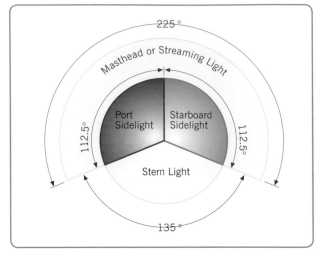

This is the 'light rose', which shows how navigation lights should be arranged to be visible around the boat.

alkaline batteries. Spare batteries are also needed. These lights are available from chandlers.

Navigation lights should be arranged with red on the port (left-hand) side, green on the starboard (right-hand) side, and white at the stern.

Sail cruisers should have navigation lights permanently installed. Instead of three separate lights, this could involve a single masthead lantern combining green and red sidelights and white stern light, connected to a 12V supply.

12V electricity

The small sail cruisers of the type covered in this book often manage with portable battery powered equipment, avoiding the complexities of 12V battery installation and charging. Equipment for short-term use, such as hand-held VHF

Below and below right: 12V batteries should be securely fixed in a purpose-made battery box and ventilated to allow explosive gases to escape safely.

radios, have rechargeable batteries. However, as some small cruisers have a 12V battery, the maintenance aspects are covered here.

The battery for use with electrical equipment should be of the deep cycle marine leisure variety rather than the type used for engine starting. Its purpose is to supply lighting, including navigation lights, and to power electrical equipment such as a VHF radio. Unfortunately, as the need for electricity increases so does the complexity of the wiring and equipment. Using electricity in a watery environment means that installation must be carried out to a high standard, preferably by someone qualified to do it. Good quality equipment must be used in order to avoid rapid deterioration, including adequate fuses and a battery isolator switch. Carrying out such installation work on a boat is covered thoroughly in several books written by electricians. Here we are mainly concerned with maintenance tasks rather than the installation of an electrical system and its associated equipment.

Problems can arise as the number of electrical devices

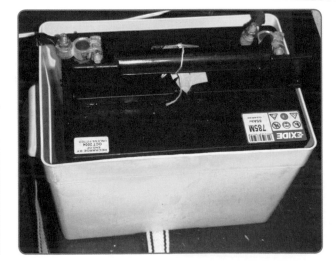

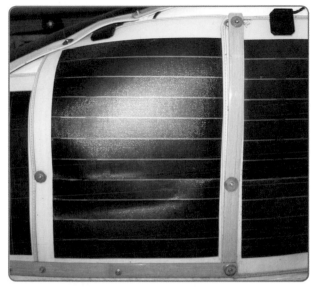

Above and *right:* Both rigid and flexible solar panels are available to charge batteries.

expands to include depth sounding, navigation and entertainment equipment, and you must take great care not to overdo things, as this can put considerable demands on the battery. If you're sailing, how do you recharge the battery? Running a noisy motor or generator to recharge it rather defeats one of the main points of quietly cruising under sail.

If the main purpose of a heavy-duty battery is to start a motor, it's vitally important to ensure that enough charge is left to do so. Having a separate deep cycle battery for electrical equipment avoids this risk.

Both batteries should be mounted in secure, suitably ventilated, purpose-designed battery boxes.

Charging – using sun and wind

Photovoltaic solar panels and wind-powered chargers have been developed for use on boats. These have become much more efficient in recent years and solar panels can generate a useful amount of electricity in daylight even without direct sunlight. However, on a small sail cruiser it's unlikely there'll be enough space to mount sufficient panels to match your electricity use during a cruise. There is, though, a good chance that a substantial recharge could be achieved on summer weekdays if the boat is used only at weekends.

If you do have enough space to mount a wind generator or solar panels, blocking diodes are needed to prevent the current flowing the wrong way. A regulator is also needed in most cases. This monitors the condition of the battery and controls the amount of charge reaching it. Without it the battery could be overcharged and damaged or could even explode.

Interesting advances with thin film solar panels by companies such as Nanosolar Inc promise to make electricity available from daylight at much lower cost in the near future.

Using mains power ashore to recharge the battery is possible if it's available at your mooring and if all the necessary equipment and safety precautions have been installed by a

suitably-qualified engineer. If shore power isn't available, removing the battery and charging it at home between cruises is likely to be necessary to be sure of a full charge.

Safety

The Boat Safety Scheme has quite lengthy regulations for electrical systems, which form part of the compulsory inspection and certification process for boats on inland waterways. The regulations are available both in printed form and online from its website at http://www. boatsafetyscheme.com.

The BSS regulations set standards that should, as far as possible, be achieved or exceeded by all boats used in coastal waters even though this isn't currently a legal requirement.

A battery isolator switch should be easily accessible and used to turn off the electrical supply when necessary.

A battery isolator switch.

Spare fuses are kept with these electrical connections, which are normally protected beneath the slide-on cover.

- Wear eye protection when working with batteries. A battery may eject drops of acid when the plugs are removed, particularly if it has been gassing during charging.
- Don't connect or disconnect any wires to the battery when it is open with plugs removed.
- Never use a naked flame near a battery.
- Have a fire extinguisher suitable for electrical fires near the battery compartment.
- Use rubber gloves when cleaning any spillage from the battery.
- Battery acid must be washed off skin and clothes immediately in order to avoid burns and damage.
- Take care to prevent salt water getting into a battery otherwise highly toxic chlorine gas can be given off.

Basic regular safety checks

Check that a 12v battery stays secured in its installed position with adequate ventilation. Ensure ventilation is not obstructed, so that the explosive hydrogen and oxygen gases that come from a battery can be vented to the outside of the boat. Gases must not be allowed to accumulate in the boat.

The battery must not be able to move as the boat heels whilst sailing, and should be enclosed in a purpose-designed battery box to contain any battery acid that might leak from it.

Sealed batteries or gel batteries can be used to prevent problems of leakage. However, gel batteries are more expensive than lead acid batteries and instructions supplied with them concerning recharging with the correct type of charger must be followed.

Never leave any loose metallic objects such as spanners near a battery, where, with the inevitable movement of the boat, they might fall across the terminals and result in sparks and a fire. A short-circuit across battery terminals can melt a screwdriver in seconds.

Fuses provided in the wiring system should always be replaced with the correct rating of fuse. Always investigate and rectify the fault that has caused the fuse to blow before replacing it. Ignoring the problem could result in a fire.

12V batteries are heavy and care needs to be taken when lifting them in order to avoid injury. Moving one from a dinghy to a boat on a mooring takes care and planning. Otherwise both you and the battery could descend into the depths.

Maintenance

Probably the most frequent cause of electrical failure, apart from a flat battery, is a loose or corroded electrical connection. A saltwater environment is inclined to increase this problem. Check, clean and tighten all connections frequently.

Keep the top of the battery clean and dry and ensure the battery terminals are clean and tight. Avoid corrosion and the appearance of the white substance that develops on battery terminals by applying Vaseline. A battery loses its charge over time whether or not it is connected. The loss

Apply Vaseline to battery terminals.

Top up the battery with distilled water when necessary.

rate can be one per cent per day depending on temperature and surrounding conditions. Dirty and damp conditions accelerate the rate of loss.

Check the electrolyte level by unscrewing the plugs on top of the battery and topping up with distilled water when necessary. In most batteries this involves covering the top edges of the plates with no more than a centimetre depth of water. Any more than this and the acid solution will leak out when the battery is charged.

Although a deep cycle leisure battery is designed to be deeply discharged, it will last much longer if it's seldom discharged below 50 per cent of its capacity. Occasionally using up to 80 per cent of its charge can be tolerated, but complete discharge will damage it and may mean it can't be recharged.

The use of an electrical meter is the easiest way to check the battery's charge. First, check that nothing is taking power from the battery. Turning off the battery isolator switch is the best way to do this. Then measure the voltage

Using an electrical meter to check the condition of the battery – in this case it's flat and needs re-charging.

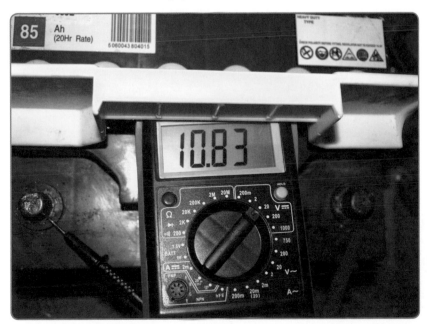

across the battery terminals. If the voltage is between 12.6 and 12.8 it's fully charged. At 12.2V it's about 50 per cent, and at 12V, 25 per cent. At 12V or less a battery is unlikely to start an engine and at 11.7V or less it's flat.

A hydrometer can also be used. This measures the amount of acid in the battery. The concentration of the battery becomes less as the battery discharges, so measuring it shows the battery's condition. A hydrometer can be obtained from a car accessory shop, but check it's the type to be used with a battery rather than the different type used to check the condition of antifreeze.

Where equipment has been installed and connected on a small cruiser it may have been connected either directly to the battery, to the battery isolation switch, to a circuit breaker, or to a point on a switch panel that incorporates fuses. Whatever the situation, the wiring should be protected by a suitable fuse. Check the ratings of all fuses and make sure you have corresponding spares. Never be tempted to bypass the fuse with a length of wire.

If it's necessary at any time to replace a length of electrical wire always use wire of the same diameter as the original or larger. Because of the amount of movement on a boat the wire must be able to flex without being damaged, so don't use single-strand wire. Always use multi-strand.

When the boat is unused in the winter, remove the batteries. Recharge them preferably every month.

The future

Hopefully, high capacity lightweight alternatives to lead-acid batteries will soon be developed and become available at a reasonable price. This will make dealing with electricity on board a sailing boat easier and help with the inevitable changeover to electric motors as the world runs out of the fuels we currently rely on.

17 Engines

Use and simple servicing

It would be marvellous if we could rely on a constant supply of wind to keep sailing boats moving, but unfortunately an alternative means of propulsion is also required. Many sailing enthusiasts manage with oars, paddles and quants, and these may well be sufficient for dinghies, day boats and very small sail cruisers in sheltered waters. Indeed, one well-known character on the UK's East Coast, Charles Stock, has covered more than 70,000 miles on coastal and inland waterways without an engine during 45 years of sailing his 16-foot sail cruiser *Shoal Waters*. When the wind drops he simply uses one of these manual methods to keep going, as explained in his book *Sailing Just for Fun* and on his website at http://shoal-waters.moonfruit.com, where much other interesting information is also available.

Motors may be regarded by some as no better than a 'necessary evil', but they can get you out of awkward, even dangerous, situations and make leaving and returning to moorings or the slipway much easier.

Most boats of the types covered by this book are much more likely to have an outboard motor than an inboard. On inland waterways and in some sheltered coastal areas electric outboard motors are a joy to use, being very quiet and extremely simple to maintain and use – more on these later – but the most commonly used motor on small boats is the petrol outboard.

Petrol outboard motors

One of the best-known makes of outboard motor used to be the Seagull. It was reliable and simple to maintain and many are still going strong. If you come across one in action, though, you'll see, hear and smell why they've largely given way to more modern, quieter and less polluting versions. Though it's more likely you'll be able to carry on a conversation with a recently made motor running, it'll still be a relief when you can stop it and let the silence of sailing prevail.

If you're keen on using an old Seagull motor, you should join the enthusiasts active on the websites at http://www.seagullparts.co.uk and http://www.saving-old-seagulls.co.uk. These provide much helpful advice, including ways of reducing the exhaust smoke from such motors.

The general points covered below provide an introduction to using an outboard motor. They will help you to understand the basic maintenance tasks to be carried out on most engines. However, because there are so many different outboard makes and models in use, of greatly varying ages, it's impossible to cover their many variations, specific details and safety precautions here.

Consult the motor's manual

It's vitally important to consult the appropriate handbook and manual for your particular make and model. This has, in the past, been a problem if the motor is second-hand and the manual is no longer published, but the Internet has made it much easier to obtain information on particular outboards.

Detailed manuals for the many makes and models of outboard motors are available from a variety of sources.

The eBay auction website is one good source and an internet search for particular manuals is also likely to produce results. Of course, outboard dealers and manufacturers can be helpful too. You may even find your outboard has been included in a book covering many models from one manufacturer, available from your local chandler.

The importance of accurate information is illustrated by the case of many two-stroke motors, which require a particular ratio of the correct type of oil to be mixed with the petrol. Don't just assume that the oil to petrol ratio is the same as for someone else's motor. An oil/fuel ratio of 1:50 has been used for a great many outboards, but it can vary from 1:10 for the very oldest outboards to 1:100 or twice that for automatic injection models.

In the case of the running in period of a new two stroke motor, the amount of oil to be added may need to be twice the amount normally used. Check the manual for the exact procedure for running-in the motor. This may also apply if parts of a motor are replaced with new ones.

Two-stroke oil to be added to petrol can be purchased at chandlers.

Preparing to set off

Check you have enough fuel. A two-stroke outboard motor will need the appropriate amount of the correct type of oil added – don't be tempted to use ordinary engine oil. Check the ratio of oil to petrol in the motor's manual.

Add fuel and oil to the tank well clear of the boat and away from any source of ignition. Have a fire extinguisher ready to hand. Never add fuel while the motor is running and always leave a small space for expansion at the top of the tank.

Very small outboards have an integral petrol tank mounted on top of the motor, so petrol and the appropriate oil should be added when the engine isn't hot. In order to mix them together the oil should be added stage by stage as the petrol is poured into the tank.

Remember that petrol produces a heavy, highly flammable and explosive vapour, and take appropriate precautions whenever dealing with it. Avoid any sources of ignition such as a smoking cigarette. Place the tank onto the boat in a well-ventilated location to disperse any vapour away from the boat.

On four-stroke outboards the oil isn't added to the petrol and a separate lubrication system is provided. The oil level for this needs to be checked and topped up if necessary.

Always have a rope tied to the outboard and fastened somewhere inside the boat so that the motor can never drop overboard. Obviously there needs to be sufficient slack in the rope to allow the motor to turn while steering. Unscrew the clamps before lowering the motor onto the transom and clamping it there. The clamps used to fasten the motor to the transom need to be tightened firmly. They can loosen with use as vibration from the motor shakes them.

Check the condition of the manual starting rope and make sure that there's no debris round the propeller. Fishing line sometimes gets wound round the propeller hub, and if not removed this can tighten and damage the seal protecting the lower gear case.

Another line, called a 'lanyard', is provided with some motors. This is attached to a stop switch and to you, so

The smallest outboards have an integral tank with the filler cap on top of the motor.

that if you fall overboard the pull on the lanyard will stop the motor.

Lower the outboard if it's tilted up. Put levers provided for lifting and tilting the motor in the 'lock' position.

With the boat in the water, point it in the direction of travel where there are no obstacles. Put the outboard in neutral to start it. If it has a separate fuel tank, connect it to the motor using the quick connect fitting, which pushes onto the appropriate point on the motor. Fuel tanks have a vent that needs to be opened by unscrewing it sufficiently to allow air to enter. This needs to be screwed down and closed to stop leakage when the tank and outboard aren't being used and particularly when it's being transported. Forgetting to undo the vent is a major cause of embarrassment, with the motor failing to start or spluttering to a stop after running briefly. On some motors there's an additional valve to open.

Gently squeeze the primer bulb in the fuel pipe leading from the tank until it feels firm. This is a hand-operated fuel pump that pushes petrol into the carburettor. Check that there's no leakage of petrol, as this could cause a fire hazard.

Pull out the choke knob and put the throttle control and gears into their starting positions. Bear in mind that on some

Check the engine oil level on a four-stroke outboard.

Clamps should be screwed tight but a rope should also be used to stop the motor dropping overboard when fastening the clamps.

of the smallest outboard motors the propeller starts turning as soon as the motor is started, so in such cases you need to be particularly careful not to move the throttle control from the start position until the motor is warmed up and you're ready to move off. The boat also needs to be securely moored and tightly tied up to prevent any movement.

Check that you won't hit anything or anyone when you pull the starting cord. Then get into a sitting or crouching position in order to avoid the exertion of starting the motor from upsetting you or the boat. Pull it steadily until you feel resistance. This is the compression building up. Now pull with more force, smoothly and firmly. With luck the motor will start first time, but a cold motor is more likely to need a few pulls. When started let it warm up for about three minutes, and once it's running well progressively push in the choke knob.

Check that cooling water is circulating by looking for water spraying out with the exhaust or coming out of a separate hole as a jet of water. If it's not coming out, stop the engine using the stop control and check for blockages or a damaged impeller, which pushes the water round the cooling system. *Never* run an engine without any cooling water circulating satisfactorily. It will soon seize up and sustain serious damage. For the same reason, an outboard

motor should never *ever* be run whilst out of the water: the impeller would be damaged in a matter of seconds, water being necessary to lubricate and cool it. Although the motor may still run when put back in the water, it will quickly overheat and seize up if the damaged impeller isn't circulating sufficient cooling water.

Check the direction you intend to travel for obstacles including other boats and swimmers. Having cast off from the mooring, move the throttle into the 'shift' position, engage forward gear and accelerate away smoothly. On a dinghy in particular you should avoid sudden acceleration – a powerful motor can suddenly push the boat so hard that it forces the stern down and powers the boat down under the waves.

Stopping

Slow the throttle back to the 'shift' position and put the motor into neutral as you approach the mooring or the shore. Some skill is needed to glide smoothly to a stop without power, but once you've mastered this it gives you a good sense of satisfaction. Any tidal flow, river current or wind can be used against the momentum of the boat to bring you to a halt without an embarrassing or damaging collision with the quay or slipway. Push the stop button and tilt the motor up before it grounds in shallow water.

If reversing is necessary to slow down or to go backwards, check no boats or obstructions have appeared behind you and put the throttle control in the 'shift' position. Smoothly put the gear lever into reverse and go slowly, using no more than half throttle unless this is an emergency stop. Reversing suddenly and rapidly can cause the boat to become dangerously unstable; it may be difficult to control and to steer a straight course when reversing.

If the motor is removed from the boat, keep it upright long enough for the water to drain out of the cooling system. Never lay it down horizontally or with its lower unit higher than the powerhead, because any remaining water might run back up the exhaust and enter the cylinders. With a four-stroke motor, check your manual for the correct side to

Undo the fuel tank vent before starting and screw it down closed after using the outboard motor.

Pull the starter cord smoothly and quite forcefully when you feel the compression causing resistance.

lay the motor down on in order to prevent oil leaking out or flowing to where it could cause damage.

Drain off any fuel remaining in the carburettor bowl before transporting the motor. It may be possible to undo a drain screw to do this and then catch the fuel in a rag. This avoids the rather risky situation of having petrol fumes in the vehicle used to transport the motor.

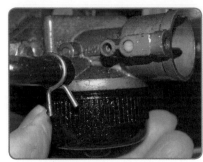

A screw or cover can usually be undone to drain fuel from the carburettor before transporting the motor.

Alternatively, whenever you're about to finish using the motor the carburettor can be drained with the engine running by simply turning off the fuel supply. The engine will stop when the fuel has drained from the carburettor.

If the motor has been used in sea water, it's important to flush the cooling system with fresh water, because salt is very corrosive and can also crystallise and block the water passages. It can be flushed through by running the motor in a suitably large and strong container of clean fresh water, after taking precautions to ensure that it's mounted safely and securely whilst it's running. The leg of the motor must be in water deep enough to cover the cavitation plate and up to the level that the motor is used on the boat. Some engines, however, have special attachments and equipment for flushing with a hosepipe. Follow the manual's instructions carefully.

It's also wise to run an outboard occasionally in clean water even if it's been used in freshwater locations, in order to remove any sand or debris in the cooling system.

Remember to close fuel tank vents and any fuel supply closures before leaving or moving the motor.

Outboard motor theft is a major problem in many areas. If the motor has to be left on the boat, tilt it up out of the water and use a suitable lockable security device to prevent it being unclamped and stolen.

Fuel additives

'Miracle' additives are often advertised for use in improving the performance of engines and to solve all kinds of problems. However, outboard motors aren't necessarily the same as other types of motor, and although some such additives may just possibly be helpful in certain engines you shouldn't risk using them.

If really necessary, only use additives specifically designed for your make and model of outboard and follow the instructions carefully. You must, of course, add the appropriate oil to fuel for a two-stroke motor, but not for a four-stroke motor because the four-stroke outboard has a separate oil circulation system similar to a car engine.

Outboard motor maintenance

The following maintenance details apply to most of the still very common two-stroke motors usually purchased with second-hand sailing boats. Additional notes are included, where necessary, to cover four-stroke motors.

If in doubt about the reliability of an outboard motor or your ability to carry out work on it, always consult and involve a qualified engineer. The following will help you to understand and discuss what needs to be done.

If you decide to dismantle parts of any motor according to the instructions in its handbook, take photographs with a digital camera at each stage as you proceed. You can then refer to these pictures photos to see how to put the parts back together again.

NB When the outboard motor is tilted up on the back of your boat out of the water – for example on a trailer – never get under the lower end of it, as it might drop onto you. Also, when carrying out inspections of the engine while it's running, keep loose clothing and hair well away from any moving parts in which they could become entangled.

Two-stroke and four-stroke motors

Two-stroke motors have proved popular because they're powerful, reasonably light and basic compared with four-stroke motors. Unfortunately, though, because oil is added to the petrol the exhaust produced is usually more polluting than is now generally acceptable, and there's a tendency for unburned oil to be deposited on the water.

The regulations governing exhaust emissions hasn't yet led to existing two-stroke motors being banned, although this could happen in future on some inland waterways as it already has on some lakes in the USA and Europe. But the sale of new two-stroke motors that don't meet today's emission regulations has already become illegal in the UK, with the result that almost all new outboards are now four-stroke motors, which don't burn oil along with the petrol. They're cleaner and somewhat quieter than two-stroke motors, although many are also heavier.

However, if you're about to buy a new outboard motor for use on inland or sheltered coastal waters, you should first read about the incredibly quiet and pollution-free electric outboards later in this chapter. With an electric outboard you can forget about 90 per cent of the following maintenance tasks and the hazards associated with petrol. Big improvements have been made in the power and efficiency of electric motors for use as auxiliary propulsion on sailing boats, particularly for the more relaxed enjoyment of cruising and leisurely trips on sheltered waters.

Check wiring and spray it with water dispersant.

Check the condition of gaskets.

Monthly checks and maintenance

Remove the engine cover and check the following.

- Check that wire terminal connections are secure. Any signs of corrosion mean that they should be disconnected, cleaned and tightened. Use an appropriate anti-corrosion/water dispersant spray on exposed electrical connections.
- If there's any corrosion developing near the cylinder head gaskets it could indicate leaky gaskets, and tightening or gasket replacement may be necessary.
- Check the fuel filters and remove any dirt and water. Take care to ensure that any washers or O rings are carefully replaced. Pump the fuel with the fuel primer bulb to check for leaks. A new filter may be needed if dirt is firmly stuck or the filter is damaged.
- With the engine running in water, operate the controls and check that they're moving smoothly. Lubricate them if necessary. Never shift the gears unless the engine is running otherwise they could get jammed or damaged.
- While the engine is running, check that no water is leaking from joints between the exhaust cover, crank case and cylinder head.
- Check whether any of the bolted-on components, such as the fuel pump, coil, voltage regulator etc, have come loose, and tighten them as necessary.
- Lubricate moving parts, including the tilt mechanism and any cable controls. The steering pivot may have a grease point that needs to have a small amount of grease inserted.
- Where zinc sacrificial anodes are fitted to become the subject of electrolytic corrosion instead of the outboard motor, check their condition. If more than half eroded away, they should be replaced.
- Clean the casing of the engine and check for scratches and damage. Do likewise with the fuel tank. To prevent corrosion, touch up in the appropriate type and colour any areas where paint is missing.
- On a four-stroke motor, check the level of engine oil and top up if necessary.

Check that bolted-on components can't move and that moving parts such as the controls can move freely. Lubricate as necessary.

The fuel primer bulb on the pipe from a separate fuel tank should be soft and flexible. Replacements are available if there's any danger of leakage.

Three-monthly checks and maintenance

These tasks are usually appropriate at between 50 and 75 hours of use or every three months, but with low usage on a sailing boat may only need to be an annual event. The above monthly tasks should be included.

The following are the basic tasks suitable for DIY. They're the tasks most commonly required for the maintenance of many outboard motors. Details will vary according to the motor you have, so consult the owners' manual as much as possible. More advanced and complicated repair and maintenance work will need special tools and the skills and knowledge of an engineer trained for your particular make of motor.

Spark plugs

When removing or replacing a spark plug take care not to damage the insulator. External sparks can result from a damaged insulator and this could ignite petrol fumes, causing a fire or explosion when the engine is started.

Use a proper spark plug socket to remove the plugs. Ideally a socket with a rubber insert should be used to reduce risk of damage to the ceramic insulator.

The electrode should be between light brown and grey if the engine is operating correctly. If it's black and damp or if it's very white in colour, ask the appropriate dealer or servicing engineer for advice on how to correct this in your particular model of outboard.

Heat and deposits on the spark plug cause it to gradually break down and wear away. Carefully cleaning the plug and electrode will help, but it will eventually need replacement. In fact replacement is often recommended instead of cleaning, which might cause damage.

Using a feeler gauge, check the gap against the recommended gap size in the motor's manual.

When refitting the cleaned plug or putting in a new plug,
use a new gasket and ensure that all surfaces and threads are clean. Screw the plug in by hand for the first few turns to make sure it seats correctly and isn't cross-threaded. Ideally, use a torque wrench to tighten to the setting specified in the manual. Alternatively, a reasonable estimate of tightness is one quarter to one half of a turn past finger-tight. Don't over-tighten it.

Where grease points are provided they should be filled with the appropriate type of fresh grease recommended by the motor manufacturer. Pump the grease in until all the old grease, along with any water, is forced out. Old grease should be wiped away as it emerges.

Check the condition of controls and any control cables. If worn, replace them before they break in use.

Disconnect the spark plug caps from the spark plugs and ensure the shift control is in neutral so that the engine can't turn the propeller. Remove the propeller and any fishing line or other debris wrapped round the shaft. If the propeller blades have any slight damage, use a file to smooth them off. Check the condition of the hub and shaft. Wipe old grease off and apply a layer of the appropriate waterproof grease.

On older and smaller outboard motors a shear pin fastens the propeller to the shaft. Check the condition of this pin, which is made of soft metal and is designed to break if the propeller hits a hard obstacle, thus avoiding damage to the drive mechanism and the propeller. When it's broken the propeller stays on the shaft but is no longer rotated by it. Spare shear pins should be amongst the spare parts and tools kit kept with the motor, so that replacement can be carried out whenever necessary. If the pin is corroded or damaged it should be replaced.

Other motors have a rubber bush instead of a shear pin. This slips on the shaft if the propeller hits something. It can get worn and will then need replacement if the system is to work satisfactorily.

Take care not to damage the white insulator when removing a spark plug.

Check the spark plug gap is correct.

Replace the gasket when fitting a new spark plug. A new gasket is usually supplied with a spark plug.

Gear oil

Gear case oil needs to be changed next. The gear case usually has two screw plugs in the side of the gear housing, and the oil will flow out when these are undone. Before undoing the drain plug, clean the skeg at the very bottom of the outboard motor. Then stick one end of a long piece of tape, such as masking tape, to the end of the skeg so that it hangs down into a container suitable for collecting the oil. After removing both screw plugs, the oil should flow down the edges of the tape into the container.

Examine the oil carefully. If a lot of water comes out before the oil emerges, or if the oil is milky, a bad seal has probably let water into the gear case. If you're uncertain, one way to check for water is to put the old oil into a transparent plastic or glass bottle or jar and leave it to settle for a couple of hours. You'll then see any water that will have settled to the bottom while the oil floats at the top. If there is water, the motor will need to be further checked by an appropriate engineer, who'll replace the seal if necessary.

The oil should be a normal brown colour, possibly with a few metal filings in it. The lower drain plug may have a magnetic pickup to collect filings; if so clean them off. The oil drain plug sealing rings should also be checked and replaced if damaged.

Be sure to use the correct type of oil according to the outboard manufacturer's instructions. Don't use oil intended for car gearboxes. The marine oil includes water-dispersant additives and in some cases may be more like the fluid used in a car's automatic transmission.

To be sure the oil goes into the gear case and fills it fully, it's most important to fill it from the bottom. If you take the apparently easier route of filling through the top hole, air is likely to get trapped in the oil. If it does, then when the oil gets hot during use the air will expand and put pressure on the seals: oil will leak out, water will get in, and the gears will be damaged.

Oil can usually be purchased in a tube like a toothpaste tube so that it can be firmly pushed up into the lower hole, but a pump may be needed to force the oil in from the bottom. This can be purchased at the same time as the oil. The oil-filling pump is inserted into the lower hole, where it should be possible to screw it onto the thread to form an oil-tight seal.

Squeeze the oil container or work the pump until oil appears at the top hole. Don't overfill, as this may result in a damaging pressure build-up when the oil heats and expands. Screw the plug into the top hole. Doing so helps to stop oil rushing out of the bottom hole when the pump or tube is removed.

Check the O ring or gasket is in place on the bottom plug and have it ready to screw in as you remove the pump. Screw in the bottom plug quickly and tighten it to avoid leakage. Wipe the area free of oil and look for any leaks.

Undo the screw-in plug used for checking the gear oil level.

Before undoing the oil drain plug stick a long piece of tape to the skeg so that it hangs down and guides the oil into a container.

Oil should be squeezed into the lower hole, with the tube firmly pushed up the hole to prevent it running out, until it appears at the top hole.

Cooling system

Thoroughly flush the cooling system with fresh water. This is best done with the motor securely mounted to run in a large, strong and stable container of water, such as a clean dustbin. Some motors have attachment points and equipment provided for flushing by other methods, such as by attaching a hosepipe and 'flush adapter' or 'flush muffs', according to instructions in the appropriate manual. Don't try these alternative methods on a motor not designed for their use, as both you and the motor could be damaged.

The impeller, which pushes the cooling water round the system, may need to be replaced. Recommendations on the frequency of replacement vary according to make. In some cases annual replacement is recommended but others advise replacing it only when it shows signs of wear. If you give the motor a lot of use in areas where sand is drawn into the cooling system, or rely on it at times when cruising offshore, the impeller should be replaced annually to be on the safe side.

Gaining access to the impeller can be quite a complicated process depending on the make and model of the outboard. The manufacturer's manual should help but you may still prefer to involve an appropriately experienced engineer.

Checking the compression of the engine is an optional task and a job for an engineer familiar with your make and model. It can be worthwhile arranging for this to be done in order to catch any developing problems before they become a serious issue. Any variation from the normal compression figures may give early warning of wear or faults that should be rectified while the engineer has the motor in his workshop.

Even if you have the equipment to do this yourself, it can still be difficult because the actual compression figures for a particular outboard aren't always easy to find, even in the appropriate manuals.

Adjustments to the ignition timing and carburettor are only needed if there are problems with smooth running of the motor. These are also tasks best left to a specialist equipped with the tools and knowledge necessary for your make and model of outboard.

Extra tasks for four-stroke outboards

As well as all the above, four-stroke outboards need some additional work, as outlined below. Four-stroke motors have an oil sump and use a pressurised lubrication system similar to that of a car.

Changing the engine oil

Warm the engine with water provided for the cooling system. This warming thins the oil so that it flows out of the sump effectively. Have a container ready to catch the old oil being drained out.

Wearing protective gloves, unscrew the drain plug, ensuring that the sealing ring comes away on the plug so that it's not lost in the oil as it drains out. The ring might need to be replaced if it's squashed or damaged.

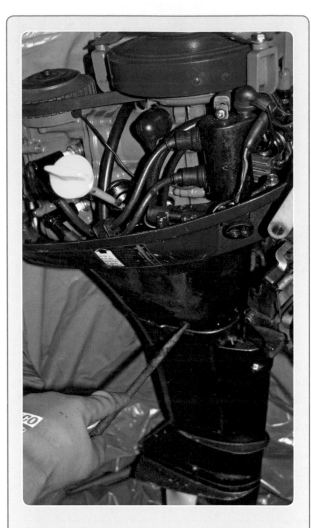

Undo the engine oil drain plug, which is usually labelled part of the way down the leg of the outboard, and drain the oil into a container.

Fill with new engine oil.

Check the belt for wear and tension.

As the oil drains out, check its colour. Any milky discolouration indicates that water has leaked into the oil. This usually means a cylinder head gasket is leaking internally. Unless you're experienced in this type of repair you should get the gasket replaced by someone who knows what they're doing. Don't ignore it, as severe damage to the motor can ensue.

There's a tendency for DIY motor mechanics to over-tighten oil drain plugs because the well lubricated plug screws easily into the hole. However, you'll want to be able to unscrew it again in the future so don't jam it in place.

The oil filter needs to be removed and cleaned next. If there's a problem finding and removing it, the manual for your outboard should help. On most outboards it can be put back after cleaning if it's not damaged. If in doubt, replace it with a new one. The filter sealing ring is likely to need replacement, as screwing a filter back onto an old seal could cause an oil leak. When tightening, get it screwed on and then tighten only an additional half to three-quarters of a turn. Don't over-tighten it.

After checking the engine is in a normal operating position, fill with the appropriate type and quantity of oil recommended by the manufacturer for your model of outboard. Run the motor with cooling water for a couple of minutes and check for oil leaks. Stop the engine and check the oil level.

Check the timing belt for wear. This usually involves removing a protective cover by unscrewing it. Belts usually last several years with the small amount of use they get on a sailing boat, but they should still be checked for fraying and excessive sideways movement.

Replacement of the belt may be a DIY task on some engines but this could once again be a job for the professionals if there are complications. Likewise, adjustment of valve clearances is really only for those who have experience in this type of engine maintenance.

Winterising an outboard motor

Before winter sets in, or earlier if the motor is to be stored unused for several months, a number of actions need to be taken in order to protect it from corrosion and other problems. A list is provided below, which includes many tasks covered in more detail earlier in this chapter. Many sailing boat owners who have little-used outboard motors do the main service at this time as well. Any developing faults that need professional attention can then be dealt with during the winter in readiness for a trouble-free sailing season the following year. As well as the general list of tasks given below, owners' manuals may have additional recommendations for particular types of motor.

- Flush the cooling system using fresh water.
- With the motor running in fresh water turn off or disconnect the fuel supply to let the carburettor run dry. In the last ten seconds spray storage oil into it.
- If a battery is used with the outboard, disconnect it, charge it and store it in a suitable dry place.
- Service the fuel filters.
- After removing the spark plugs, squirt a small amount of outboard oil into the cylinders through the holes. Turn the engine over by rotating the flywheel to distribute the oil and then replace the plugs.
- Wash and clean the outside surfaces of the motor, touch up any scratches in the paint and when the paint is dry spray the motor with a water dispersant such as WD40. Any salt-encrusted crevices should be scrubbed with an old toothbrush.
- Remove and inspect the propeller. Grease the shaft before replacing it.
- Check the sacrificial anode and replace it if more than half used.
- Lubricate all moving parts and grease points.
- Check the manual starter rope and replace if necessary.
- Drain out and replace gear oil.
- On a four-stroke motor, change the engine oil.
- Check the fuel supply pipes and replace them if showing signs of deterioration.
- Petrol can deteriorate over time, particularly when mixed with oil. Enquire about local facilities for the safe disposal of old fuel – a local car-servicing garage may help with this. The tank should be drained very carefully, avoiding any sources of ignition.

Storage

Having completed the above, mount the motor upright in a lockable garage or reasonably frost-proof shed. Clamp it on a support where it can't fall over, preferably organised so that it doesn't rest on its skeg. Cover the motor with a cloth to keep out dust.

Mice have been known to take up residence under the cover of an outboard motor and then feast on its insulation and sound-proofing. If this is likely to be a problem take suitable precautions, such as the use of a trap or two.

A Minn Kota electric trolling motor may provide sufficient power to reach a mooring in sheltered waters.

An electric motor and 12V deep cycle battery can provide several hours of very quiet cruising on sheltered waterways in a sailing dinghy when the wind drops.

Electric outboard motors

If you use an electric outboard you can forget most of the maintenance tasks covered above. Other advantages are very easy starting, very quiet operation, no exhaust fumes, no risky petrol fumes, and the motor itself being lighter, easier to carry and quicker to prepare for use. Use of electric motors is environmentally friendly to the location where the boat is used.

In recent years big advances have been made in the efficiency and power of electric outboards. Increased popularity, and regulations banning petrol motors on some waterways, have made them more widely available and more competitively priced. Originally, most electric outboards were actually 'trolling' motors for use when fishing, particularly in the huge number of lakes in North America, 'trolling' involving motoring quietly along whilst towing fishing lures. Their quiet operation also suits them to auxiliary use when the wind drops in inland and sheltered coastal locations, because if you've been quietly slipping along under sail starting a petrol outboard utterly shatters the peace and tranquillity.

An amusing aspect is the appearance of achieving the impossible. An electric outboard can be so inconspicuous that, when used whilst actually sailing – motor sailing – onlookers aren't aware of the motor. The expressions of amazement at the speed and unlikely manoeuvres of the boat are most entertaining! Jocular suggestions of 'cheating' have been made in such situations, but combining sailing with electric outboard motoring can be most enjoyable.

A disadvantage is the need for a 12V deep cycle leisure battery. Lead-acid batteries are heavy but the combined weight of the electric outboard and the battery needs to be compared with the total weight of a petrol outboard plus fuel, spare parts and tool kit. It's a pity we still rely so much on lead-acid batteries, and the development of high capacity lightweight alternatives, available at a reasonable price, is long overdue; but progress is being made with lighter alternatives, as in the case of Torqeedo electric outboards.

Comparisons between electric and petrol outboards are difficult because most electric outboards have the motor mounted next to the propeller, providing direct drive without the loss of power involved with the gears and transmission in most petrol outboards. The electric outboard's thrust is usually measured in pounds of thrust rather than horsepower.

Minn Kota is particularly well-known for its 'trolling' motors in the USA, and a wide range is imported for sale in the UK. Other makes have also become more widely

Minn Kota Riptide motor for seawater use.

Left: The Torqeedo Cruise motor, suitable for a small sail cruiser.

Right: A Torqeedo Travel motor in use.

available. Although trolling motors were originally intended to be used on fresh water and for just a few hours at a time, there are now more powerful versions for use in sea water, such as the Minn Kota 'Riptide' series running on 12, 24 or 36V depending on size and thrust required. These can be used on the majority of sailing dinghies and smaller sail cruisers in sheltered coastal waters. For the open sea and strong currents, however, a petrol outboard motor still has the advantage of greater power against strong winds and tides.

Torqeedo electric outboards, which have become available from Germany in recent years, may be more expensive than trolling motors but they demonstrate big advances in efficiency. The smaller Torqeedo Travel motors fold neatly into

Torqeedo Travel electric outboard motors with their removable black battery packs mounted on top.

a waterproof bag and are supplied with advanced lithium-manganese batteries. The larger Torqeedo Cruise is advertised as having the power of a 6hp petrol motor. In fact the overall cost of buying and using this motor, although substantially higher than less powerful electric outboards, is not much more than many 6hp four-stroke petrol motors, which cost much more to run and service. Torqeedo outboards do produce a little more noise than trolling motors but they're still quieter than most petrol outboards.

Remember, with electric outboards there's no expenditure on petrol and oil, and virtually no expenditure on servicing and spare parts such as spark plugs. Recharging a standard 12V leisure battery is a fraction of the cost of just one litre of petrol and a suitable battery should have a life of about 200 to 300 charge/discharge cycles. It may last five years or more if well looked after.

The deep cycle leisure battery used with electric outboards should have a rating of at least 85 amp hours. Running at full speed can use the capacity in an hour or two, but easing back to half throttle makes the battery last much longer. You can, of course, use two batteries connected in parallel for longer-range expeditions.

Inland waterway authorities are keen to encourage the use of environmentally friendly electric motors on boats and offer discounts on annual navigation licences to encourage their use – a significant saving, applicable, for example, to those boating on the River Thames.

Servicing is mainly concerned with keeping the leisure battery (or two batteries, in the case of 24V motors) in good condition, with prompt recharging and topping-up as necessary.

The propeller should be cleaned of weeds and fishing line. Remove the propeller, following the procedure in the motor's instruction manual for removal and replacement, and cut off any fishing line that may have wound round the shaft, which could damage the seal protecting the underwater motor. Keep the leading edge of the propeller blades smooth by sanding with fine sandpaper.

Washing off dirt and salt, light lubrication of the few moving parts and checking the electrical connections are tight completes all the regular attention that's required.

This boat engine, exhibited at boat shows by Lancing Marine, is painted to show parts of the engine more clearly than may be seen in the confined space on a boat, and was used in some of the following photographs.

Inboard engines

Although most boats of the size covered by this book are much more likely to have outboard motors, some more substantial small sail cruisers may have diesel inboard motors. Consequently this section provides an introduction to the use and servicing of inboard motors that will help you to understand the basic tasks that need to be carried out.

Whole books have been written on the maintenance of such engines, and manuals are available for most makes and models, of which there are many. The appropriate manual should be consulted for more detailed information, including maintenance and repair work plus appropriate safety precautions. The Royal Yachting Association runs courses for those who are keen to do much of the work involved in maintaining their own boat engine.

Unfortunately, in the confined space of a boat's engine compartment it can be difficult to reach parts for servicing. If in doubt about the reliability of an engine or your ability to carry out work on it, always consult and involve a qualified engineer. The following guidelines will help you discuss what needs to be done.

Although you have sails to get you home, the wind can drop and you may have to rely on the engine to get you out of a hazardous situation. When going out to sea, a cautious approach would be to have an outboard motor in addition to the inboard in case of engine failure.

Checks before starting the engine and setting off

Many of the safety points covered in the section on outboard motors above apply equally to work on an inboard diesel engine. Diesel fuel may be less of a fire hazard than petrol but it can still burn fiercely when it's ignited.

Take care not to get hair and clothing entangled in moving parts, and wear suitable protective gloves when handling oils and other liquids and chemicals.

All fuel-burning engines produce harmful exhaust gases, which can dangerously accumulate in a boat. Fit smoke detecting and carbon monoxide detecting alarms in cabins and ensure adequate ventilation. A 'bilge blower' fan can help to remove hazardous gases and should be operated for a time before starting the engine and during operation.

When reaching down into a cramped engine compartment there's a risk of falling head first into it. Some people have had to be rescued from this situation after their legs have been spotted waving frantically in the air. It's therefore a good idea to have a mobile phone in your pocket at such times!

Tools and small items that you've taken apart also have a habit of dropping down and disappearing into inaccessible corners in the bilges. It's much easier to find them if the bilges are clean, and positioning a container under the parts being unscrewed helps to catch anything that attempts to escape.

■ Check the engine oil by removing the dipstick. Wipe it clean, re-insert it, remove it again and check that the level comes up to the marker. Top up as necessary. Check the gear oil level in the same way.

Use the dipstick to check the oil level.

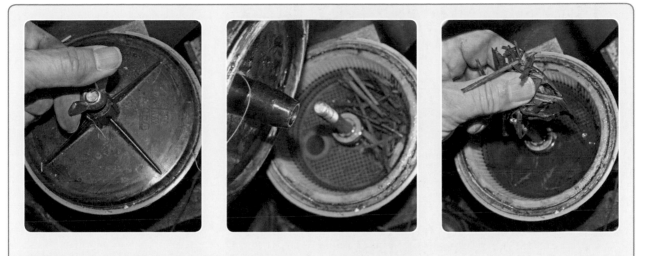

The water filter cover should be unscrewed and all debris removed.

- Both oils should be a dark colour. If there's any change in the colour, and in particular if it's turned milky, this should be investigated, as water is likely to have contaminated the oil.
- Depending on the type of cooling system, it may be necessary to check the level of coolant in the freshwater reservoir while the engine is cold.
- Open the seacock, which is a tap allowing water to be pumped into the cooling system.
- Check for leaks of oil, water or fuel in the bilges and investigate if necessary.
- Check the fuel filters and water filter. It may be necessary to clean the filters and remove dirt from the filter units.
- Check all belts are tight and not worn.
- Ensure all cables, hoses and connections, etc are secure.
- If fitted, operate the stern gland lubricating dispenser where the propeller shaft passes through the hull.
- Check nothing is likely to get caught up in moving

parts in the engine compartment or round a drive shaft, such as a cleaning rag, rope or an empty container.
- Look outside the hull for any trailing ropes that might wrap round the propeller.
- Open the fuel shut-off fully.
- Operate any fuel primer device.
- Turn on the battery isolation switch.
- Check you have twice the amount of fuel likely to be needed and, in any case, that the tank is at least half full.
- Operate the pre-heat for 15 seconds.
- With the engine in neutral and the boat securely moored, start the engine and allow it to warm up fully before moving off. A diesel engine benefits from being worked quite hard and should not be stopped until it's reached full working temperature.
- Check that cooling water is flowing and coming out of the hull.
- If all is well, check that the course ahead is clear of boats and obstacles, untie from any mooring, engage forward gear and accelerate smoothly away.

If appropriate, while the engine is cold check the level of coolant and top it up if necessary.

The fuel shut-off usually opens with a lever.

The place where you add the engine oil should be easy to find, although it won't necessarily be as obvious as this.

Regular maintenance

The checks covered above should be carried out plus the following.

Lubrication

Changing the engine oil and filter at least as often as stated in the handbook is an essential task. This will mean doing so annually, even though the engine may have had little use. The oil contains additives that stop corrosion but have a limited lifespan. An oil drain pump is fitted to many types of engine. Alternatively a dipstick tube oil drain pump can be purchased.

The gearbox oil should also be changed. Check the type required as it may be different from the engine oil.

Old oil should be disposed of where a suitable facility is

available. Refuse disposal sites run by local authorities usually have a container to receive old oil. A car servicing garage may also take the old oil for disposal.

The cooling system

In a freshwater cooling system, the coolant should be changed every second year, including sufficient antifreeze/summer coolant, which has corrosion inhibitors.

Seawater-cooled engines should have the system drained in winter. To prevent frost damage they should be flushed and then filled with a mixture of 50 per cent antifreeze and fresh water.

Any sacrificial anodes in the cooling system should be checked annually and replaced if more than half has gone.

The water pump impeller should be checked and replaced annually. It may be necessary to use two screwdrivers at the same time to extract the impeller, but a special tool for this can also be purchased. Take care not to leave any broken bits behind in the cooling system.

Check the condition of the water injection point of the exhaust system. This can corrode and leak exhaust gases and water into the bilges.

Fuel system

There are normally two filters in the fuel system: the primary filter and the engine fine filter. The primary filter should have a transparent bowl giving a view of any dirt or water. If fuel is contaminated, this should be tackled urgently – by an engineer, as it could involve cleaning the inside of the fuel tank, which unfortunately can be difficult to reach in many boats.

The annual changing of the fuel filters is followed by 'bleeding' the fuel system to remove air and get the fuel flowing smoothly. This should be explained in the manual for your make and model of engine and it's worth knowing

The cover should be unscrewed to access the water pump impeller. Take care not to damage the gasket and remember to include it when screwing the cover back on.

Removing the impeller.

Many primary fuel filters have clear bowls so that dirt and water in the fuel can be seen and removed.

how to do it in case it becomes necessary during a cruise. One way to learn is to ask the engine dealer or engineer to do the job and show you how it's done.

Air system
The air intake filter should be cleaned or changed annually.

Electrical system
Clean and check the tightness of all electrical connections. The battery should be kept clean and dry. Grease the battery terminals with petroleum jelly – Vaseline or similar – to prevent corrosion. Remember, batteries contain harmful acid, so wear suitable eye and hand protection when dealing with them.

In a sail cruiser the engine's battery can get neglected, so if it's unused for any length of time remember to charge it every month or two. A small 12V solar panel connected to the battery can help to stop it losing its charge.

Winterising an inboard engine

Many of the above servicing tasks will be relevant for winterising most types of diesel engine.

A major enemy of engines – particularly in a watery environment – is condensation, which will cause corrosion. When you lay up your boat for the winter, block the holes where moist air can enter and condense on cold metal surfaces. These include intake and exhaust ports.

Changing the oil before running the engine for the last time at the end of the sailing season will help to give the moving parts a fresh coat of protective oil. Use of a lubricating water-dispersant spray will also help.

Shut the cooling water seacock and ensure water is drained out of the engine by opening any drains. Close them after draining out. Put a suitable antifreeze mixture into the cooling system to ensure that all parts are protected from frost. The exact procedure for this will depend on the type of cooling system.

Remove the battery and charge it regularly during the winter. Check the engine's manual for additional winterising tasks.

Most importantly, before using the engine again in the spring you must remember to re-commission it by removing the blockages you put in the air intakes etc, replacing the impeller and battery, and restoring the cooling system and other winterised components to their normal operating condition. Fixing a reminder list of these tasks somewhere prominent is a good precaution.

Air filters vary but this type is accessible by unscrewing the bolts.

The filter is replaced between the securing mesh before bolting the cover back on.

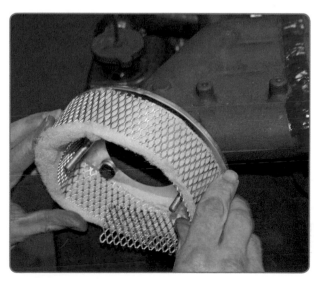

Clean and check the tightness and condition of all electrical connections, drive belts, hose clips, all other fastenings and the engine mounts.

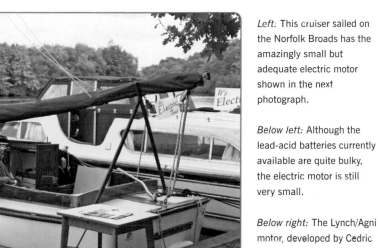

Left: This cruiser sailed on the Norfolk Broads has the amazingly small but adequate electric motor shown in the next photograph.

Below left: Although the lead-acid batteries currently available are quite bulky, the electric motor is still very small.

Below right: The Lynch/Agni motor, developed by Cedric Lynch for use in boats, is displayed along with its controls in a boat show display case. This is an indication of future trends in boat propulsion and motors for transport generally.

Electric inboard motors

As is the case with electric outboards, most of the above work isn't needed on an electric inboard motor. Electric motors are amazingly small compared with diesel engines: even when the controls and batteries are added, they can still take up less room than the fuel tank and all the parts of a diesel engine.

Substantial advances have been made with electric motors for boats. In particular, the Lynch motor (also known as the Agni motor) is surprisingly powerful and very compact, as can be seen in the photographs.

Although they're still more suited to inland waterways such as the Norfolk Broads and the River Thames than the open sea, further developments are progressing rapidly, and there should soon be electric motors suitable for use on seagoing sail cruisers. In the meantime hybrid diesel/electric motor systems are suitable for this. These have the reserve power for seagoing situations along with the advantage of silent and exhaust-free electric motoring in calm conditions when sailing isn't possible. A purpose-built vessel, the Swiss catamaran *Sun21*, recently crossed the Atlantic Ocean using only electric motors powered by solar panels.

Extensive details on all matters concerning electric motors on boats can be found on the Electric Boat Association's website at http://www.electric-boat-association.org.uk. Membership of the association gives access to many opportunities to become involved in the quiet and relaxing world of electric boating.

Electricity supply companies provide 'green energy' schemes to supply electricity from wind turbines, so if the electricity used to charge the batteries comes from wind turbines it makes electric boating almost as environmentally friendly as wind in the boat's sails. The use of solar panels or a wind turbine to charge the batteries is also beneficial to the environment and helps to conserve resources.

18 Boating equipment and accessories

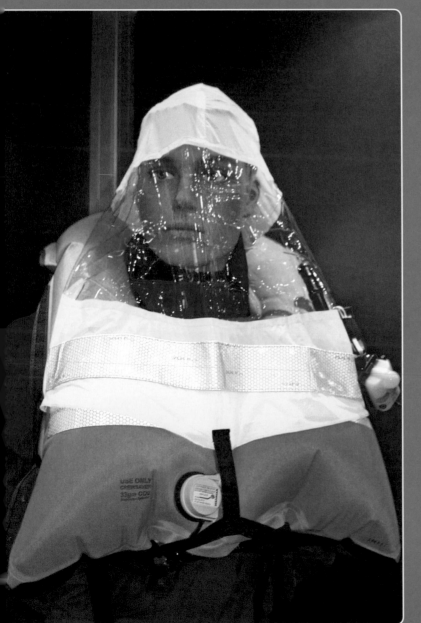

An inflated lifejacket with spray hood and reflective strips that make it much easier to see someone in the water at night.

The huge range of equipment available for boats fills catalogues with many more pages than this book. The range and variety is fascinating but can be confusing, and some of it is desirable rather than essential. Sailing magazines regularly include reviews of equipment, and articles from back issues can be ordered via their websites, listed in the Appendix.

This chapter concentrates on essential items and some strongly recommended items of equipment, where storage space allows. Some equipment has already been covered in earlier chapters.

Equipment in a day boat and sail cruiser

In a day boat and small sail cruiser the amount of equipment will be dictated to some extent by the storage space available. The list below mostly covers items that are important from the safety point of view. Very cautious people might say they're all essential. Realistically, though, the inclusion of some items will depend on what you can afford, the size of the boat, how far from land you expect to cruise and for how long. Practical aspects concerning some of these items are covered further on in this chapter.

In addition to the items for a dinghy listed above, basic equipment should include:

- Lifejackets with crutch straps
- Distress flares
- First aid kit and sunscreen cream
- Safety harness and clip-on lifeline, often linked with lifejacket
- Horseshoe lifebuoy with floating line and light
- VHF radio, fixed and/or hand-held
- Mobile phone
- Hand-operated signalling horn and whistle
- Fire extinguishers
- Fire blanket
- Smoke alarm
- Carbon monoxide alarm
- Boat hook or two to pick up moorings
- Adequate waterproof and windproof clothing and non-slip shoes
- Sleeping bags and pillows in waterproof bags
- Tool kit including knife and tools to match the boat's fittings
- Motor fuel and motor spares, including shear pins, propeller pins, oil, spark plugs and spanners
- Bilge pump as well as bailer and bucket
- Oars and rowlocks
- Fenders
- Compass – fixed and hand held
- Anchors
- Spare ropes
- Navigation lights

Equipment in a sailing dinghy

Little room is available for storage in a sailing dinghy used for a few hours at a time. It's therefore important to keep it clear of clutter so that you can move around quickly and unhampered. In addition to the obvious parts of the boat, including sails, rigging, rudder and dagger board, the basic essential equipment includes:

- Buoyancy aids (preferably with crutch straps)
- Bucket, bailer and sponge
- Paddles or oars
- Sailing knife
- Pliers
- Screwdriver
- Lengths of rope and cord
- First aid kit
- Anchor and rope

You'll also need a range of spare parts that might include:

- Shackles
- Rigging links
- Sail ties
- Cable ties
- Sail battens
- Nuts, bolts and screws to match those on the boat
- A selection of tools to fit the above
- Cork or rubber bungs

- Torches, batteries, 12V spotlight
- Temporary hull repair materials, eg bungs and epoxy putty
- Binoculars
- Charts of waters to be navigated
- Tide tables
- Copy of insurance details
- Illustrated table of emergency signals
- Echo sounder to measure depth
- GPS (Global Positioning System) to establish position at sea for navigation purposes
- Wristwatch
- Barometer
- Radar reflector
- Padlocks, security devices and their keys

Food and drink will also be needed according to your personal preferences. The quantity will depend on the length of your cruise, but you should always take some with you even on a brief trip, in case you go aground and get stuck out on the water – or mud – for longer than expected. An emergency drinking water supply, in addition to the cruiser's own water supply, is strongly recommended.

Buoyancy aids.

Even a dog can have a buoyancy aid, complete with a handle to lift him back on board.

Lifejackets and buoyancy aids

True lifejackets and buoyancy aids are both often just referred to as 'lifejackets' for brevity, but there is a difference.

A buoyancy aid is like a padded waistcoat. Its built-in foam will help to keep someone afloat who's conscious and can swim. The padding of the buoyancy aid will also help to keep them warm. This type is ideal for dinghy sailors who expect to get wet. Buoyancy aids also tend to be cheaper than lifejackets, and some people are happier to rely on their permanent built-in buoyancy than on the quick inflation of a lifejacket.

Modern lifejackets are usually of the inflatable type and are designed to turn an unconscious person onto their back in order to keep their face out of the water. It's often regarded as the best life preserver for people on a boat who don't normally go into the water. A tube is provided for the wearer

Illustration of an inflatable lifejacket with crutch straps from a Crewsaver lifejacket display. This is the make of lifejacket used by most lifeboat crew members.

to inflate it and there may be a gas cylinder inflator that can be activated by pulling a cord. In addition to the pull cord and inflation tube, self-inflating lifejackets have a device that activates the gas cylinder automatically if it gets wet.

The RNLI's advice is very thorough on the subject of life preservers and encourages the wearing of crutch straps between the legs to prevent the jacket or buoyancy aid rising up and over the head. It also recommends having a spray hood with a lifejacket. This helps to keep spray and waves off the face in order to make breathing easier without inhaling or swallowing water, and preserves some body heat. A whistle, reflective tape and possibly a light fixed to a lifejacket all aid location during search and rescue.

Buoyancy is measured in Newtons (N). There are four European standards for life preservers:

- A 50N buoyancy aid is recommended for dinghy sailors. It doesn't have enough buoyancy to protect those unable to help themselves and is unlikely to turn a person over from a face-down position in the water.
- A 100N buoyancy aid/lifejacket is recommended for those in sheltered and calm water. It may not have enough buoyancy to protect a person who's unable to help themselves and may not roll an unconscious person onto their back, particularly if they're wearing heavy clothing.
- A 150N lifejacket is recommended for general use on coastal and inshore waters when sailing, including rough weather. It should turn an unconscious person onto their back so that their face is clear of the water. Its performance may be affected if the user is wearing heavy and/or waterproof clothing.
- A 275N lifejacket is recommended for offshore cruising. It's intended primarily for extreme conditions and those wearing heavy protective clothing, which could stop lesser lifejackets turning an unconscious person onto their back.

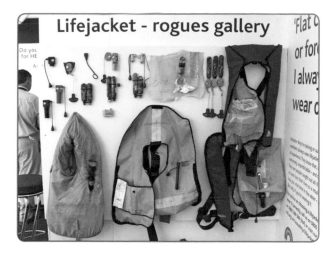

The RNLI's Lifejacket Rogues Gallery showing useless and dangerous equipment.

Corroded gas cylinders found attached to lifejackets that would not automatically inflate when most needed.

Many lifejackets are fitted with a harness, which can be clipped via a safety line to suitably strong points on the deck of a sail cruiser. This helps keep you from losing balance on the deck of a cruiser and should prevent a 'man overboard' situation. Additionally, traditional good advice is 'One hand for yourself and one for the boat' – in other words, hold on to something with one hand whenever doing something for the boat with the other.

Selecting lifejackets for children requires special care in order to ensure a good fit. In particular, the buoyancy aid or lifejacket mustn't be able slip up over the child's head when in the water.

Even though many choose not to wear one unless sea and weather conditions are risky, putting on a lifejacket when boarding a boat should, ideally, be as automatic as fastening a car seat belt.

Lifejacket maintenance

A buoyancy aid can be checked visually for wear, chafing, splits and loose stitching. It can be tested by wearing it and going for a swim. This also helps to show how effective and how good a fit it is – a particularly important consideration as children grow up and possibly pass theirs on to a younger sibling.

Manually-inflated lifejackets can be tested by inflating them to the correct pressure and leaving them for 24 hours. There should be no loss of pressure. To release the air completely, press the valve in the inflating tube and press the jacket down on a flat surface.

Older lifejackets, such as those obtained when buying a second-hand boat, must be checked and serviced. The RNLI Lifejacket Rogues Gallery displays some life-threatening lifejackets and equipment that should have been discarded and replaced long ago.

Inflatable lifejackets should be checked for abrasion, splits and wear every month and professionally serviced at least every two years. Don't forget to check the straps and fastenings.

The automatically-inflating type of lifejacket has a small CO_2 cylinder, which must be replaced after it has inflated the lifejacket and at regular intervals according to the manufacturer's recommendations and instruction manual. All too often this cylinder is neglected and corroded. Check regularly that the cylinder is screwed in hand-tight.

Trained RNLI volunteers demonstrate at boat shows how to inspect lifejackets, including the inflatable types. The accompanying photographs are from a display and demonstration at the Southampton Boat Show. Procedures vary according to make and type so it's most important to follow the instructions provided with the appropriate kit of parts sold by the manufacturer. If you have the slightest doubt about replacing a lifejacket's cylinder yourself, arrange for the manufacturer or dealer to do it for you.

Kits for replacing inflation cylinders on lifejackets are available from manufacturers and dealers. The instructions must be followed carefully, or else someone qualified to do so should replace the cylinder.

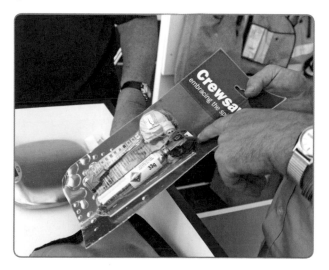

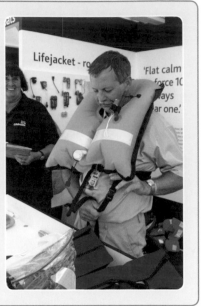

Obviously a jacket can't be test-inflated using its cylinder as this would discharge it, but the jacket should still be test-inflated regularly using the manual inflation tube. Leave it for 24 hours to check that it remains fully inflated and that there are no leaks.

Right: An inflated lifejacket in position, with crutch straps in place to prevent it rising up and over the wearer's head.

Lifejacket manufacturers and dealers have websites with servicing information. Examples include http://www. lifejackets.co.uk and an online video for the Crewsaver make of lifejackets at http://www.crewsaver.co.uk. Click on 'Inflatable Lifejacket Manual'.

Ensure the crew never use lifejackets as cushions, always dry them after use, and always store them in dry conditions.

Horseshoe lifebuoy with floating line and light

A lifebuoy mounted on the rail of a sail cruiser should be easily accessible to throw to someone in the water so that they can be pulled towards the boat. 'Man overboard' rescue procedures are taught and practised on sailing courses.

Distress flares and signals

The following may seem rather alarming but you shouldn't let it put you off sailing. Most distress flares never need to be used, but they should nevertheless be part of a boat's safety equipment.

If you get into difficulties while sailing you need to be able to attract attention and call for help. One recognised method is, if possible, to stand and slowly raise and lower both outstretched arms. However, audible signals are more effective. If you're near the shore or other boats shout for help or give the SOS signal using a whistle or hand-operated signalling horn: three short blasts, three long blasts, and three short blasts.

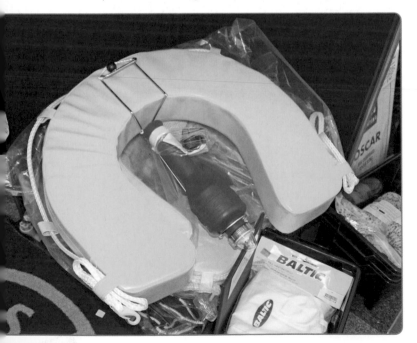

Left: Horseshoe lifebuoy with floating line and light.

Right: Hand-operated signalling horn.

Hand-held red flare. Used to show the location of a vessel in distress.

Orange smoke flares, hand-held and floating. The dense orange smoke signals your position, *eg* to an aircraft.

Distress flares should be used in an emergency situation, to attract attention and pinpoint your position. A white flare isn't a distress signal but is used to warn other boats of your presence and to avoid a collision. Other types of flares include packs of mini flares compact enough to be carried when dinghy sailing, and red parachute rocket flares.

Flares show the lifeboat and helicopter where you can be found and rescued.

A VHF radio can be installed in the cabin where 12V electricity is available on a sail cruiser.

Portable VHF radios with rechargeable batteries are an alternative.

When first boarding a boat, instructions concerning emergency equipment and procedures, including instructions provided with each flare, should be read by all members of the crew, and followed carefully in the event of an emergency.

Each flare will have an expiry date, and it needs to be replaced at this date otherwise it may not work when you most need it to. In fact an out-of-date flare may misfire and cause damage and injury. For this reason as well as the obvious risk of giving a false alarm, old flares should never be used as part of a firework display.

Out-of-date flares must be disposed of properly according to the regulations current at the time. When buying replacements, ask the seller for the current procedure regarding disposal. He may even be able to dispose of your old ones for you. The local coastguard or fire station should also be able to provide advice on disposal facilities.

More detail on choice and use of flares can be found on the RNLI website and the Pains Wessex website at http://www.pwss.com.

Mobile phone and VHF radio

The RNLI strongly advises the use of a VHF radio rather than a mobile phone. The radio needs to be licensed before it is used. The fact that it's also necessary to gain a qualification and licence to use a VHF radio is good because it helps to ensure that radios are used properly. However, there's a tendency for this to put some boat owners off owning one. RYA-approved sailing schools and many sailing clubs arrange the short courses and tests necessary for this qualification.

Harbour masters and coastguards listen for calls on VHF radio and can be contacted for advice and information about navigation, hazards, weather, moorings and marina berths, etc.

In an emergency a mobile phone is useful as a back-up device, to call 999 and ask for the coastguard if there's a problem with the radio. But this isn't as effective or reliable as sending a Mayday call on a VHF radio. With VHF transmissions, rescuers can pinpoint the location of a vessel and other boats can hear the distress signals and come to its aid. A fixed VHF radio will have more range than a mobile phone and has the substantial power of a 12V battery behind it. A mobile phone by contrast has limited range, poor signal strength and much less battery power.

Where 12V power is not available a hand-held VHF radio, using internal batteries, can be used. A wide range of these is available, including radios that are waterproof and can even float if accidentally dropped. A hand-held VHF radio also provides a backup to a fixed radio and can be used in a tender away from a sail cruiser.

The RNLI often provides demonstrations on the use of emergency equipment and procedures, and the RYA and many sailing clubs provide courses that are essential to gain the qualification to use a VHF radio.

Navigation lights

Navigation lights are covered in Chapter 16.

Bilge pumps

In a sail cruiser with a 12V electricity supply an electric bilge pump can be installed. This can have an automatic float switch that turns the pump on when water accumulates in the bilges, which is particularly useful when a boat is left afloat. It removes rainwater that may get into the bilges and helps reduce the risk of sinking if a leak occurs.

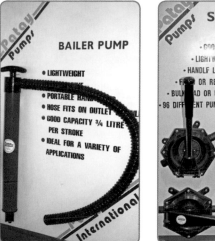

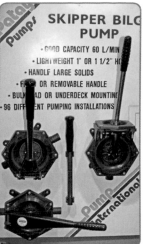

A 12V electric bilge pump kit with automatic float switch.

Hand-operated bilge pumps.

The belt and braces approach is appropriate here. Even with an electric pump it's wise to still have a manually-operated pump and one or two buckets for bailing, just in case the battery is flat or gets swamped with water.

Fenders

Few boats are built with sufficient fendering or rubbing strips to cope with mooring alongside quays and other boats. Horrible grinding noises as GRP rubs against concrete or steel can be avoided with sufficient carefully

placed fenders. Most plastic fenders are inflatable and should be reasonably firm but not rock hard. If you can press your finger about half an inch (1.5cm) into the middle of a fender it should be about right for absorbing shocks without itself harming the boat.

Fenders that are dirty with mud and grit can scrape the gelcoat, so it's best to keep them clean. Some boat owners use fabric covers on fenders to further reduce any risk of chafing.

A selection of inflatable fenders.

GPS

Global positioning systems or 'satellite navigation' devices have become widespread and their mass production has reduced their price. If you have the necessary electricity supply on a sail cruiser they certainly aid navigation. In fact a portable hand-held GPS with alkaline batteries is worth considering if 12V power isn't available on a day boat.

The very sophisticated systems displayed at boat shows are quite expensive and more appropriate for ocean-going vessels, although high tech enthusiasts may have fun with them – and why not, if this improves their boating experience?

Clothing and footwear

On warm summer days with a light breeze, plenty of people wear ordinary casual clothing to enjoy sailing on inland or very sheltered estuary waters in the more stable types of boat. However, non-slip footwear is essential, along with clothing that'll maintain sufficient body heat, bearing in mind that it's almost always considerably colder out on the water than inland. A waterproof outer layer should always be taken on the boat in readiness for a sudden unexpected downpour. If there's the risk of a capsize the purpose-made clothing described below becomes necessary, as getting very wet can lead to hypothermia, even in summer.

Dinghy sailors often wear wetsuits (or drysuits if they can afford them), and plenty of purpose-made waterproof jackets and trousers are available for cruising.

Sailing clubs may insist on all sailors wearing wetsuits for races in cold weather. These work by trapping a layer of water under the neoprene material of the suit, next to your skin. Body heat then warms the water, providing protection from the cold. Wetsuits are available in various thicknesses, the thickest – mainly for winter use – being called 'steamers'. A wetsuit must fit well in order to work properly.

The more expensive drysuit is fully waterproof, with watertight seals around openings for neck, wrists and feet. Thermal layers need to be worn under this suit to keep you warm.

Wet boots made of neoprene work in the same way as a wetsuit. They need to be strong to cope with the use of toestraps and have good grip when moving about the boat.

Sailing gloves can also be made of neoprene. As well as providing warmth, gloves reinforced with leather protect the hands from the chafing caused by pulling on ropes and can provide extra grip.

The range of recently devised highly specialised clothing for sailing, including dinghy sailing, is expensive and it's possible to spend more on the latest clothing and fashionable accessories than on buying a good second-hand boat. However, the latest 'hiking pants' (for use when sitting out on a dinghy) and breathable waterproof drysuits make life more comfortable and may be considered worthwhile by an enthusiast who sails and races at every opportunity whatever the weather.

Navigation is much easier with GPS equipment.

The most important feature of boating footwear is secure non-slip soles and heels.

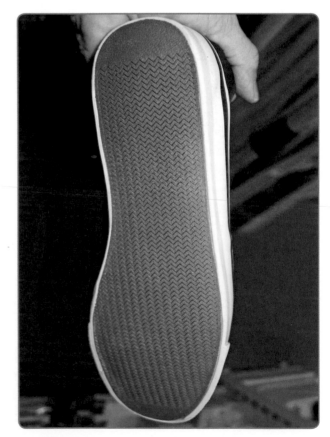

Windproof and waterproof clothing is available for sail cruising. A hood or hat is strongly advised, as much body heat is lost via the head. You may also need a hat for sun protection.

Wetsuit care

The following tips will help prolong the life of a wetsuit and similar neoprene garments for many years:

- Never clean the wetsuit in a washing machine, and don't dry-clean it. Rinse it by hand in clean fresh water to remove salt and dirt. Stains can be removed with a mild shampoo or special wetsuit cleaner.
- Dry it away from direct heat, suspended on a large thick hanger that will spread the load and not cause distortion.
- Zips that get stiff or clogged can be cleaned gently with an old soft toothbrush and lubricated by rubbing them with a candle or beeswax.
- Avoid contact with petrol, aerosols, oil and solvents.
- Take care not to damage the material with a broken or sharp fingernail.
- Check for tears in the neoprene. Small repairs can be made using neoprene glue. It may be possible to repair larger tears with neoprene material glued and stitched with strong polyester thread.
- Store the suit unfolded in dry, well-ventilated conditions.
- A wetsuit not often used may lose its elasticity and seem to have shrunk. Elasticity can be restored by soaking the suit in lukewarm water and then drying it thoroughly away from direct heat.

Locks and security devices

Unfortunately, outboard motors and other equipment are sometimes stolen from boats left on moorings and in less secure storage facilities. This varies considerably according to the location. In some areas boat owners leave outboard motors, trailers and equipment without any security devices at all and seem to have no problems, but elsewhere anything not securely fastened soon gets stolen.

It's better to be safe than sorry. If the outboard motor can't be removed and locked away, use a purpose-made security device, locked as in the accompanying photographs. Try to put loose equipment where it's under lock and key or else take it home. Clearly, it's as important to lock the cabin of a sail cruiser as it is to lock the doors of a car. A range of outboard motor locks is available from OML Ltd, and there's plenty of useful information on their website at http://www.outboardmotorlocks.co.uk.

This simple cylinder lock is slid onto the outboard motor clamps and locked in place.

Check what your insurance company requires regarding locks and the precautions that should be taken against theft. A trailer needs to be locked with a hitch lock or wheel clamp when left, whether or not the boat is on it.

Like neighbourhood watch schemes on land, there are boatwatch schemes in harbours and at waterway mooring locations. Enquire from the local police station, harbour master or marina office what applies locally and get your boat and outboard motor, etc, registered with whatever scheme is available.

A battery-operated burglar alarm in a cabin may help, but only if there's someone available and willing to respond.

Boat shows and boat jumbles

Boat shows provide not only the opportunity to see equipment and compare prices and specifications but also to learn from the experts how to use all the items displayed. Special reduced price offers are usually available for some equipment.

A cheaper alternative is the boat jumble, described in Chapter 4. The mixture of second-hand and reduced price new equipment found at such events is fascinating, and the atmosphere is invariably friendly. Having said that, caution needs to be exercised if you're considering the purchase of items affecting safety. You need to bear in mind all the points raised in this book about the strength and reliability of equipment you'll rely on when the wind and waves increase unexpectedly. Bear in mind too that some people believe equipment stolen from other boats sometimes finds its way into boat jumbles, though the regular presence of police at such events has reduced this risk.

Websites such as eBay and those that advertise boats for sale, as described in Chapter 4, also have sections containing a large range of used and reduced price chandlery. Although a huge amount of equipment is purchased in this way, it's important to be sure it's safe and fit for its purpose.

New and second-hand equipment is available quite cheaply at boat jumbles, but you should check the quality and reliability carefully.

Echo sounder or fish finder

The electrical device originally called an echo sounder is now often referred to as a fish finder. This indicates the increased sensitivity of such devices not only to the seabed but also to fish, making them particularly appealing to boat owners who want to do any fishing. For actual sailing, a clear indication of depth and the shape of the seabed helps to avoid running aground.

A fish finder gives a clear indication of depth below the boat.

19 The future

Boats owned and sailed by Ian and
Christine Davies.

The Halcyon 23 sail cruiser.

Ian Davies in his well-equipped cabin, ready for cruising.

Selling and trading up to a bigger boat

Plenty of boat owners start with a sailing dinghy and then, after several years of enjoyable sailing, decide to move up to a more substantial boat for cruising sheltered coastal waters and staying aboard overnight. It may be possible to achieve this by buying a bargain 'project' boat requiring improvement and then selling it at a small profit after carrying out the necessary work and sailing it for a season or two. In this way it's possible to finance, at least partly, the move upmarket to a bigger boat.

An inspiring example

Ian and Christine Davies started with various small boats and sailing dinghies bought at bargain prices and improved. They enjoyed sailing them – often with their children – for many years, particularly in a scenic North Wales estuary.

A Halcyon 23 sail cruiser was later purchased, when advertised at a bargain price because it needed substantial improvement. The hull, sails and the structure of this project boat were in basically sound condition. Many of the tasks described in this book were then carried out. They replaced wire and rope rigging, cabin windows, hatches, doors and many of the fittings. Parts of the structure, such as the keel bolts, were replaced and reinforced to improve strength and safety. Substantial work throughout the winter rendered the cabin dry and comfortable and greatly improved the overall appearance of the boat through painting and polishing, etc. In addition Ian's knowledge of engineering helped bring a seized-up inboard engine back to life.

In this way they've become the proud owners of a very smart and well-equipped sail cruiser worth substantially more than the total cost of purchase and renovation. Some of the photographs in this book were taken on board, and the picture on page 197 shows the 23ft sail cruiser.

Selling a boat

Preparation for selling a sailing boat involves carrying out many of the tasks described in this book in order to present it in a way that will be most appealing to a buyer willing to pay a fair price. Bear in mind in particular the advice on buying a second-hand boat outlined in Chapter 4. A buyer may well arrive with a copy of this book under their arm and check those very points!

It may seem obvious but it's surprising how many boats for sale haven't been cleared of personal possessions, rubbish and dirt. A good clean and polish makes a big difference. It shows that the boat's likely to have been well cared for. Pay particular attention to cookers and toilets. Tidy up the rigging and coil ropes neatly.

The hull of a sail cruiser may well look mottled and shabby at the end of the sailing season but a coat of antifouling primer makes a big difference to that important first impression.

The first thing anyone sees on stepping down into a cabin is the floor, so make sure it's clean. A new floor covering makes a difference. The next thing to hit a potential buyer is the smell, so provide enough ventilation and deal

with anything causing an off-putting odour. A sailing boat may well be perfectly sound but the above points can be a serious obstacle to a sale – particularly if a critical family member accompanies the buyer.

Paperwork

Have the necessary paperwork ready to answer questions – and prove your answers – about ownership, receipts, VAT, costs of mooring and insurance, professional repairs and servicing and any surveys that you or a previous owner had done, along with details of work that may have been carried out to satisfy the surveyor.

A future buyer will want to see the necessary European Recreational Craft Directive documentation for a qualifying boat built since June 1998. Anyone selling a boat without the necessary paperwork to prove this compliance risks prosecution.

The latest rules and procedures for compliance should be available at http://www.berr.gov.uk. Put 'European Recreational Craft Directive' into the search box.

Advertising

An advertisement including the phrase 'Well equipped; ready to sail away', helps to inspire confidence. Put adverts in as many websites, magazines and notice boards as possible at the same time. Many of them, such as the http://www.boatsandoutboards.co.uk website, take adverts free of charge. One or two photographs can usually be included. Give as much information as possible in the space allowed and then make it clear that extra pictures and full details can be provided before buyers view the boat. The extra photographs can be put on your own website or emailed to enquirers. They could even be printed and posted by snail mail.

This approach is an effective way to avoid wasting the time of both seller and buyer. If a potential buyer has detailed information and plenty of pictures showing different views of the boat – including the inside – they'll only travel to view it if they're very seriously interested. In fact, some have been known to say, even before viewing, that they'll definitely buy the boat if it's exactly as in the photographs and description. They may want to reserve it on the basis of 'first refusal'.

Future ambitions

Those with a small sail cruiser often become more ambitious and adventurous, having gained substantial experience of sailing in a variety of weather and tidal conditions, and may want to exchange their boat for a larger cruiser, able to cope with longer voyages.

Opposite: A most unusual way to advertise a boat for sale!

Right: Plenty of opportunities exist to trade up and cruise further afield.

This is an exciting and rewarding challenge. However, owning and sailing a larger cruiser, and embarking on offshore voyages further afield, requires much greater knowledge and skills than are covered in this book or on basic sailing courses. It's essential to gain the extra skills and knowledge by crewing with experienced and qualified skippers. This can be an enjoyable process in itself but should be combined with Royal Yachting Association approved courses, in order to gain the skills necessary for navigating offshore. You will also learn about the appropriate rules, regulations, and paperwork. For example, many countries require a Certificate of Competence to be produced on arrival. This can be obtained by completing an appropriate RYA course.

Sailing boats of various sizes provide a choice of ways to escape into a different environment for relaxation, enjoyment, pleasure and – if you so desire – excitement and adventure. The choice is yours.

Appendix

This is a list of contact details for the sailing boat information, products and services mentioned in the *Sailing Boat Manual*. Sadly, space doesn't permit the listing of every one of the many organisations and companies involved with boating.

The majority of people have access to a computer at home or at work and Internet access is now available to all, with assistance, through public libraries and other facilities. Putting the name of a product or service into an Internet search engine will produce plenty of contact details. Additionally, the first group of organisations listed below maintain their own detailed lists of sailing organisations and commercial companies.

Sources of information and contact details

Royal Yachting Association
An extensive range of information and contact details is available, including sailing clubs, boat owners' associations and training courses.
RYA House
Ensign Way
Hamble
Southampton
Hampshire SO31 4YA
United Kingdom
Tel 023 8060 4100
http://www.rya.org.uk

Boats and Outboards
A very comprehensive boat advertising website and magazine. On the website, select 'Services' for companies according to categories, and 'Directory of Marine Traders' for an alphabetical list.
Friday-Ad Ltd trading as Boats And Outboards
London Road
Sayers Common
West Sussex BN6 9HS
Tel 01646 680720
http://www.boatsandoutboards.co.uk

Yachting and Boating World
IPC Country & Leisure Media Ltd publish several boating magazines including Practical Boat Owner, Yachting Monthly, Yachting World and Classic Boat. Magazine subscription offers, marine directories, boats for sale, articles and forums are included on their website.
IPC Country & Leisure Media Ltd
The Blue Fin Building
110 Southwark Street
London
SE1 0SU
Tel 020 3148 5000
http://www.ybw.com

British Marine Industries Federation
This is the trade association for the UK marine leisure industry.
Marine House
Thorpe Lea Road
Egham
Surrey
TW20 8BF
Tel 01784 473377
http://www.britishmarine.co.uk

Inland Waterways Association
A source of information and publications concerning canals and rivers, including the safe use of these and their facilities.
PO Box 114
Rickmansworth
WD3 1ZY
Tel 01923 711114
http://www.waterways.org.uk

Sources of safety information and other boating information

Royal National Lifeboat Institution
West Quay Road
Poole
BH15 1HZ
Tel 0845 122 6999
http://www.rnli.org.uk

HM Coastguard and Maritime and Coastguard Agency
Spring Place
105 Commercial Road
Southampton
Hampshire
SO15 1EG
http://www.mcga.gov.uk

Boat Safety Scheme – For inland waterways.
64 Clarendon Road, Watford
Herts WD17 1DA
Tel 01923 201278
http://www.boatsafetyscheme.com

European Recreational Craft Directive
Paperwork that has to accompany boats built since June 1998 should provide the necessary information on this directive, which sets statutory standards of boat construction. If you want all the latest information on the regulations, put 'Recreational Craft Directive' into the search box on the website.

Ministerial Correspondence Unit
Department for Business, Enterprise & Regulatory Reform
1 Victoria Street, London SW1H 0ET
Tel 020 7215 5000
http://www.berr.gov.uk

Magazines

Magazines are an excellent source of up-to-date information, news and articles. Most are available through newsagents, but it's well worth visiting their websites for discounted subscriptions, boating news, archived articles, reviews and reports on boats and equipment, discussion forums and advertisements for second-hand boats. Many of the boat owners' associations and clubs listed on the Royal Yachting Association's website (see above) also publish very informative and entertaining magazines and newsletters.

All at Sea
http://www.allatsea.co.uk

Anglia Afloat
For East Anglia.
http://www.angliaafloat.co.uk

Boat News
http://www.boat-news.co.uk

Boat and Yacht Buyer
http://www.boatandyachtbuyer.co.uk

Boats and Outboards
http://www.boatsandoutboards.co.uk

Classic Boat
http://www.classicboat.co.uk

Dinghy Sailing Magazine
http://www.dinghysailingmagazine.co.uk

Electric Boat News (and Association membership)
http://www.electric-boat-association.org.uk

Practical Boat Owner
http://www.pbo.co.uk

RYA Magazine
http://www.rya.org.uk

Sailing Today
http://www.sailingtoday.co.uk

Watercraft Boatbuilding Magazine
http://www.watercraft.co.uk

What Boat?
http://www.whatboat.com

Yachting Life Magazine
For the north of England, N Ireland and Scotland.
http://www.yachtinglife.co.uk

Yachting Monthly
http://www.yachtingmonthly.com

Yachting World
http://www.yachting-world.com

Yachts and Yachting
http://www.yachtsandyachting.com

Companies mentioned in this book

Andy Seedhouse Boat Sales
2 Quayside
Woodbridge
Suffolk IP12 1BH
Tel 01394 387833
http://www.andyseedhouseboats.co.uk

Blakes Paints/Hempel
Swanwick Marina
Swanwick Shore Road
Southampton
Hampshire SO31 7EF
Tel 01489 864440
http://www.blakespaints.com

Calor Gas Ltd
Calor Gas Ltd
Athena House, Athena Drive
Tachbrook Park
Warwick CV34 6RL
Tel 0800 626 626
http://www.calor.co.uk

Chris Somner Dinghy Services
Sailing dinghies built and ready for self-completion.
40a Salterns Road
Parkstone, Poole
Dorset BH14 8BN
Tel 01202 736704
http://www.cserve.co.uk

Churchouse Boats Ltd
For Drascombe boats.
Apsley Sawmill
Andover Road, Whitchurch
Hampshire RG28 7SD
Tel 01256 896292
http://www.drascombe.org.uk

Eagle Boat Windows
Unit 2, The Sidings Business Park
Engine Shed Lane, Skipton
North Yorkshire BD23 1TB
Tel 01756 792097
http://www.eagleboatwindows.co.uk

Essex Boatyards Ltd
Essex Marina
Wallasea Island
Essex. SS4 2HF
Tel 01489 576888
http://www.essexboatyards.com

Henkel Loctite Adhesives Ltd
Including Plastic Padding marine products.
Technologies House
Wood Lane End
Hemel Hempstead
Hertfordshire
HP2 4RQ
Tel 01442 278100
http://www.loctite.co.uk

International Paint
Akzo Nobel Decorative Coatings Ltd
Crown House
Hollins Road
Darwen
BB3 0BG
Tel 08447 7094444
http://www.international-paints.co.uk

Jordan Boats
Kits for self-build.
8 School Wynd
East Wemyss
Kirkcaldy
KY1 4RN
Tel 01592 560162
http://www.jordanboats.co.uk

Lancing Marine
Lancing Marine
51 Victoria Road
Portslade
Sussex
BN41 1XY
Tel 01273 410025
www.lancingmarine.com

Marinestore Chandlers and Mail Order
Marinestore Chandlery
Shipways Yard
North St
Maldon
Essex CM9 5HQ
Tel 0845 241 2313
http://marinestore.co.uk

Pains Wessex Ltd
Distress flares.
Chemring Marine Ltd
Chemring House, 1500 Parkway
Whiteley
Fareham
Hampshire PO15 7AF
Tel 01489 884130
http://www.painswessex.com

Trident UK
Sailing dinghy equipment including Mirror dinghy self-build kits.
Trident Quay
South Shore Road
Gateshead
Tyne and Wear NE8 3AE
Tel 0191 490 1736
http://www.shop.trident-uk.com

Whisper Boats
Kits for self-build
1 Home Farm Cottages
High Street
Babraham
Cambridge CB2 4AG
Tel 01223 832 928
http://www.whisperboats.co.uk

Glossary of terms

If you're new to sailing don't let all these terms put you off – our long seafaring traditions have resulted in a large and sometimes strange vocabulary. The words are listed here not because you have to learn them all before going sailing but in order to help you when you come across them. Some other relevant terms and abbreviations are also included.

About Used in the expression 'going about', meaning to change direction through the wind by tacking.

Aft At or towards the back of the boat.

Amidships In the centre of the boat.

Anchor well Storage facility for an anchor.

Astern Travelling backwards or referring to what is behind.

Backstay The part of the rigging fixed to the stern and the top of the mast, to support it.

Bail To remove water from the boat.

Batten A thin flat length of wood or other material slipped into a sleeve to stiffen the leech (back edge) of the sail.

Beam The widest part of the boat.

Bear away To alter course away from the direction the wind is coming from.

Beat To sail to windward (closer to the wind).

Beaufort Wind Scale Used in measuring wind strength.

Blistering Water can penetrating the gelcoat surface of a fibreglass boat, causing blisters through osmosis.

Block Pulley used on a boat.

Boat pox American term used when a fibreglass hull has a 'rash' of many blisters in the gelcoat.

Boltrope A rope along the edge of the sail to reinforce the edge where it slides into the appropriate slot along the mast or boom.

Boom A horizontal pole attached to the foot of the mainsail.

Boot A protective plastic fitting, one of which is fastened on to each end of the spreaders to prevent chafing on the mainsail.

Boot top A line painted along the waterline of the hull.

Bowline Knot for making a loop at the end of a rope.

Bowsprit A spar fixed to the bow of the boat to allow a bigger or additional foresail to be used.

BSS Boat Safety Scheme. The inspection of cruisers on inland waterways is legally required, the examiner issuing a four-year certificate if satisfied.

Bulkhead Vertical partition across the width of the boat.

Bumpkin A spar fixed to the stern of the boat to allow an additional small sail to be rigged.

Buoy A floating object used as a marker and for mooring.

Burgee Triangular flag displaying a sailing club's identity.

Cage The structure surrounding a sheave or pulley.

Capsize To turn a boat over.

Catamaran A boat with two hulls.

Centreboard Board lowered through the hull, usually pivoted, to stop sideways movement.

Chainplates Attachment points for standing rigging that holds up the mast.

Cleat Fitting on a boat for securing a rope.

Clew The bottom back corner of a sail.

Close hauled Sailing as close as possible to the wind.

Cockpit The area at the rear of the boat where the crew can control it.

Cone terminals Another term for stainless steel 'swageless' terminals for DIY fitting on the wires of standing rigging that holds up the mast.

Cringle Metal eye in a sail for a rope to go through.

Cruiser A boat suitable for making journeys by water and staying aboard overnight, usually having accommodation in a cabin.

Cuddy A small shelter on a boat not big enough to be called a cabin.

Dagger board A board that can be lowered and raised through a slot in the hull of a dinghy, similar to a centreboard.

Day boat A boat used for one-day excursions; usually bigger and more stable than a racing dinghy and with space to accommodate a number of people quite comfortably for a whole day.

Dinghy Small rowing or sailing boat.

Displacement The weight of water a boat displaces when it is afloat.

Dodgers Rectangular sheets of fabric either side of a sailing cruiser's cockpit, intended to provide some shelter from the wind and spray.

Draught The depth of a boat below the waterline.

Ebb tide The tide going out towards the sea.

Echo sounder An electrical device that uses sound echoes to find the depth of water.

Ensign The maritime flag of a country.

Fairlead A fitting that guides a jib sheet (rope) towards the stern of the boat.

Fender Pad or pads fixed round or hung from the boat to protect it from damage against harbour walls, other boats, etc.

Fiddles A framework of steel rails round the burners on a cooker to hold pans in place when the boat moves.

Fin keel A thin, deep, single keel projecting from the hull of a sailing boat to stop it moving sideways and to enable forward movement.

Fish finder An electrical device that uses sound echoes to find the depth of water; similar to an echo sounder but with the increased sensitivity necessary to show fish on its screen.

Flaking The zigzag folding down of a sail for storage.

Flood tide Tide rising as it comes in from the sea.

Flukes The blades of an anchor.

Foils A collective term often used for centreboards, dagger boards and rudders on sailing dinghies.

Foot The bottom edge of the sail.

Forestay The part of the rigging fixed to the bow and the top of the mast, to support it.

Freeboard The vertical distance from the water's surface to the gunwale.
Furl To roll up a sail.

Gaff A spar attached to the top edge of the sail used in gaff rig.
Gate A device that holds the lower end of the mast on some sailing dinghies.
Gennaker A sail used when sailing downwind, often described as a cross between a genoa and a spinnaker. It is asymmetrical like a genoa but is rigged like a spinnaker and tends to be most popular for use in racing.
Genoa A sail used in front of the mast but big enough to extend back beyond the mast and overlap the mainsail.
Go about Change tack so the wind comes over the other side.
Gooseneck Fitting that fixes the boom to the mast.
Goose winging Sailing downwind with the mainsail and jib out on opposite sides.
GPS Global positioning system, used in establishing position at sea for navigation purposes.
GRP Glass-reinforced plastic. The term 'fibreglass boat' is often used to refer to a GRP boat.
Gudgeon Fitting on the rudder that hinges on the pintle.
Gunwale (pronounced 'gunnal') The top edge all round the sides of the boat.
Gybe To change course whilst sailing downwind so that the stern moves through the wind and the sail swings across to the other side of the boat.

Halyard (or halliard) Rope which is used to hoist a sail.
Hank A clip for attaching a sail to the forestay.
Head The top corner of a sail; also the toilet on a sail cruiser.
Headsail A sail, such as the jib, attached to the forestay.
Head up Turn the boat more towards the wind.
Heave to Stop the boat by adjusting the sails and rudder.
Heel Leaning over to one side away from the wind.
Helm The tiller or wheel that's gripped in order to steer the boat. Sometimes used to refer to the person who does this.
Hiking out (also called 'sitting out') Leaning out over the side of a dinghy to balance it against the pressure of the wind on the sails.
Hounds Points where rigging is fixed to the mast to hold it up.

In irons The boat stops when trying to tack with the bows pointing into the wind and sails flapping.

Jib Triangular sail attached to the forestay.

Keel A weighted extension of steel or some other heavy material below the boat, designed to stop it moving sideways and enable efficient forward progress.
Ketch A boat with two masts.
Kicking strap A device (sometimes called a vang) that holds

down the boom and keeps the correct shape in the mainsail.
Knot Unit of speed – one nautical mile (2,000yd) per hour.

Lanyard A thin rope used for holding things in place.
Lee The side of a boat away from the wind. 'In the lee' means sheltered from the wind.
Leech The rear edge of a sail.
Lee shore Shore onto which the wind is blowing from the sea.
Lifting keel A heavy type of centreboard on some sail cruisers and larger dinghies. It can be winched up for shallow water.
Log A book for recording a boat's movements, speed and distance travelled, or a device for measuring the speed and distance.
Luff The leading edge of a sail.
Luff groove The groove in the rear of some masts into which the luff of the sail is inserted.
Luff up To change a boat's course by turning into the wind.
Lug sail A sail with four sides that extends a little way forward of the mast.
Lunch hook A small anchor for use in calm conditions for a temporary stop.

Mainsheet The rope used to control the mainsail.
Mast step The place on the boat where the bottom end of the mast rests.
Mooring Permanent anchorage or place to tie up a boat.
Moused Binding of a shackle with wire to stop it coming unscrewed.

Neap tides Tides with the smallest range of rise and fall.

Offshore wind A wind that blows away from the land.
Onshore wind A wind that blows towards the land.
Outhaul A rope that pulls something, such as the clew of a sail towards the end of the boom to tension the sail.

Painter Rope secured to the bow of a dinghy to tie it up for mooring or for towing behind a cruiser.
Pinching Trying to sail too close to the wind, resulting in the boat losing speed.
Pintle A pin-shaped part of the rudder hinge that the gudgeon fits onto.
Planing Skimming over the surface of the water when the wind is strong enough to lift the boat sufficiently.
Point of sail Direction of sail compared to the wind direction.
Port side The left-hand side of a boat when looking forwards.
Pram dinghy Mainly used to describe a dinghy that has a blunt bow instead of a pointed one.
Pulpit Metal guard-rail fitted at the bow.

Quarter The rear end of the side of a boat.

Rake The slight slope of the mast when adjusted for best efficiency.

Range of tide The difference between high and low water.

Reach To sail with the wind from the side or slightly behind the side.

Reef To reduce the area of the sail as wind strength increases.

Rig All of the equipment for capturing energy from the wind, including mast, spars, sails, control ropes and supporting ropes and wires.

Rigging screw A threaded fitting for adjusting the tension of standing rigging that holds up the mast.

RNLI Royal National Lifeboat Institution

Rode The rope and chain attached to an anchor. Sometimes called a warp.

Roller A cylindrical revolving fitting over which rope or chain can run smoothly, as in the case of a stem head roller, which is used with an anchor chain or rope.

Roller reefing Reducing sail area by rolling the mainsail round the boom or rolling the jib round the forestay.

Rond anchor A type of anchor used to moor to the bank on inland waterways.

Rowlocks Fittings used as receptacles and guides for oars.

Rudder Device for steering, mounted at the stern and controlled with a tiller or steering wheel.

Run To sail with the wind coming from behind.

RYA Royal Yachting Association.

Sacrificial anodes Lumps of zinc attached to the hull near metal fittings, beside propeller shafts, and to the underwater casing of outboard motors. Zinc gets attacked by electrolysis before the other more 'noble' metals, thereby protecting them from corrosion.

Samson post Strong attachment point for ropes for mooring and anchoring.

Scope The length of the rope used with an anchor.

Seacock Tap that controls the flow of water for cooling an engine or flushing a toilet on a boat.

Sea rails Term sometimes used instead of 'fiddles' for the steel rails round the burners on a cooker to hold pans in place.

Shackle Metal fitting used to join chain or parts of rigging.

Sheave A pulley over which a rope runs.

Sheet A rope used to control the movement of a sail.

Shoal An area with shallow water.

Shroud The standing rigging used to support the mast on each side.

Sitting out (also called 'hiking' or 'hiking out') Leaning out over the side of a dinghy to balance it against the pressure of the wind on the sails.

Skeg A fixed fin on the hull of the boat designed to keep it moving in a straight line and, on some boats, to protect and support the rudder or propeller shaft.

Slack water The period when the tide hardly moves between high water and low water.

Sleeve A receptacle or pocket for a sail batten.

Sloop A sailing boat with a mainsail behind the mast and another sail forward of the mast.

Spar A term that includes masts, gaffs, booms and bowsprits.

Spinnaker A lightweight, very full sail attached forward of the mast when the boat is running with the wind coming from behind.

Spreaders Struts of metal or wood fixed horizontally high up the mast to provide better angles of support for the shrouds holding up the mast.

Spring tide The tides with the greatest range, including the highest tides of the regular four-week tidal cycle.

Springs Mooring ropes used in addition to the main bow and stern lines, to stop the boat swinging and moving excessively when tied up.

Stanchion A post supporting a lifeline at the edge of the deck on a sail cruiser to prevent crew falling overboard.

Standing rigging Wire rigging used to hold up the mast.

Starboard side The right-hand side of a boat when looking forwards.

Stays The wires supporting the mast fore and aft – the forestay and the backstay.

Stem head The fitting at the bow over which mooring and anchoring ropes pass.

Stern The back of the boat.

Sunstrips Protective strips of material fixed to foresails to protect them from sunlight damage when rolled onto the forestay.

Tabernacle A type of mast step usually found on sail cruisers.

Tack Sailing in a zigzag course towards the wind by swinging the bow across the wind, causing the wind to strike the sail from the other side. 'Tack' is also used as a name for the lower forward corner of a sail.

Tackle A combination of pulleys and ropes designed to make it easier to pull or lift.

Telltales Small strips of material fixed to the shrouds or sails to show the direction of the wind, making it easier to trim the sails.

Tender A small boat used to get to a boat on a mooring.

Thwart A seat arranged across the boat.

Tiller A spar fixed to the rudder for steering.

Toe-straps Straps fastened along the floor of a sailing dinghy under which feet can be placed when sitting out over the side of the boat.

Topping lift A rope used to support the far end of the boom.

Topsides The external area of the hull above the waterline.

Trampoline The space between the two hulls of a catamaran where an area of mesh is used to support the crew.

Transit A navigation term used to describe the observation of two or more objects in line.

Transom Flat, near vertical stern of a boat.

Trapeze A harness or seat suspended from the top of the

mast, used by crew when sitting out to help right the boat when heeling at speed.

Traveller A track along which the mainsheet fixture slides to allow for the movement of the sail.

Trim To change the setting of the sails in order to get the best performance from them.

Trimaran A boat with three hulls.

Trip line A length of line attached to the crown of an anchor with a float at the other end of the line. This can be used to free the anchor if it gets stuck.

Trysail A small sail used in very strong winds instead of a mainsail.

Turnbuckle Device for adjusting the tension in rigging, also known as a rigging screw when used with shrouds.

Twin-bilge keels Two parallel keels attached to the hull of a boat to stop it moving sideways and enable efficient forward progress.

Una rig Boat rigged with only one sail.

Vang Another name for a kicking strap.

Veer To turn away from the wind; or the wind changing direction.

Warp A rope used when mooring a boat.

Whipping A binding of twine on the end of a rope to stop it fraying.

Winch A device used to wind in ropes.

Windlass A type of winch normally used to raise an anchor.

Windward Towards where the wind is coming from.

Yard A spar supporting the top of a sail, similar to a gaff but with part of the spar going across the mast.

Yaw Unintentional swinging of the boat off course from side to side, often caused by waves.

Further reading

This list includes the books referred to in the text along with other suggested reading that expands on the topics covered. Books on skills involved with sailing and navigation are best read in conjunction with sailing courses and crewing with experienced skippers.

Anderson, Bill. *RYA International Regulations for Preventing Collisions at Sea* (Royal Yachting Association, 2007).

Bartlett, Tim. *RYA Navigation Handbook* (Royal Yachting Association, 2003).

Bartlett, Tim. *RYA VHF Handbook* (Royal Yachting Association, 2006).

Bate, Brian. *The Trailer Manual* (J.H. Haynes & Co, 2006).

Calder, Nigel. *Marine Diesel Engines: Be Your Own Diesel Mechanic – Maintenance, Troubleshooting and Repair* (Adlard Coles Nautical, 2006).

Campbell, Geoffrey. *The Good Launch Guide* (CSL Publishing, 2005).

Clymer. *Outboard Motor Manual* series (Clymer Publications).

Cunliffe, Tom. *RYA Manual of Seamanship* (Royal Yachting Association, 2005).

du Plessis, Hugo. *Fibreglass Boats* (Adlard Coles Nautical, 2006).

Dye, Margaret. *Dinghy Cruising: The Enjoyment of Wandering Afloat* (Adlard Coles Nautical, 2006).

Elvstrom, Paul. *Paul Elvstrom Explains the Racing Rules of Sailing* (Adlard Coles Nautical, 2004).

Featherstone, Neville. *Reed's Practical Boat Owner Small Craft Almanac* (Adlard Coles Nautical, annual publication).

Garrod, A.E. *Practical Boat Owner's Electrics Afloat: A Complete Step by Step Guide for Boat Owners* (Adlard Coles Nautical, 2001).

Glasspool, John. *Open Boat Cruising* (Nautical Books, 1990).

Gougeon Brothers. *Wooden Boat Restoration and Repair* (West System and Gougeon Brothers, 1990).

Hahne, Peter. *Sail Trim: Theory and Practice* (Adlard Coles Nautical, 2005).

Imray. *Nautical Charts series and Pilot books* (Imray, Laurie, Norie & Wilson Ltd, regularly updated).

Judkins, Steve. *The Complete Knot Pack: A New Approach to Mastering Knots and Splices* (John Wiley & Sons, 2003).

Mellor, John. *Cruising: A Skipper's Guide* (John Wiley & Sons, 2000).

Poiraud, Alain; Ginsberg-Klemmt, Achim; and Ginsberg-Klemmt, Erika. *The Complete Anchoring Handbook* (International Marine, 2007).

Ransome, Arthur. *Swallows and Amazons* (Red Fox, new edition 2001).

RNLI. *Sea Safety – The Complete Guide* (Royal National Lifeboat Institution, 2007).

RYA. *Boat Safety Handbook* (Royal Yachting Association, 1994).

Seddon, Don. *Diesel Troubleshooter* (John Wiley & Sons, 2001).

Stock, A.C. *Sailing Just for Fun: High Adventure on a Small Budget* (Seafarer Books, 2002).

Tibbs, Chris. *RYA Weather Handbook* (Royal Yachting Association, 2005).

Index

Acknowledgements

Much help, guidance and advice has been gratefully received from the following:

The many friendly and helpful people involved with boat shows, boating activities, boating product supply, boat building and maintenance, marinas and sailing clubs.

The late Maurice Perry, my uncle – a lifelong sailing and boating enthusiast from whom I gained much of my knowledge of boating matters.

My wife, Rita, who has shared my enthusiasm for sailing, and read the proofs.

My son, David, for his great help with the work on our boats and with information technology.

Louise McIntyre of Haynes Publishing, for her helpful advice and guidance in writing this book.

People building and improving their own boats
Ian Davies (Halcyon 23)
David Pertwee (Northumbrian Coble)
Tim Pettigrew (Drascombe Lugger)
Max Campbell (The Secret)

Advice and technical assistance
Nick Barke of Essex Boatyards Ltd
Martin Ingram, Technical Services, Blakes Paints/Hempel
Rob McKelvey of Eagle Boat Windows
International Paints
Max Campbell of Whisper Boats
Stewart Brown of Churchouse Boats Ltd
Chris Somner Dinghy Services
Henkel Loctite Adhesives Ltd
Marinestore Chandlery and Mail Order
Alec Jordan of Jordan Boats
Trident UK

Photography
All photographs are by the author with the exception of those (and some of the information in their captions) kindly supplied by:
Nick Barke of Essex Boatyards Ltd: photographs of GRP deck repairs, page 119
Tim Pettigrew: photographs of repairs to his Drascombe Lugger, pages 78, 96, 125 and 126
Max Campbell of Whisper Boats and Simon Tomlinson: photographs of the building of Secret sailing boats, pages 7, 84, 85, 86, 87 and 88
Stewart Brown of Churchouse Boats Ltd: photographs of the construction of Drascombe boats, page 93.
Chris Somner: repairs to a J24 sailing boat, page 109 and construction of a sailing dinghy, page 92.
Pains Wessex Ltd: photographs of flares in use, page 189.
Front cover main image: David Harding/SailingScenes.com

Project Management: Louise McIntyre
Page design: James Robertson
Copy editor: Ian Heath
Index: Penny Brown